THE GREAT PHONOGRAPH IN THE SKY

THE GREAT PHONOGRAPH IN THE SKY

SELECTED WRITINGS OF JOHN A. KEEL

Edited by Andrew B. Colvin

METADISC PRODUCTIONS, SEATTLE

NEW SAUCERIAN BOOKS, POINT PLEASANT, WEST VIRGINIA

Books by John A. Keel

Jadoo!

Operation Trojan Horse

Strange Creatures From Time and Space

Our Haunted Planet

The Mothman Prophecies

The Eighth Tower

Strange Mutants From the 21st Century

Disneyland of the Gods

The Complete Guide to Mysterious Beings

Flying Saucer To the Center of Your Mind

The Outer Limits of the Twilight Zone

The Book of Mothman

Searching For The String

The Invisible Diet

The Best of Pursuit Magazine

The Best of Anomaly Magazine

The Fickle Finger of Fate

The Great Phonograph In The Sky

ISBN-13: 978-1508516606

ISBN-10: 150851660X

© 2015 John A. Keel

PUBLISHED BY: New Saucerian Books
Point Pleasant, West Virginia

"Man must be prepared to accept notions of the cosmos, and of his own place in the seething vortex of time, whose merest mention is paralyzing. He must, too, be placed on guard against a specific, lurking peril which, though it will never engulf the whole race, may impose monstrous and unguessable horrors upon certain venturesome members of it."

-H.P. Lovecraft

CONTENTS

INTRODUCTION

When Ivan T. Sanderson founded the Society for the Investigation of the Unexplained over a decade ago, he put forth some very intelligent ground-rules including a ban on "any aspects of medicine or psychology; the social sciences or law; religion or ethics." At that time, those subjects seemed remote from the typical Fortean interest in unknown animals, meandering nocturnal lights, geographic anomalies, and archaeological conundrums.

The past decade, however, has seen a dramatic change in the overall approach to these matters. Psychiatrists, psychologists, and sociologists are now deeply involved in UFO research. All of the once-strictly-physical sciences are merging into a superscience that is actively exploring "inner space," as well as the visible universe. Even religion is being absorbed into this superscience.

Behind the closed doors of scientific academies all over the world, learned men are discussing parallel universes, antimatter, the possibility of extraterrestrial life, and the nature of reality itself. Realms that were once the exclusive domain of a handful of Fortean researchers are now public property. A "golden age" of Forteana has arrived, with surprising and unexpected suddenness.

Ufology, once considered to be the hobby of cranks, has attained respectability. Popular books, such as the phenomenally successful *The Bermuda Triangle* by Charles Berlitz, are turning a large segment of the population into amateur Forteans. Television and motion picture documentaries on Fortean subjects are assaulting the public's senses. Newspapers are filled with sober accounts of new breakthroughs at Loch Ness, and in Abominable Snowman research. Occult subjects sneered at a few years ago are now being studied at major universities.

We could choose to ignore this explosion and go about our quiet way, collecting "angel hair" and cataloging the mischievous appearances of kangaroos in the American countryside. But we must bend in the winds of change. Certain aspects of psychology and parapsychology (or paraphysics) do seem to belong in the pages of the Fortean journal. The exciting exploration of inner space has become a natural extension of our other interests. Even the important new studies of religious apparitions demand our attention.

The sociological impact of UFOs may prove to be more important than the UFOs themselves. The psychological effects of monsters and sea serpents on their witnesses may provide us with the most valid clues to their exact nature. Fish falling from the sky may tell us something about the eccentric composition of space, time, and parallel universes.

Above all, a coordinated effort to explore all of these seemingly disparate fields, in a cohesive manner, may well uncover some remarkable new facts about the human race itself, and its ultimate place in the cosmos.

-John A. Keel, 1977

Dear Editor:

It is imperative that we discuss at some length various misconstruances and false impressions that may be engendered by the divers articles by Mr. John Keel, et al.

I speak now only of my own group, not wishing to be uninvited spokesman for the other groups working here, especially those whose policies differ vastly from our own, and indeed have caused intense friction between us...

My group, which shall remain unidentified because our identity is of no consequence to you, has been working in total secrecy on your planet since 1895.

During our long presence on your planet, we have at no time interfered with your way of life, nor imposed ourselves upon you. We have indicated our presence to you in no way, and we shall continue to maintain this policy.

We use no spacecraft such as flying saucers, since all transportation to and from this planet is done by rather specialized forms of electronic matter transmission, which you have often called teleportation – something far beyond your own technical capacity.

All communication is carried out on frequencies and via modulation techniques that render them beyond the scope of your receiving equipment. You might be interested to know that it is an adaptation of the laser principle, on frequencies far beyond the ultraviolet.

Our major purpose in communicating with you at this time is to assure you that we are in no way involved with those occurrences that Mr. Keel has described, at length, in the past months.

We are here purely as observers. It may not please you to know that your own fate is entirely immaterial to us, but that is the plain fact of the matter. We know that, left to your own devices, you will inevitably destroy your race and your planet. We will consider it unfortunate, but it will cause no consternation among us, as you are, in fact, no more than curious laboratory specimens.

Your planet is but one of a multitude under study by our group, and we accord you no more attention than the others. We have neither the desire nor the need to enter into cultural and trade relations with you, since you have very little to offer us, and anything which we might be willing to deliver to you is beyond your own level of development – verily, beyond your very comprehension.

This is not to assert or to flaunt our superiority over you. Our development is thousands of years beyond your own simply because we started earlier, and for no other reason. In the equivalent expanse of time, you would surely be as advanced as we – allowing that you did not exterminate yourself in one of your absurd wars, a fate that seems, by all observations, to be as certain as death.

Yet, you do mean nothing to us, either way. We are neither hostile nor amicable to you, because you are an order of life totally alien to our own species, much as an anthill is to your own. It is the same passive interest that you have in the social order of these insects that we have in your race and your world.

We live amongst you purely as a scientist might live amongst aborigines – for study, research, and information. At such time as we have accumulated the required data, we shall withdraw our forces, and leave a few observers here to report on anything major that might be of some interest to us, such as your self-imposed extinction.

We will inform you that there are other forces at work here, from divers places, of both hostile and friendly inclinations. We have no contact with them, and what they achieve to either end is of no concern to us, except as part of the overall effect they have upon your race.

At such times as we might find expedient, we will again communicate with you. At this time, our communication is complete.

You may know me as VOK, which is an acronym.

This original, or a copy, should be forward to Mr. Keel for his information.

CHAPTER 1

My specialty is magic, the "forbidden arts." My favorite hunting grounds are the back hills of Africa and the savage plains of India. My story sources are witch doctors, fakirs, lama sorcerers, and men who claim they can kill you with a hypnotic glance, or cure your troubles by donning a grotesque mask and shaking a gourd over your head.

Jadoo is my stock in trade. Notes about this jadoo, about the black world's darkest secrets, have been piling up in my battered old suitcases. Perhaps this is as good a time as any to put them all down in tangible form, to write a history of the dying age of mystery, magic and superstition; an age being smothered to death by civilized skepticism.

Even though your mind is conditioned to accept the daily miracles of color television, supersonic flight, and atomic fission, you may tend to dismiss the proceeding cases as impossible. But they are all carefully authenticated. All of these things have happened, and are still happening today!

This is not a work of fiction. It is a work about magic and the "impossible."

For the "impossible" belongs to the magicians, the odd men who have earned their living by defying the laws of reason and the laws of the physical universe; who have given depth to fantasy and reality to legend. Men like Merlin, Cagliostro, and Houdini. Men like the *gali-gali* of Egypt, the *sannyasin* and fakirs of India, the lamas of Tibet. This is their story. The story of the "impossible" – and how it's done.

Sheikh Shemes, the first man I ever saw who would eat a snake alive, professes to be a man of faith. His strange powers, he says, are the result of secret prayers and mystical incantations. He had visited me in Zamalek, Egypt, to invite me to a private demonstration in his home, promising me some unusual pictures.

To reach his house, I had to follow intricate paths weaving through the teeming street bazaars in the ancient, crowded Darb El Ahmer district. He lived near the Citadel, the huge Muslim mosque made from slabs of granite and alabaster taken from the side of the Great Pyramid.

The Sheikh's house was old and broken, with shuttered windows and time-stained walls. When I plunged from the bright sun into the gloomy blackness of the place, my nostrils were hit with the sickening odor of hashish. A small, barefoot boy in striped pajamas (which he wore day and night) ushered me into a bare, windowless room, furnished only with a thick, worn carpet. He motioned to me to sit down, and disappeared through a door. After a moment, he reappeared with a smoky oil lamp, closely followed by Sheikh Shemes.

There is nothing dramatic about the Sheikh. He's not a showman like the Gali-Gali magicians. A stolid and stoical man of medium height, he was dressed in the usual galibeah with a tight, white *boab's* cap on his head. His eyes were penetrating, but in the swarming streets, his appearance would command little attention.

"I usually only eat snakes during certain times of the year," he explained. "At religious festivals and on special occasions, such as the birthdays of great Sheikhs. When I'm eating snakes during the festivals, I can eat little else. Sometimes I eat as many as ten large snakes in a two-week period."

Shemes' technique for snake-eating was simple. He pulled a reptile of a common, nonpoisonous variety out of a bag, and coiled it around his hand. It was about three feet long, its head darting back and forth, its thin tongue flickering in the air.

Suddenly he popped the ugly skull into his mouth, clamping his sharp teeth down on it. I could hear the sickening crunch of bones! Gripping the snake firmly in both hands, he twisted it, wrenching off its head, chewing it up and swallowing it! Blood oozed between his lips. He stared at the ceiling and gnawed at the headless, squirming thing in his hands.

Finally, only the narrow, pointed tail flapped between his lips; then it, too, was gone. There was no trick to it. The Sheikh really ate the snake alive. All it takes is strong teeth and a strong stomach.

Sheikh Shemes received fifty piastres from me for posing for the pictures. We had a long talk over little cups of thick saleb, Turkish coffee, during which I complained about how few real "mysteries" I'd been able to find in Cairo. He started talking about the "Way of Rafai" and the miracles its members could perform.

Before I left him that day, he'd promised to take me to one of their secret meetings. Numb with wonder and anticipation, I battled my way back to Zamalek through the trains of camels and screeching donkeys, swirling crowds of veiled women, and robed men.

Out on the eastern desert, beyond Cairo's imposing, forbidden Citadel, there lies a range of dirty hills laced with deep caverns, and topped with crumbling old temples and tombs. Civilization, with its highways, railroads, and irrigation canals, has bypassed this place. And for good reason.

This is the land of the old men; the bearded Jews ostracized by Arab society, the witch doctors and sorcerers and Gali-Gali men run out of the city by the law or their own lawless elements. Above all, this is the land of Rafai, where the followers of the "Way of Rafai" gather every so often to practice their strange rituals.

One bleak, moonless night in October of 1954, I sat among these bearded old men around a line of low fires and sputtering lanterns, against a backdrop of chipped columns and broken temple walls.

Few of them spoke English, and my Arabic at that time was confined to a few stock phrases such as, "Emshee!" ("Go away!"), the first word every traveler in Egypt learns. And "Allah yahanen aleik!" (May God give you pity!"), usually used as a polite brush-off for persistent beggars. But jadoo, like love, has a language of its own, and the men of Rafia speak it eloquently.

Snakes were everywhere that night. When the old Sheikh beside me opened the meeting, he held a long reptile in his hand and muttered a prayer in Arabic while everyone repeated some of the phrases after him. Then the evening's "entertainment" began.

One old man threw a four-foot-long snake on the ground and when it started to crawl away he shouted, "Andak!" ("Stop!"). And it stopped! Another command made it turn and crawl back into its bag.

Then one came forward with a long stick in his hands, his eyes watching me closely. He stood in front of me with a slight smirk on his face and held the stick rigidly toward me. I reached automatically, thinking he wanted me to take it. But he pulled it back sharply, went into a little shuffling dance, and then suddenly threw it on the ground. Instantly, it changed into an enraged cobra, rearing up and coming straight at me! As the hissing, flat serpent weaved toward me, the Sheikh beside me scooped it up and handed it back.

When members of the Rafai called on me afterward, at Zamalek, they explained how this stick trick was done. It's the same trick Moses used to impress the Pharaoh. The snake is known as the *naje haje*, and by pressing a nerve on the back of its head the charmer paralyzes it completely, making it rigid. The shock of being thrown on the ground restores it to its normal, repulsive self.

After I'd recovered from this trick, a plump little man, clean-shaven in contrast to the others, stepped into the flickering ring of light, flourished a long, thin-bladed knife, and suddenly stabbed it completely through his throat. He did it for me again in Zamalek a few days later. The wound didn't bleed, and I couldn't find any evidence of trickery.

Then suddenly everyone quieted down. All eyes turned to me. The old man next to me smiled and patted my arm. My turn had come! I was expected to perform some feat to qualify myself for this mystic circle.

The silence grew expectantly. Nervously, I struggled to my feet with my back to the temple wall, fumbled for a moment, then produced four billiard balls from the air and made them vanish. The silence continued for a moment, and then everyone started applauding. It was the first applause of the evening. They kept it up until the old Sheikh nudged me to do it again.

There's an old magician's rule never to do the same trick twice before the same audience, because the second time, they know what to expect and might catch on. But I had no choice. I repeated it, with variations, until I'd exhausted my limited repertoire of manipulations. Then I was sworn into the "Way of Rafia" amidst a wild, frenzied chanting, in a bizarre ceremony, the details of which I've vowed to keep secret. When it was all over, the meeting degenerated into a brawl. Some men grabbed sticks – not naje hajes – and did the Sudanese Dance, a sort of male belly dance.

By two o'clock in the morning, most of the old wizards had drifted away, and the fires were going out. Before they started staggering across the desert to their huts and homes, I made appointments with several of them, and invited them to a little jadoo party in Zamalek.

The old Sheikh walked back to Cairo with me, over those hills and through the solemn Qaitbai cemetery, with its mud mausoleums and round-domed tombs. On the horizon behind us, the early streaks of dawn were appearing. Ahead of us Cairo, was coming alive with the chant of morning prayers from the minarets of the mosques, and the lonely howls of donkeys. The world seemed touched with antiquity and mysticism.

I went through the Muski one afternoon to meet the only man in modern Egypt who earns a living by operating a black market in mummies. The mummy dealer was a nervous little Egyptian dressed in a soiled galibeah, with a cheap tarbush perched on his head. He studied my letter, and then surveyed me suspiciously.

"You interested in antica?" he asked, tilting his head appraisingly, like a sly squirrel.

We were standing in the doorway of his hut. Some putrid odor was pouring out, mixed with heavy incense. He looked up and down the busy street cautiously, and with a slight nod of his pointed head, motioned me inside.

"My friends said you had mummies for sale." I looked at him expectantly.

"Mummies are very expensive," he said softly.

"How much?"

"Five hundred pounds," he announced, watching for my reaction. I whistled and frowned.

"That's $1,500 dollars!"

"It is difficult… I take my chances…" He shrugged apologetically.

Actually it was cheap for a real mummy. Too cheap, I thought.

"Let's see one."

He led me into a corridor again, past a doorway where a wrinkled female face bobbed momentarily, then disappeared. The smell was getting stronger. We came to a narrow flight of stairs leading downwards.

I followed him into a basement. The odor was now almost overwhelming. There, in the flickering glow of his lamp, I saw a terrifying sight.

Seven old, half-decayed coffins were scattered about the floor or leaning against the walls. And every one of them contained a withered brown mass of bones and leathery flesh loosely wrapped in moldy linen. They looked like rigid ghosts, ready to step out of their cases. Each one was fifteen hundred dollars worth of ancient death.

I examined one closely. The shopkeeper seemed to have the jitters.

Suddenly another thought hit me coldly. This mummy didn't smell! It was a little musty, perhaps, but that wretched stink wasn't coming from the mummies! What I was smelling were fresh corpses!

"My God!" My voice must have been a shrill whisper. "This is a fake, like those statues upstairs!"

The Egyptian narrowed his eyes and glared at me warily. My friend had just told me he sold mummies. Not that he *made* them!

"You…" I choked out, "you make these mummies here, don't you?"

I moved toward him, toward the closed door, fascinated with horror.

"Please," there was an alarmed quiver in his voice. "These are genuine mummies from Saqqara!"

Now I knew why he was so nervous. Bootlegging relics is a serious crime in Egypt. But manufacturing mummies must be punishable with life imprisonment, or maybe even death.

"Look," I said reassuringly, "I don't care if you boil babies. Your secret is safe with me. But what's behind this door?"

"Nothing!" he blurted, standing spread-eagled in front of it. I gave him a quick shove and slid the heavy bolt, throwing the door open.

That smell burst out like a shotgun blast. A gasoline lamp hung from the low ceiling, filling the room with a blaze of light. A large vat sat in the center. And standing over it, a huge muscular Egyptian stared at me in surprise. With a fierce, ugly look, he came at me slowly, hunched like a wrestler. I glanced hopefully toward the little shopkeeper. He stepped forward, speaking a few words in Arabic in a hushed, disturbed voice. The big man stopped, studying me defiantly.

"Here is where we prepare the mummies," the shopkeeper confessed worriedly. "You tell no one?"

"No, I won't tell anyone," I promised. Then I talked smoothly, trying to win his confidence and get the inside story of his weird business. Finally, in hesitant, broken English, he answered my questions, hoping, I suppose, to satisfy my curiosity so I would go away. Later, with further research in the library of Cairo's American University, I pieced together these facts about mummy-making.

Four hundred years ago, you could buy "Egyptian Mummy" in any apothecary. It was a coveted cure-all during the Middle Ages. Ground-up bodies hauled out of Egyptian crypts were considered good for everything from a hangnail to a knife wound. For this reason, hundreds of priceless tombs were rifled by profit-hungry merchants, and undoubtedly many records and relics of immense historical value were stolen or destroyed. Eventually the heavy traffic in mummies exhausted the supply, so the merchants had to start manufacturing more.

Getting fresh bodies from the jails and hospitals, they filled them with bitumen, wrapped them tightly with cheap cloth, and put them out in the hot desert sun for short periods. The resultant mummies, when ground up (into "occultum" dust), easily passed for the real thing.

Since most of them were made from corpses that had died from the worst kinds of diseases, their medicinal value was questionable. In the end, the Egyptian government slapped a very heavy tax on the sale of the grotesque merchandise, and the once-flourishing market died out.

But not completely. Mummies are still smuggled out of Egypt, to China and India, where they are still used for medicine. And they are still sold to collectors of strange curios. That is where my friend came in. He didn't waste his time using the genuine method of mummification; that took a lot of work and preparation. My friend in the basement was using some crude, foul smelling liquid that sped up the drying process. He had inherited the formula from his father. Even this ghastly trade was a family affair.

His big accomplice gruffly showed me their particular mummification technique, while I battled nausea. The terrible odor was searing my lungs. Tossed in a cruel pile in a corner of the room, several stiff, brown bodies lay waiting their turn in the vat. Flies clustered over them like animated inkblots.

"First we cut them open," the Arab explained with a craftsman's pride, "then we pull out their insides." He pointed toward a pile of red and white innards.

"We stuff them, just as the ancients did, and put them in this for a few weeks." He patted the vat lovingly, "After we take them out, we wrap them in old, treated linen, and bury them in the desert to ripen."

Suddenly I felt sick. I leaned against the wall, and pulled my handkerchief out of my coat pocket. My Egyptian press card popped out, too, and fell on the floor. It was a little green folder with the name of a government ministry official written in Arabic on the cover. The big native stooped and picked it up. A violent oath rolled from his lips. The shopkeeper looked at it, and terror crossed his face.

It took me a moment to realize what as happening. Suddenly, my feet were dangling as the giant lifted me by the collar, thrusting his vicious face into mine.

"I'm not a government agent!" I exclaimed. "I'm a journalist! That's a press card!"

He dropped me and I stumbled backwards, falling against something hard and cold: the bodies.

For one desperate moment, I tried to gather my strength. I sucked in my breath and raised my hands defensively. The giant seemed eight feet tall.

My arms were weak, my stomach was heaving, and my throat and nostrils were burning. I shoved one fist forward, and it hit something as solid as a brick wall. Then I saw the native pull his arm back and make a sudden movement. There was a moment of savage pain; then the terrible smell went away.

An army of boot-wearing ants seemed to be marching through my head, going in one ear and coming out the other. My first thought on regaining consciousness was: "I'm still alive!" The shopkeeper congealed out of the mist at the corners of my vision. His frightened face came very close to mine.

"Are you all right?" he asked anxiously. "Ahmed hurt you?"

A pair of strong hands lifted me to my feet.

"The bodies…where do you get the bodies?" I asked the one great question on my mind.

"We buy them. Dig them up." He read my thoughts. "No! We do not kill! We are not murderers!"

Baghdad, far to the northeast of Cairo, had a terrible climate. It was unbearably hot in the summer, and fiercely cold in the winter. I remember one bleak, frigid afternoon in February, when I was sitting on a rough wooden bench in one of the city's "first-class" cinemas. Suddenly, the picture went out of focus. I rubbed my eyes and it got worse. Finally I stumbled over the Arab legs stretched in the aisle, and fumbled my way to the exit.

Back in the unheated hotel, I sat at my favorite table in the bar, reading – or trying to read – while I absently manipulated some coins. I slowly became aware of a tall, robed man watching me, his jaws agape.

He smiled sheepishly, and I motioned for him to sit down. "You magician?" he asked. He spoke fragmentary English in a deep, commanding voice.

"No, newspaperman." I made typing gestures. He understood.

"Me Shaikh," he said proudly. "Shaikh Abdullah Haj."

That's how our conversation began. Before it ended, he'd invited me to visit him and his Yezidi tribe.

"You come," he declared. "We give you good horse, a big house, virgins."

The next day, I packed my bags and stored them with the hotel, along with my typewriter. Then I started going through some books about Iraq given to me by the Press Ministry. Suddenly I came across one short, curt sentence in a folder about the "People of Iraq." It explained everything.

"The Yezidis in the hills north of Mosul have a religious formula centered around the propitiation of the principle of evil."

I had accepted an invitation to spend two weeks with a tribe of devil-worshippers!

From Baghdad, the Shaikh and I traveled four hundred miles northward on an unexpectedly comfortable train to Mosul, a gigantic, sprawling city of sagging mud huts, intricate one-way streets, and minarets so old they tilt dangerously toward the ground like the tower of Pisa.

A few miles farther north, on a huge mound overlooking the Tigris Valley, are the ruins of the ancient walled city of Nineveh, one of man's earliest attempts at communal living. Today it is just a haunted shell, inhabited by lizards and vultures. Far beyond it, deep in the "cradle of civilization," was our destination – the secret cities of the Yezidi tribe.

The Yezidis have a reputation for being cold and inhospitable to outsiders. They live in a world of armed suspicion. The deserts around their villages are dominated by fierce bandits. Foreign oilmen traveling through the area are usually accompanied by heavily armed police guards. But the Shaikh told me repeatedly not to worry.

Shaikh Addi was a loose little village tossed helter-skelter across rocky valleys and ravines, and set off with twin temples, white and prominent against the drab background. Their fluted spires were like inverted ice-cream cones thrust boldly up against the gray sky.

Though it was hardly a paradise, Shaikh Addi seemed to be much cleaner and much more picturesque than the other towns we had passed through. Half the population had turned out to welcome the bus. Some of them were grotesquely ugly, with hard, desert-worn faces and unkempt beards. Yezidis believe God gave man a beard to distinguish him from women, so their custom forbids shaving. But they all managed to give me a warm smile as they shook my hand, western-style.

The "big house" Abdullah promised me turned out to be a small mud hut, very clean but very empty, except for a sleeping mat, a water pitcher, and an incongruous "European-style" chair of ancient vintage. Abdullah was very proud of that chair, and during the big feast held in my honor that night, he insisted I sit in it while everyone else sat around on the floor. When I entertained the Shaikhs with some magic tricks, I used it for a table and that pleased Abdullah very much. Maybe he thought some of the magic would rub off, and he would have a "magic chair."

The feast was held in Abdullah's big one-room house, a couple of miles over the hills beyond Shaikh Addi, amid all kinds of cheap tapestries, colored blankets, and clay pottery. It was a fancy house by Yezidi standards; a house that was lived in – a happy house by any standards. Abdullah's wife was a slim, good-looking woman whose proudest possession was a nylon blouse he had bought for her in Baghdad.

Guests for the feast arrived at sundown from all over the area. Tall shaikhs, short shaikhs, old men and young, all wearing their gaudiest finery and carrying their Sunday-go-to-devil-worshipping khanjers and swords.

The fare was limited in variety, but not in quantity. There was roasted chicken, a great slab of scorched mutton, a mountain of boiled rice, dates, bitter tasting local fruits, eggs broken raw onto slabs of bread, and endless cups of chi.

When the food was gone and the air filled with satisfied belches (their etiquette demands a hearty belch to show you approved of the dinner), the older Shaikhs rose, one by one, to welcome me with long-winded speeches.

At the end of the speeches, I stood up and gave my performance, turning a handkerchief into an egg, producing and vanishing billiard balls, and doing all my other simple pocket tricks. They watched with quiet wonder, and begged me to start all over again when I'd finished.

It was early morning before the party ended, and Abdullah escorted me to my "big house."

Four good-looking teenaged Yezidi girls were there – the promised virgins.

"They serve you," Abdullah explained, casting his eyes at the floor, "but better you do not touch."

In other words, they'd better still be virgins when I left! He gave them some sharp orders, and they fussed with the blanket on my sleeping mat. He smiled, shook my hand, and went out.

The girls crowded around me, attempting to undo my zebun, and disrobe me. They acted so hurt when I pushed them away that I wearily let them peel me down to my shirt, then I shook hands gravely with them.

I slept more contentedly that night than I had in weeks. One afternoon, after I had tried repeatedly, and vainly, to get permission to enter one of the peaked temples of Shaikh Addi, I was trying to pry more facts from Abdullah about the religion when he suddenly said, "I cannot tell you.

That is forbidden. I will show you."

He had decided to take a great risk and smuggle me into a secret ceremony taking place that night in a temple. Promptly that evening, we started out for the forbidden temple. It was nestled between bare, rocky hills a few miles north of Shaikh Addi.

In the dim light of early evening, I could distinguish strange, snakelike symbols carved in the marble around the doorway. There was no sign of life anywhere about. The only sound was the quiet trickle of water.

I started to speak, but the Shaikh put his finger to his lips. From there on, absolute silence was the rule. Pushing open the heavy door, he stepped carefully over the threshold. It was considered bad luck to step on the threshold. I followed him into the gloomy, black interior of the temple. The floor was soft, damp earth and the ceiling was out of sight in the darkness overhead. Three or four lonely oil lamps hanging down from the roof supplied the light. Their thin, flickering wicks were like blinking eyes.

Pushing one of the drapes aside, the Shaikh revealed a flight of stone steps leading downwards. As we descended, the sound of the water grew louder. At the bottom, a single oil lamp was glowing. Its naked light showed a long, narrow chamber with a stream of water flowing through it. For some reason that the Yezidis themselves can't explain, they always build their temples over a river or a stream.

The water was extremely cold against my bare feet, and the stream wound into a tunnel so low that we had to stoop over. Soon, we'd left the light behind, and were groping ahead in complete and chilling darkness.

After a couple of minutes, the tunnel began to get noticeably warmer. Suddenly, we emerged into a larger tunnel, stepping out of the water onto a narrow path.

Then Abdullah stopped. "Wait here…" he whispered, "then follow. Sit not near me."

He vanished toward a faint, eerie glow visible at the far end. I waited a minute, then felt my way after him. Finally, I came out into a large cavern filled with a fantastic spectacle.

About thirty or forty Yezidi men were squatting along the walls, facing several pits ablaze with roaring fires. Oddly, there was little or no smoke. The fires must have been burning natural gases. In the crimson light and dancing shadows, the men looked bizarre and unworldly. Their weird wide turbans and fierce beards contributed to the hot atmosphere of secrecy and mystery.

I squatted in a vacant spot between two furry-faced Shaikhs and waited breathlessly for the ceremonies, whatever they were, to begin.

After a few minutes of silence and waiting, an old priest dressed in colorful ceremonial robes made his appearance from the far end of the cave. He strode past the fires and stood in the center of the Yezidi circle. In one hand, he carried a small peacock, in the other a long khanjer. He stood silently sniffing the air for a moment, as though something unwholesome had entered his temple. Then he carefully scrutinized each face in the gathering. When he came to mine, he stopped!

Breaking into a cold sweat, I drew my sparsely bearded chin deeper into the folds of my zebun, praying the shadows would hide my pale skin. But he wasn't fooled. He lifted his arm slowly and pointed at me with his knife. All eyes turned angrily toward me.

Not a word was spoken. The whole horrifying drama was acted out in pantomime. He just stood there pointing me out while the others glowered and fingered the blades in their sashes. There wasn't much I could do except brazen it out.

I sat stock still until the priest took a step toward me and muttered something softly in Arabic. It sounded like "Rooh!" ("Go!"). Slowly, I rose to my feet and gathered myself together to rush for the exit.

Most of the men in the cave knew me or at least had seen me around. I relied hopefully on their friendliness and respect. Two or three jumped to their feet, watching me silently, their hands on the handles of their khanjers.

Still there was not a sound except the low roar of the fires. I stepped out of the circle and backed slowly toward the tunnel. Not a man moved. Reaching the gaping black mouth, I hurriedly turned and felt my way out of that place. No one followed me, but I could feel all those angry eyes until my feet were back in the trickle of water.

A few minutes later I was outside, breathing heavily against the icy night air.

Somewhere, deep in the cave under the secret temple, the men of the Yezidi tribe were resuming their secret rites – rites that may never be seen by any white man. At least not by me.

Satan played a nasty trick on me the next morning when I went to the Shaikh's tent for a breakfast of chi, bread, and raw eggs. As I was returning, I saw a young Yezidi slip out of my tent and disappear among the lounging camels. Thinking he might have stolen something, though there wasn't much to steal, I rushed through the flap and stopped!

A girl was kneeling on the sleeping carpet, hurriedly arranging her clothing! She couldn't have been more than fourteen years old, with the usual prominent Iraqi nose, full sensual lips, and soft dark eyes. Those eyes looped up at me, surprised and ashamed. Then she flashed past me.

After she left, I was gathering up my briefcase of tricks when, suddenly, a tall, ugly man with glowing eyes appeared at the flap. Without a word, he whipped out his khanjer and came at me! With equal suddenness, other men appeared behind him, and grabbed him while he burst into a stream of profanity.

The Shaikh, hearing the disturbance, strode into the tent, tossed me a quick reassuring smile, and spoke to the ugly man. My own Arabic was too limited to follow the fast, angry dialogue closely, but I understood I was being accused of the worst crime of all.

"He says he saw his wife leave your tent," the Shaikh said, turning accusing eyes toward me.

I tried to tell my side of the story but my Arabic failed me. The quick-witted Shaikh managed to grasp what I said.

"I believe you," he said at least. "But you had better leave as quickly as possible. I will stay here and make sure he doesn't try to overtake you."

So I left, fast and unheroically, laying the whip to my horse until I was well away from the devil worshippers.

Jadoo also hovered over Hyderabad, India. It was a city of mosques and great domed temples, where women collected the dung from the sacred cows roaming in the streets, worked it with their hands into little patties, and dried them in the sun to use later as fuel. On the outskirts of the city, there was a little straw hut where the jadoo concentrated. Government officials had closed it, because it was supposed to be haunted by what we call a "poltergeist," a playful ghost who throws things, sets fire to cloth, and so on.

I spent a night in it, sitting up on a straw mat, waiting for the ghost to appear. It never did. But the next morning, a lot of curious natives gathered outside to hear my report, and among them was an amazing old yogi.

He sat cross-legged in front of me, reached a wrinkled hand up to one of his eyes, dug his fingers into the socket, and pulled the eye out until it was hanging on his cheek, supported by the raw, red muscles and purple nerves!

There was no trick to it. Since childhood, he'd worked on that eye, gradually loosening it. By the time he'd reached adulthood, the nerves and muscles were stretched and numb, and the eye was totally blind. He was earning a living with this grisly trick, sitting in the marketplaces with his eye hanging out, flies clustering around it.

In Egypt, along the banks of the muddy Ganges, great crowds of pilgrims, beggars, and lepers gather to wash off their sins (and diseases) in the holy water, while shouting mobs of yogis, fakirs, snake charmers, and jadoo artists vie for baksheesh. I roamed the city alone, and there, by the Ganges, I discovered the secret of the human pincushions.

The young man who revealed the secret to me was squatting in front of an old temple near a foul-smelling funeral pyre, thrusting long steel needles through his cheeks. Other pins and needles poked into his shoulders, chest, and legs, while his eyes rolled vacantly towards the sky.

This young fakir seemed to be in a trancelike state. He didn't appear to notice me until I dropped a one-rupee coin into his bowl with a flourish. Then his eyes flickered.

"If you can teach me the words so I can do it myself, you can have this," I said pulling out a crisp ten-rupee note. He hesitated for a moment, and then led me into the temple.

When we were alone, he gave me a lot of mystical mumbo jumbo, tongue-twisting words to repeat to myself, "secret" prayers to recite before and after the trick, etc.

The fakir said that, after preparing myself with the holy words, I should feel around the inside of my cheek with my tongue until I found a spot between the muscles. The point of the needle is then placed in the mouth and a sharp blow on the opposite end will drive the steel through the cheek.

I examined his needles carefully. They were just ordinary hatpins with artificial pearls on the blunt end. They'd seen a lot of use and were dark and slightly bent.

Nervously, wondering if I wasn't crazy to attempt it, I held two needles over a candle, hoping to sterilize them a little. Then we were ready to act out what might be described as a dramatic farce. I moved my tongue against my cheek and found what seemed to a soft spot between two lumps of muscle. Then I carefully placed the point of one of the hatpins in my mouth. It pricked and I winced.

"Think of the holy words," he said softly.

I braced myself and slammed the palm of my hand against the round end of the pin. There was a flash of pain as it went into my cheek and another pain as it came out the other side. Then there was no pain at all.

"See," the fakir grinned triumphantly, "the holy words protect you."

When I drew the pin out again, the wound didn't bleed, and the puncture was hardly discernible.

The "holy" words were nonsense, of course. Later, when I recited them for an Indian friend, he broke into laughter.

"Those are Bengali swear words!" he said.

Sikkim is a land where orchids sprout wild among the weeds, and loafing tigers yawn in the faces of unarmed travelers. Hidden among the tallest mountains on Earth, the country should be a Garden of Eden, a safe refuge for men as well as beasts. But it isn't.

My guide left me at the village of Dikchu, about fifteen miles beyond Gangtok. There I had a dinner of tukpa, a kind of noodle soup, in a little stall, and performed a few tricks for the curious crowd gathered around me. I made a big impression, and several of the natives held a conference, came to a decision, and led me through the village to a little shack. In front of it was a human skull filled with dirt, and a little plant growing in it.

"Dhami!" An old man tried to explain, pointing first at the skull and then at a worried looking young native, who stared at the plant in terror.

The door of the hut was locked, but I understood that there was a witch living inside. They wanted me to meet her. I beat on the door, but there was no answer. All of these villages have a dhami, a female witch doctor, who dispenses love potions, chases evil spirits, and levels curses of her own.

The dhami had put a curse on the youth. When the plant in the skull withered and died, he would die, too! It was purely the power of suggestion.

Turning away from the door, I pulled my tiny plastic wand from my pocket and made a couple of "magical" passes over the skull. Then I picked it up with a dramatic flourish, wrenched the plant out by the roots, and ground it under my boots.

The young man turned pale and rocked back on his feet, while everyone gasped with alarm. But he didn't drop dead. After a stunned moment, he realized he was all right and broke into a grateful grin. Then the awed, excited crowd became very still.

The dhami's door was creeping open, and a dark face was peeking out!

Jamming my foot into the opening, I threw my shoulder against it and forced my way into the hut. It was one small room with a crude table in the center. Shelves along the walls were sagging with bottles filled with murky liquids. Assorted yak tails, rhino horns, and the implements of witchcraft were scattered all over. The witch herself cowered in a dark corner, studying me with frightened eyes.

Somehow I had expected an old hag with a wart on her nose. But this was no hag! It was a lovely girl, not older than twenty-five, with glossy black hair.

As I stood there awkwardly, I became almost embarrassed, feeling like an intruder. I managed to stifle a smile and assume a hard, menacing look, stepping over to her while palming the wooden egg I used for a handkerchief trick. The silent crowd pressed around the doorway, watching the whole comic scene breathlessly.

I made some clucking sounds, trying to tell them the witch was an old hen. Then I produced the egg from her knot of hair. She cried and ran to another corner, trembling and sobbing. The crowd burst into laughter – laughter that must have stung deep into her.

The witch of Dikchu was disgraced forever.

After a long and arduous trek south, back to civilization, I docked for four days in Rangoon harbor. I stayed ashore most of the time, exploring the fringes of Burma.

In the park near the 326-foot-high Shwedagon pagoda (where four hairs from the sacred head of Lord Buddha are supposed to be buried), I stumbled unto a gruesome demonstration by a beautiful young snake-charmer. She turned a twelve-foot cobra loose in the grass, sat down in front of it, and carefully brought her head forward. Then she pressed her lips to the snake's mouth for a long kiss.

This snake-kissing is an art confined exclusively to Burma. It is practiced by pretty young girls who take a two-year course in the "School for Snake Charmers" at the village Nagale. Once they have learned it, they make a good living, albeit a short one.

I had realized most of my dreams on this quest, but now, new dreams were springing up to take their place. I would have liked to have remained in the Far East longer, to have jumped from island to island across the Pacific, but I had more than sufficient material to keep my typewriter busy for a long time. My trip had been hard, but fruitful.

CHAPTER 2

After centuries of calling the Moon a dead body in space, scientists are now telling us that it's really a sister planet to Earth. What they haven't explained yet are the pictures taken of the surface showing strange "domes," mysterious "lights," and odd "craters" that look suspiciously like our own ICBM silos!

If you had been sitting beside a "canal" on the planet Mars on July 14, 1965, and had happened to look upwards, you would have seen a very peculiar object gliding silently overhead, sweeping from pole to pole at incredible speed. And if you had a powerful telescope, you probably would have been able to make the huge letters "United States – NASA" emblazoned on its silvery sides. Perhaps if you had faithfully reported your sighting to the Martian Air Force, they would have scoffed at you and issued a formal announcement explaining the thing away as "swamp gas."

But it was a mighty expensive hunk of "swamp gas," representing not only millions of dollars from the pockets of U.S. taxpayers, but also a centuries-old dream of all Earthmen. On that date, we finally photographed the surface of the Red Planet from the relatively short distance of 6,118 miles.

What did the 22 pictures really show? And why is it that we haven't heard much about them since the first burst of triumphant publicity on July 15th? Today the average man in the street thinks simply, "They showed a lot of craters, no signs of life," and dismisses them. However, there is more to the story than that. Much more.

On November 28, 1964, after several delays and failures, the technicians at Cape Kennedy held their breaths, crossed their fingers, and watched Mariner IV roar skyward, balanced on the end of a huge firecracker. They had planned to launch it the day before, but a last-minute problem with the craft's transmitter delayed the shot.

Weighing only 575 pounds, the tiny Mariner IV contained over 138,000 different parts. Naturally, there were a lot of things that could go wrong with such a system. Earlier attempts had failed, because one tiny transistor had become temperamental, or one thin wire had accidentally been grounded.

But this time, everything seemed to be going perfectly. Now the satellite was on its way at last, and during the long trek through the blackness of outer space, it responded to 79 different commands broadcast from Earth, altering its course slightly, feeding back sundry bits of information.

Finally, 228 days after launching, it closed with Mars and the order was sent out for the picture-taking to begin. The specially designed TV camera focused on the surface of the planet, turning the reflected light into electrical impulses or "pixels" for each picture, and then broadcasting them back to the Earth where elaborate devices at Tidbinbilia, Australia and Goldstone, California would convert them into photographic images.

Then something went wrong! The signals from the hitherto perfectly operating satellite were being jammed! The technicians at Tidbinbilia, sealed inside their mammoth control rooms, frantically jabbed at switches and twirled dials. Something was amiss. But what? A desperate check of all the equipment indicated that everything was in order.

A few miles away, at Canberra Airport, six men in the traffic control tower were facing another puzzle. A strangely glowing metallic object was hovering about 5,000 feet overhead. It was plainly visible to everyone on the ground – and no one could identify it. The men in the tower placed a series of phone calls. One of them was to Tidbinbilia.

Reporters at the tracking station went outside for a look. They could see the thing, too, and some of them allegedly took photographs of it. (Although these photos were mentioned in the wire stories, none of them were ever released.) Then an Air Force plane was sent up to identify the object. As the plane neared it, the thing simply disappeared.

And once it was gone, the signals from Mariner IV began to pour into the tracking station!

Slowly the pictures from Mariner IV came back. The great computers straightened out the jumble of signals and reassembled the photographs, while groups of astronomers stood by in anxious expectation. Every scientist had his own theory on what we would find there. Some thought the planet was capable of supporting life; others said it had to be a frigid emptiness.

When the first Martian photograph spewed out of the computer, the astronomers who supported the "it has an atmosphere" theory patted each other on the back. There on the edge of the planet (astronomers call it the "limb"), a cloudlike smear was rising some 50 miles above the surface. But their elation was short-lived, for as picture after picture emerged from the machine, it became clear that Mars was strangely pockmarked with craters, looking more like the Moon than anything else.

Furthermore, a preliminary examination showed no signs of the famous "canals." The learned men of science muttered in their beards. How could this be?

Over the past century, a great many strange things have been observed about Mars by highly distinguished astronomers. All of the men gathered at the Goldstone Tracking Station had hoped that the Mariner IV pictures would help to explain some of these unusual observations. Instead, the photos only posed new questions.

Although Mars had been carefully studied by hundreds of astronomers since the invention of the telescope, no one apparently noticed the two Martian moons, Deimos and Phobos, until 1862.

Long and thorough examination of these two bodies has led most astronomers to the conclusion that, because of their curiously unnatural orbits and speeds, they may be hollow, and may even be artificial constructions.

The celebrated "canals" were first charted by the Italian astronomer Schiaperelli, in 1877, and have been a center of controversy ever since. Some astronomers stubbornly maintain that the "canals" do not exist at all. Others insist that they have seen them, and that there is no question of their existence.

For some very strange reason, astronomers have kept this controversy alive to this day, and have quietly kept secret the fact that the "canals" were first plainly photographed over 15 years ago, and have been photographed again and again since.

Yet these photos have not been published in any scientific journals, however obscure.

Why are they keeping the pictures of that "canals" of Mars a secret? No one has been willing to answer that question.

There are numerous other mysteries about our nearest neighbor in space. In 1900, the famous astronomer, Lowell, reported seeing a large beam of light shoot up from the surface of the planet, like a gigantic beacon. He reported that it remained in view for several hours. In 1937, and again in 1954, astronomers said they saw a series of brilliant flashes of light on the surface. These flashes were far brighter than any volcanic activity could have been, according to *Sky and Telescope* magazine. What were they then?

Strange gray clouds were also observed on the planet in 1909, 1911, and 1950. And astronomers still cannot explain the origin of the huge,

W-shaped cloud, some 350 miles in diameter, which appeared there in 1954.

The possibility of life on Mars has been a favorite topic of the Sunday supplements and science-fiction writers for years. However, the U.S. Air Force took it quite seriously back in the late 1940s, when they assigned Dr. J. E. Lipp and others to study the possibility that the "flying saucers" might be coming from the Red Planet. These scientists quickly discovered that saucer reports usually hit a peak during "oppositions" – when Mars was closest to the Earth. This pattern, according to NASA astronomer Jacques Vallee, still continues.

A few months ago, Dr. Carl Sagan, the loquacious Harvard astronomer who has repeatedly dismissed the possible existence of "flying saucers," announced that he had studied the photos and data from the Mariner IV mission, and that he believed Mars had an atmosphere capable of supporting life.

In December, 1965, one of the world's leading astronomers, Dr. Clyde Tombaugh, the man who discovered the planet Pluto in 1930 and who believes that UFOs are spaceships (because he has seen one), held a press conference, at which he said that he had found traces of those elusive "canals" in seven of the 22 Mariner IV photographs. He claimed that these markings coincided with studies he had made by telescope. Dr. William Pickering, the head of the Jet Propulsion Laboratory in California, backed Dr. Tombaugh and admitted that some "canal-like" markings were, indeed, visible in the photos. The markings were most noticeable, they said, in pictures #11 and #12.

Astronomers remained sharply divided however, on what these "canals" might actually be. Laid out in perfectly straight lines radiating from hubs or "oases," the canals suggest some kind of planned, intelligently conceived construction. But they could be giant cracks and fissures, or belts of vegetation.

Writing recently in the British journal *Orbit*, one James Goddard unveiled his own careful analysis of the Mariner IV photos. He claims to have detected several minute geometric formations, including triangles and circles, which seem to be laid out in an organized manner. Other astronomers, both amateur and professional, have had a field day with the pictures. All have found something in them to support their own pet theories.

Dr. Gerard de Vaucouleurs of the University of Texas examined the pictures by a special process that canceled out the blurring caused by the

Martian atmosphere, and he uncovered the long straight line or "canal" called Pyriphlegethon. Two other men, Dr. Robert P. Sharp and Dr. Bruce C. Murray, both from the California Institute of Technology, say that the craters of Mars show signs of erosion. Their rims have been worn down – but by what?

As near as can be determined, there are no eroding elements on Mars such as rainstorms, wind, or flowing water. Or are there? Dr. Murray speculates that there may be a lot of moisture in the Martian soil, which freezes during the cold nights there, and then thaws during the day, causing an endless cycle of expansion and contraction that could produce changes in the planet's surface.

The atmosphere of Mars is estimated to be as thin as the earth's atmosphere at 130,000 feet. Yet several different groups of scientists recently declared that they have found traces of methane gas ("swamp gas") over the Red Planet. Others insist that the Martian air consists mostly of carbon dioxide. Still others ignore the clouds that have been seen – and the extensive spectrographic studies that have been made – and stubbornly stick to the notion that the gravity of Mars is not strong enough to hold onto any kind of an atmosphere.

When you sum up all of the learned scientific papers that have been spewed out of the world's observatories and universities, you can only conclude that we really don't know a damned thing about Mars. The scientists responsible for this endless outpouring of speculation and contradictions are the same men who were arguing that the moon was not solid enough for a rocket landing.

They continued to argue right up until our first lunar vehicles touched down there. Then the diehards said that we were "lucky" that the vehicles had just happened to land on solid spots.

These are also the same men who soberly insisted for generations that the planet Mercury revolved on its axis only once for each complete revolution around the sun, thus "explaining" why one side of that planet was burned to a crisp, while the other was a frozen wasteland. This, they insisted, was a scientific fact, and it was taught to millions of schoolchildren.

Then, two years ago, radar experiments discovered that Mercury was actually revolving slowly and steadily, and was not the "half and half" world the scientists had long considered it to be. Last year, these same profound gentleman suddenly decided that Jupiter was not a planet after all, but was a dead star! Next year, they may tell us that the rings of Saturn are really a swarm of fireflies.

Science is not infallible, and many of our scientists are hog-bound by dogma and tradition. They accept only what fits into the neat little theories they favor at the moment. When something turns up that doesn't fit in with their notions, they brand it as "erratic," and sweep it under their laboratory carpets.

If Mars should have an atmosphere of carbon dioxide (a combination of oxygen and carbon, both necessary to sustain life) then it may very well have many forms of plant life and, possibly, animal life. Methane, on the other hand, is a gas that is deadly to oxygen-breathing forms of life. It is made up of carbon and hydrogen, and here on Earth, it is created by the decay of vegetable matter; thus it is found in swamps. And flying saucers have shown a definite preference for our earthly swamps. Some ufologists have suggested that they visit our swamps so that they can refill their tanks with methane gas.

Life is a tenacious and adaptable thing. Here on our planet, there are millions of varieties of living things existing in conditions of extreme heat, extreme cold, and great pressure under the oceans. There is even a microbe that lives in granite, and actually feasts on it. It is not altogether unlikely that some form of life could develop in a methane atmosphere. We have, after all, learned to live in an atmosphere that is 80 percent nitrogen and less than 20 percent oxygen.

"There can be no life on Mars as we know it," the scientists have been chanting for years. But "life as we know it" is a freaky thing. Our planet is 80 percent water, and a large part of the land surface is either barren deserts or frozen wasteland, barely capable of supporting life. Our atmosphere is charged with electricity and great masses of shifting air, which give many areas a foul climate. The earth's crust is unstable, constantly moving and producing destructive earthquakes.

Now, to top it all off, we are rapidly polluting both our air and our water. Traces of DDT have even been found in fish caught in the Antarctic. In short, "life as we know it" isn't much. We may be living on one of the more hostile planets in the universe – an uncommon planet employing uncommon gases to support life.

Mars and the other planets in our solar system may possibly be swarming with forms of life compatible with those existing conditions. We were surprised to find craters on Mars. Perhaps the Martians, if there are any, would be surprised to find craters on Earth.

Those Martian craters in pictures #11 and #12 of the Mariner series have produced another mystery – one with staggering implications. A group of scientists in Spain discovered it when they studied the photos. Recently, they published their incredible findings in *The Strolling Astronomer*, a small technical journal.

Two men, Antonio Ribera and Jose M. Oliver, claim that picture #11, the one in which Dr. Tombaugh discovered traces of the canals, is almost identical to pictures of the Clavius Crater on the Moon.

This may not seem very sensational at first, but it is an incredible coincidence that goes far beyond the laws of chance. These men painstakingly drew maps from photos of Clavius and the #11 picture of Mars and found that the two areas – on two widely separated bodies in space – share many common features.

In fact, the similarity of the features and formations of these two areas was greater than 50 percent. In other words, it would be like discovering an exact duplicate of the Grand Canyon on, say, Venus. Unless identical conditions of terrain, erosion, etc., existed on both planets, it would be impossible for identical formations to appear.

A mathematician named Don Feliu Comella examined the results of the Ribera-Oliver study and came up with a lot of complicated computations, which proved that the chance of similar (if not identical) groupings appearing on both Mars and the Moon was 21,280,000,000,000,000,00 0,000,000,000,000,000,000,000,000,000 to one! It would be almost impossible, he concluded, for a grouping of features similar to the Moon's Clavius Crater to appear on Mars naturally.

Other astronomers have agreed with the Spanish findings. No one has even tried to explain this astonishing coincidence. This is a fact: Mariner IV sent back a photo that either closely resembles similar photos of the Moon, or it actually sent back a photo of the Moon instead of Mars. No matter how you examine this puzzle, you are confronted with only three possible explanations:

1. This is a formation on Mars that resembles Clavius to a remarkable degree – in defiance of all the laws of chance.

2. The Mariner IV pictures were intercepted in some manner, and at least one Moon picture was deliberately substituted for the Martian photo recorded and transmitted by the satellite This "phony" Martian picture was relayed on to our tracking stations, where it was accepted by our flabbergasted scientists.

3. Someone at NASA deliberately removed picture #11 from the series, after the fact, and replaced it with a Moon photo.

What are we left with? What gambler would bet on odds of 2128 followed by 53 zeroes? Are you willing to accept such a coincidence at those odds?

But the second possible explanation is equally hard to accept. Who or what could intercept the Mariner IV transmissions and successfully substitute a set of new signals for the ones being broadcast? We do know that a UFO was hovering over the Australian tracking station when the signals were being received, but only a wild-eyed fanatic would dare propose that the UFOs possessed the knowledge of our communications necessary to successfully intercept and substitute one signal for another.

Furthermore, what would be the purpose of such an operation? The only possible answer: to conceal what is actually on the surface of Mars – something that the UFOs do not want us to see. It is an almost insane concept. Or is it?

The third hypothesis is also difficult to consider seriously. Why should NASA, or anyone at NASA, want to substitute a Moon photo for a Mariner IV picture? This would imply some kind of conspiracy to conceal certain features of Mars not only from the public, but also from the scientific community. Would this make any sense at all?

I suppose one could argue that it was part of our paranoid Cold War strategy to keep as much information from the Russians as possible, for as long as possible.

Unfortunately, NASA officials are, indeed, paranoiac, especially when it comes to the subject of unidentified flying objects. In his best-selling book, *Flying Saucers – Serious Business*, newsman Frank Edwards accused NASA of classifying as "secret" one of the 4,320 pictures of the Moon sent back by the 1964 Ranger series.

Later, when the picture was finally released to the press, it showed only some white lumps or "domes," which NASA explained away as "rocks." Then why did they bother to classify the picture in the first place? Today, NASA officials deny that they ever did.

NASA is not above censoring pictures. While James McDivitt and the late Edward White were orbiting the earth in Gemini IV, in June 1965, they radioed that they had sighted a circular object with arms projecting from it. They were taking pictures of it.

After they had successfully completed their mission, NASA officials blandly told inquisitive reporters that "those pictures didn't come out."

Several months later, a series of three of those nonexistent photos were quietly released, but they went unnoticed by most of the nation's press.

A few years ago, many NASA officials talked freely about UFOs and the numerous sightings around our rocket launching sites. Nowadays, all questions about flying saucers are shrugged off. Reporters are told, "Only Mr. Webb (head of the space program) can make statements on this subject." But Mr. Webb isn't talking.

It is well known that pilots of the X-15 rocket plane saw and photographed UFOs during their flights in the early 1960s. Today, those photos are allegedly kept at the CIA's Lookout Mountain facility in California, where they are inaccessible to reporters.

The one-time official spokesman for the Air Force's UFO investigating "Project Bluebook," Al Chopp, is now a top man in the NASA public relations office at the Houston Space Center. For years, Chopp was an outspoken believer in UFOs. He endorsed the work of Major Donald E. Keyhoe, head of NICAP, and issued a number of statements expressing the belief that flying saucers were machines controlled by intelligent extra-terrestrial beings.

A few months ago, however, he publicly declared that he no longer believed in UFOs. "I use to believe in Santa Claus, too," he said.

Does all of this mean that NASA is covering up something? And is that something so important that they would dare switch pictures in the Mariner IV series? We can only point to the above facts.

Actually, as we all know, the best way to hide something is to put it right out in the open where it will be overlooked. Perhaps this is NASA's current policy. They have released some amazing photographs of the Moon containing details that NASA's astronomers simply cannot explain. These pictures have been widely published in the national press, along with bewildered captions, but then the newspapermen and the public forgot about them.

However, a few people did pursue the subject. Their conclusion? There is something on the Moon – something no one has been able to explain. Astronomers are currently juggling a whole collection of new theories to answer the mysteries revealed in the photos.

For over 400 years, astronomers have been reporting strange lights on the Moon. Scientists at the Goddard Space Center have admitted that there have been more than 200 sightings of "bright spots" and strange moving lights around the craters of the moon in recent times.

On October 29, 1963, for example, astronomers at the Lowell Observatory in Flagstaff, Arizona, watched a weird group of 31 objects moving about the surface of the Moon in organized geometric formations. Some of these objects were estimated to be three miles wide. About that same time, the Soviet astronomer Nikolai Kozyrev was observing a very bright light in the crater Aristarchus.

What were these things? Today we are told that it was all "volcanic activity." The Moon, it seems, is blessed with walking volcanoes.

A total of 35 space probes have been fired at the Moon since 1958. Fourteen of these, seven American and seven Russian, have been successful. For centuries, man believed that the craters on the Moon were caused by meteor impacts, in spite of the fact that although millions of man-hours have been spent studying the Moon since the invention of the telescope, not one single astronomer has ever reported seeing such an impact.

For centuries, also, scientists have been convinced that the Moon is nothing but a dead hunk of rock trapped in the earth's gravitational field. Now, suddenly, these "facts" are being dumped. Now these same men are telling us that the Moon is actually a planet – a sister planet to the earth – and that it is alive with volcanic activity. Again, millions of photos have been taken of our "sister planet," and not a single one has caught a volcano in the act of blowing its top.

Scientists at the Douglas Aircraft Company who have studied the lunar photos have finally come up with an explanation for the mysterious "domes" that appear all over the Moon and have baffled scientists for years. These domes, they tell us, are volcanic mounds of moon crust, forced up by the pressures of gases underneath.

It's a comfortable theory until you examine a large number of lunar photos and realize how many of these domes there are. The Moon is literally covered with these bubbles, indicating incredible seething beneath its surface. If the Moon really had all of the volcanic activity currently being blamed on it, it must be a molten mass inside, ready to explode.

For these reasons, many astronomers refuse to "buy" the volcano explanations. And why would NASA have bothered to "classify" an early photo showing one of these domes?

Before you get too confused, let's take a look at some of the other lunar photos. On November 22, 1966, NASA released a blow-up or a photo covering a small section of the Moon, measuring only 750 by 550 feet. In this picture, there is a series of long, pointed shadows, such as a church spire might cast when the sun is low in the sky. NASA estimates the largest of these objects, the one in the center, to be 50 feet wide at its base, and from 40 to 75 feet high.

What's so exceptional about this? First of all, such tall slender spires of stone are quite rare, and are found on Earth in areas where there has been centuries of erosion – wind, rain, etc. So far as we know, there are no eroding factors on the Moon. So the first mystery is how these spires were formed.

Obviously, this picture was taken from almost directly overhead. If so, the tall, narrow spires would have reflected very little light, and would have been somewhat darker than the other, flatter features in the picture. But at the base of each shadow, you will see a very bright spot – brighter than any of the other features. How come? No one at NASA can answer that question.

This picture was widely published when it was released. However, most newspapers cropped out the most interesting feature – the small white cross. According to NASA, this cross is a "reference mark used by scientists in photographic measurements." Oddly enough, when the author went through hundreds of photos in the NASA files in Washington, D.C., recently, this was the only picture containing such a cross.

True, some of the lunar photos did have crosses on them, but they were big and black, and sharply angular. Since this particular picture is an enlargement of a section of another photo, the cross must have been almost microscopic originally. When closely examined, this cross appears to be a three-dimensional object rather than a simple "reference mark."

One scientist who examined this picture said that he thought the long shadows were falling the wrong way. That is, all the other formations in the picture were casting their shadows opposite to the pointed spires. What are these things really? They hardly seem volcanic. Are they real or has NASA hired the same photographic technician who pasted Lee Harvey Oswald's head onto a photo of a larger man holding a rifle?

(Oddly, during his string of odd jobs, Oswald worked alongside various people who later worked for NASA. And Fred Crisman, another JFK suspect, was involved in the first major UFO case in 1947, at Maury Island, Washington. Crisman's interest in UFOs has continued up to today.)

On December 14, 1966, newspapers across the country carried another interesting lunar picture. This one showed the broad limb of our "sister planet," and revealed that the terrain was covered with several groups of well-defined craters. But these craters are unlike those that appear in many other Moon photos. These are perfect circles. When carefully studied and measured, they prove to have lips that are all the exact same height from the surface.

Even more intriguing, these circular features are all aligned in neat rows. Some of the rows pass from east to west, and intersect the rows going from north to south. When studied with magnifying glasses and plastic grid sheets, we find that these "silos" are laid out in an intelligent pattern, not in the random, haphazard patterns of nature. In short, these "silos" do resemble our underground ICBM silos, and appear to be deliberate constructions, spread at planned intervals over a large portion of the surface.

Volcanoes and meteors rarely, if ever, form perfect circles. Nor do they produce an organized sequence of features. NASA blithely ignores these "silos" and points out, instead, that the mounds of "domes" that are also in the picture "confirm the fact that the Moon has had a long and complicated history of volcanic activity."

The area covered by this picture is roughly the size of the states of Massachusetts, Connecticut, and Rhode Island combined. This would mean that the "silos" are actually miles apart from each other.

Back in 1952, a UFO researcher named Albert K. Bender suggested that there might be flying saucer bases on the Moon, and that these bases might take the form of "silos," with launching platforms that could be lowered out of sight when not in use. Bender became a legend in the flying saucer field, when, in 1953, he suddenly destroyed his files and discontinued his research, claiming that he had been warned or threatened by "government agents."

Naturally, no one can really say what's up there on the Moon. Future picture-taking satellites will almost certainly come up with new mysteries for us to ponder. Unfortunately, many people do have the uneasy suspicion that if NASA did actually take a photo of a flying saucer base on the Moon, or Mars, or anywhere else, our chances of seeing that picture would be slim to nil.

For some unascertainable reason, the government does seem determined to conceal hard data on unidentified flying objects from the American public, and from the world at large, even though it is spending millions of dollars in space projects and in UFO research.

Of course, in the end, we may find out that Mars does look just like the Moon, and that all of the peculiar features on the Moon were created by natural forces. But that still wouldn't explain the mystery of the unidentified flying objects, or tell us why the worldwide "flap" of UFO sightings began anew on July 14, 1965, the same day that Mariner IV swept over Mars. That "flap" continued unabated through 1966, and is still going on.

Perhaps when our astronauts finally set down on the Moon, they will find some of the answers.

Back in 1957, Dr. V. Davydov, of the USSR's Sternberg Astronomical Institute hinted at what the astronauts might discover. "If visitors from outer space wished to leave some token of their presence," he said, "they would place it not on Earth, but on our Moon, where the destructive action of wind and water is absent."

From the steadily mounting mass of evidence, our astronauts should not be too surprised if they discover that some unknown extraterrestrial "Kilroy" has reached the Moon before them.

CHAPTER 3

AIR FORCE STATISTICS: A PROBLEM OF ACCURACY – *FLYING SAUCERS #64* – JUNE 1969

In 1966, I collected all of the available U.S. Air Force statistical reports on unidentified flying objects, and spent many long hours comparing their figures for various years, rechecking all of their calculations on an adding machine. The results were very intriguing. It was obvious that the Air Force statistics had been wantonly juggled from year to year, and that their total reliability was nil. The tables in the 1966 Project Blue Book report, for example, contained no less than 22 blatant mistakes in basic arithmetic.

Apparently no one in the Air Force can even add. More perplexing, perhaps, is the fact that many UFO researchers have repeatedly published these erroneous figures in their publications, without ever bothering to check the statistics out. These false tables have also been published, over and over again, in newspapers throughout the world, and in other governmental publications dealing with UFOs.

I compiled a most extensive breakdown of these incredible discrepancies, and wrote a 6,000-word analysis, complete with graphs, charts, and tables that fully demonstrated how the Air Force figures have been manipulated. This article has floated from publisher to publisher for two years, and was rejected by everyone from *True*, *Argosy*, and *Saga* to more obscure "scientific" publications. The usual reason for rejection was that the piece was "too technical." Mass magazines were afraid of boring their readers with an article that dealt purely with statistics and mathematics.

However, I do feel that this study is of prime importance to ufologists, and so I will summarize the results here. You can check my findings with your own Blue Book files. I hope you will use this material as "ammunition" in your own lectures, radio and TV appearances, and publications. By emphasizing the total inaccuracy and unreliability of the Air Force calculations, we can diminish the validity of the government's anti-UFO claims.

I am grateful to several independent researchers who provided me with earlier Blue Book releases for this study.

For years, Project Blue Book told us that a mere 79 UFO reports had been received by the Air Force in 1947. Actually, over 500 sightings were published in newspapers from coast to coast during the single *two-week period* of late June and early July 1947. Mr. Ted Bloecher compiled and published 200 of these reports last year.

In Blue Book's 1966 report, the 1947 figure was suddenly changed from 79 to 122. Somehow, apparently, an additional 43 sightings from 1947 had turned up 19 years later. In their 1966 listings, they unaccountably increased the number of sightings for each year (except 1949, 1952, and 1954).

In my *Saga* article of October 1967, I noted that the report of the "Top Secret" CIA Panel on UFOs, issued in 1953, declared that there had been 1,900 sighting reports received in 1952. Blue Book's 1966 report lists only 1,501 sightings for that year. What happened to the other 399?

In their "Special Report #14," issued in 1955, Project Blue Book openly stated: "Official reports on hand at the end of 1954 totaled 4,834." Yet Blue Book's 1960 report offered the following breakdown of totals up to 1954:

1947 – 79

1948 – 143

1949 – 186

1950 – 169

1951 – 121

1952 – 1501

1953 – 425

1954 – 429

3,053 Total

It looks as it a whopping 1,781 UFO cases were misplaced somewhere between 1955 and 1960 (4,834 compared with 3,053). But before you start worrying about those missing files, 297 of them apparently turned up again in 1965-66. Here are the official Air Force statistics for those same years, as published in 1966:

1947 – 122

1948 – 156

1949 – 186

1950 – 210

1951 – 169

1952 – 1501

1953 – 509

1954 – 487

3,340 Total

Blue Book *Special Report #14* stated that a total of 3,201 cases received from 1947 to 1952 were used in their tabulations. But if you added up the 1966 figures for those same years, you will find that they total only 2,344.

Somewhere in the Pentagon, a strong wind blew away 857 clouds of swamp gas between 1955 and 1966. If you add up the 1955-1966 figures and compare them with the earlier figures, you will find that a total of 1,494 sighting reports have been juggled out of existence. And that's only a starter. They've also been adding as well as subtracting.

Blue Book's 1960 report claimed that a total of 6,312 reports were received between 1947-59. But when you check their 1967 figures for that same period, you arrive at a total of 6,578. Somehow, in recent years, another 266 ancient cases have turned up. Another enigmatic 121 cases were added to the years 1953-59 in the 1966 report. In 1960, the Air Force total for those years was 4,113. In 1966, it jumped suddenly to 4,234.

If you do not have a copy of the Blue Book release for 1965-66, you can find an accurate reproduction of these tables in Captain Loftin's book, *Identified Flying Saucers*, pages 233-236. Compare it carefully to the earlier tables as reproduced in the Condon Report. Add up the column of "Total Sightings" – 1947-66 (Loftin, page 233). While the Air Force total is 11,003, the actual total is 10,903. The figure for 1965 is given as 886. Later this was changed to 887 by the Air Force, as per Table 1 in the Condon Report.

In the Air Force's own Blue Book *Special Report #14* (1955), Table A-1 presents a complete breakdown of the sighting reports evaluated in that study. These were from the years 1947 to 1952 exclusively. A total of 2300 reports are represented. Of these, 689 are listed as "unknown." Elsewhere in Report #14 (page viii), it is stated, "Official reports on hand at the end of 1954 totaled 4834. Of these, 425 were produced in 1953 and 429 in 1954… The period January 1, 1955 to May 5, 1955 accounted for 131 unidentified aerial object reports received."

Now compare the above Air Force figures with the figures published in the tables in the Condon Report, and in Loftin's book.

A total of 434 "unknowns" were selected for the Report #14 study. A total of 689 were definitely classified as "unknown." Yet in 1966, we were told that the grand total of "unknowns" for the past 19 years was only 659. Thirty less than the 1952 total!

Are you confused and bewildered? You were meant to be. The simple truth is that the Air Force statistics are not worth the paper they're printed on. The figures are deliberately juggled from year to year. The compilers may have safely felt that no one would bother to add up and compare all of those digits. Traditionally, people only look at the final column in statistics – the totals. Few ever bother to check all the columns.

Someone connected with the Condon Project did bother to check out the Air Force table, it seems. So they deliberately deleted all totals from all columns when they reproduced the 1966 figures on Table 3, page 521 of the Condon Report. These erroneous totals have been widely published.

The very basic validity of the Air Force figures is in doubt. The 1949 Project Grudge Report claimed that a total of 375 UFO sightings were received and studied between 1947 and 1949. This figure was widely published. When we add up the 1960 totals for those years, we get 408. The 1966 total for those same years is 464. Thus, we have three distinct official totals for the same three years – 375, 408, and 464. The figures for "unknown" sightings has also proven to be widely variable over the years – so variable that they cannot be taken seriously.

In previous articles, I have offered my own calculations, based upon extensive field studies of my own, which have led me to conclude that as few as 2% of all UFO witnesses actually bother to report directly to the Air Force. The Condon study substantiates my findings.

This means that the Air Force statistics, even if they were accurate – which they're not – would be dealing with a sampling too small to provide any conclusive data. It also means that we must multiply each claimed Air Force statistic by almost 100 in order to really ascertain the scope of any particular flap. Thus, if the Air Force did receive 536 UFO sightings in July 1952, as claimed, then the actual total number of sightings that month was closer to 50,000!

Considering all of the visible discrepancies in the Air Force statistics, it is highly probable that the Pentagon has been deliberately reducing the figures all along, matching their statistics to the amount of publicity a given flap received. The flap of 1952 was well publicized, so they were forced to submit relatively high figures. Other, lesser-known flaps were ignored; for them, the official Air Force figures were set at absurdly low numbers, like 12 or 15.

The table on page 514 of the Condon Report is purportedly a breakdown of the monthly sightings received by the Air Force from 1950 to 1968. I must point out that 1949's Project Grudge Report terminated official Air Force interest in the subject. Project Blue Book was not established until later in 1951. Therefore, the figures for 1950-51 are automatically suspect.

In 1958, Blue Book claimed that it had received a total of 414 reports for the month of November 1957 alone. Table 1, page 514 of the Condon Report lists only 361 sightings for November 1957. So another 53 cases have vanished from the Air Force files over the years.

We can conclude that the Air Force statistics are a complete sham, and always have been. They do not responsibly reflect the scope of the phenomenon, and any scientific study of the published Air Force data is impossible.

CHAPTER 4

A hunter is splashing alone through a swamp. Suddenly, his dog begins to howl, flips his tail between his legs, and runs off. The brush ahead of the startled hunter stirs, and a great hoary shadow rises up, uttering an unearthly screech. It towers above the man by two or three feet. He is too surprised and too paralyzed with fear to raise his rifle. The thing shuffles off into the blackness of the swamp, only to turn up elsewhere, months later.

This drama has been acted so many times over the years that the basic job of simply cataloging such incidents is almost impossible. The Abominable Swamp Slob (ASS) is not necessarily a special breed of monster, though. In most cases, the descriptions are very similar to our mountaineering Abominable Snowman (ABSM). While the ABSM thrives in forests and high places, the ASS prefers low-level marshes and bayous.

There's hardly a respectable swamp in the Deep South that does not boast at least one ASS. As usual, our local historical experts, the Native Americans, have many legends and stories about the swamp creatures. It would seem that all wet, dark, forbidding places are inhabited by unspeakable monsters of some sort.

Frequently, our swamp slobs blunder unto highways, dripping with water and an ungodly stench, and try to flag down passing motorists. Perhaps one of these slobs served as the original inspiration for the popular horror movie of some years ago, *The Creature from the Black Lagoon*.

At 7:30 p.m. on May 19, 1969, young George Kaiser was walking towards a tractor on his farm, when his dog began to growl and bark. He looked up and saw a grotesque figure standing about 25 feet away. Whatever it was, it was the size of a man, and covered with black fur.

"I watched it for about two minutes before it saw me," young Kaiser told investigator Bonnie Roman:

> It stood in a fairly upright position, although it was bent over in the middle of its back, with arms about the same length as a normal human being. I'd say it was about 5'7" tall. It had a very muscular structure. The head sat directly on the shoulders, and the face was dark black, with hair that stuck out on

the back of its head. It had eyes set close together, and a very short forehead. It was all covered with hair, except for the back of the hands and the face. The hands looked like normal hands, not claws.

George was transfixed with shock and fright for a moment, and then he made a move to get into the family automobile parked nearby. The creature made "a strange grunting sound," turned, jumped over a ditch, and ran down the road at high speed, quickly disappearing out of sight. Footprints were found in the dirt by the ditch. They showed three small toes, plus a big toe. Plaster casts were later made of these prints.

Back in 1931, an "escaped ape" was running around Long Island, only a few minutes from New York City. In June of that year, half a dozen persons at Lewis & Valentine's Nursery near Mineola, Long Island, excitedly reported the sudden appearance and disappearance of a fleet-footed "apelike, hairy creature – about four feet tall."

"Monster mania" struck Long Island. The police received so many alarmed calls that the Nassau County Police Department sent out ape-hunting details armed with shotguns. No circus was in town. A head count was taken of the gorillas in the nearest zoos. Nobody was missing. Still, the hairy little fellow kept pouncing out of bushes, scaring Long Islanders half to death.

On June 29, Captain Earle Comstock organized a dozen heavily armed police patrols. Twenty hardy citizens armed with pitchforks and other weapons joined them. The four-foot-tall hairy thing must have seen the mob coming, as all the monster-busters found were a lot of footprints: "The prints seemed to be solely those of the hind feet and were about the size and shape of a man's hand, though the thumb was set further back than would be the case with a man's hand."

The "ape's" final appearances were in the middle of July. A nurseryman named Stockman reported that his family had seen a "gorilla" thrashing about in the shrubbery near Huntington. Soon afterwards, a farmer three miles away called in to report seeing the thing. Police found tracks at both places and tried to follow them, but lost the trail in the nearby woods. That was supposedly the end of the Long Island "ape."

Or was it? This particular section of Long Island, with Huntington in the north, Mineola in the east, and Babylon in the south, constitutes a very interesting UFO "window." We have spent many days there in the past three years, talking to flying saucer witnesses and collecting some very odd information.

There have been numerous monster sightings in a rather desolate hilly and wooded section south of Huntington since 1966. Necking couples parked in an area known – appropriately enough – as "Mount Misery" claim to have been terrified by a giant seven-foot, human-shaped something. It turns up periodically in a place where many low-flying, glowing, saucer-shaped and cigar-shaped objects have been seen.

The leading expert in Mount Misery is a young lady named Jaye P. Paro. Miss Paro is a reporter and radio broadcaster, and has been studying the history of the area for years. She has made efficient and responsible investigations into many of the UFO and creature sightings. In January 1969, she succeeded in photographing a very unusual being in the secluded woods on the top of the Mount. Fortunately she had a witness with her, Richard Demartino, and he signed the following statement:

> At 8 a.m. on Sunday, January 12, 1969, I drove with Jaye P. Paro and Barbara LaMonica of Huntington, New York, to the area of Mount Misery for the purpose of taking photographs of the landscape. We pulled our car into a partial clearing on the left side of Mount Misery Road, then decided to photograph an area that was located about five hundred feet from our car.
>
> Jaye was ready to take her first shot when, through the corner of my eye, I caught a glimpse of a moving black object. Knowing we were completely alone in this desolate area, we were very scared. Immediately, Jaye turned and snapped the first two pictures. The three of us were horrified to see the figure of something that resembled a human, with a disfigured face, long, wild black hair, and dressed in a long black garment.
>
> It retreated immediately further into the bushes. It made no sounds, and made no attempt to communicate with us. Frozen in her tracks, Jaye dropped her camera. I picked it up and shot the two remaining pictures. Barbara started to run to the car. Jaye and I followed and we took off in a cloud of dust.

What was it? A practical joker lying in wait on a bitterly cold Sunday at 8 a.m.? Not very likely. A hermit? There are no rumors of a hermit living around Mount Misery. The photo depicts a dark blob with a very bushy head of hair extending a pale, long-fingered hand.

To demonstrate our theory that these events tend to recur in the same "window" areas year after year, and even century after century, we will present a catalog of monster sightings summarizing many of the major and minor incidents of the past few years. We have organized this material by states, to give you some idea of the geographical dispersion of these reports. We have not tampered with these stories in any way. We present the facts as originally reported.

We have, of course, greatly condensed each item. Some of these reports cover many pages. Some have included photographs, plaster casts, and lengthy tape recordings of the witnesses. Others are based upon lengthy newspaper stories written and published by competent local reporters.

We have not, for example, attempted to present even a fraction of the California "Bigfoot" sightings, and we have weeded out the hundreds of sightings involving only the discovery of inexplicable giant footprints. We have also omitted, or tried to omit, the many unconfirmed or "hearsay" reports that flood our mail, but a few have been included and properly identified as such. As any statistician will tell you, a sampling must be random if any valid conclusions are to be reached.

Alabama

A "Booger," as the locals called it, created quite a stir around Clanton, Alabama, in the fall of 1960. Several witnesses reported seeing a tall, hairy creature around Walnut Creek. A posse was formed, and they found footprints that resembled those of "a giant ape." Shortly after the posse quit the chase, the Reverend E.C. Hand saw the monster near Liberty Hill, grabbed his shotgun, and pursued it. But it got away.

"I can make my dogs catch a mule, Reverend Hand said, "But I could not get them to venture out toward the 'Booger'."

As time passed, there were more reports. Some witnesses claimed the animal made a sound "like a woman screaming." Others said it sounded more like an elephant. It also prowled peach orchards, apparently sampling peaches. A cement cast was made of the track, about the size of a person's foot, but looking more like a hand. The cast is still somewhere in Clanton.

California

"It ran upright like a man, swingin' long, hairy arms," said Ray Kerr of McKinleyville, California, as he described his sighting of 'Bigfoot' on Sunday, October 12, 1958. He was near Bluff Creek when he saw it. "It happened so fast, it's kind of hard to give a really close description. But it was covered with hair. It had no clothes. It looked eight to ten feet tall to me."

Roy Wallace said he had seen a similar creature a short time earlier. It was hairy, walked stooped over, had long dangling arms, and was "four feet across the shoulders."

The mutilated bodies of four dogs were found in the area by Curtis Mitchell, a Native American, on the evening of Kerr's sighting. "They looked as if they had been ripped apart," he said. "One of them had apparently been slammed against a tree." The bodies were still warm when they were discovered off the Elk River Road, about five miles south of Eureka, California.

Charles Wetzel was driving home in Riverside, California, on Saturday night, November 8, 1958, and as he neared the point where North Main Street crosses the Santa Ana River, something leaped in front of his car.

"It had a round, scarecrowish head," he said, "like something out of Halloween. It wasn't human. It had a longer arm than anything I'd ever seen. When it saw me in the car it reached all the way back to the windshield and began clawing at me. It didn't have any ears. The face was all round. The eyes were shining like something fluorescent, and it had a protuberant mouth. It was scaly, like leaves."

Wetzel reached for the .22 pistol that he carried in the car, and stomped on the gas. "The thing fell back from the car and it gurgled. The noise it made didn't sound human. I think I hit it. I heard something hit the pan under the car."

There were long sweeping scratches on his windshield, but nothing was found at the site. The next night, a six-foot-tall black thing leaped out of the bushes near the Wetzel site and frightened another motorist. The Wetzel story was widely circulated by the wire services and has become a monster "classic."

Late in July 1966, two frightened teenaged girls reported they had been in a car near Lytle Creek outside of Fontana, California, when a "bush beast" suddenly stood up beside their vehicle. They described it as being seven feet tall, with brown hair and covered with moss and slime.

Their report kicked off a monster epidemic, and over 250 people, most of them armed to the teeth, poured into the area on a massive monster hunt. The Bernardino County sheriff's office said that amateur "bush beast" hunters were swarming nightly over the barren foothills, filling the night with wild gunfire. The slime-covered creature got away.

Florida

In 1963, several persons on a ranch outside of Holopaw, Florida, said they had seen an apelike creature running across a field. A "prominent cattleman and citrus grower" claimed he was in a group that been within a few feet of the creature, and that "it was definitely an ape of some kind."

In 1966-67, the Holopaw "ape" was back. Eugene Crosby said it was five feet tall, hairy, very broad, and walked on two feet. It threw a tire tube at him. Other stories described how a six-foot-tall "ape" attacked two hunters on the Desert Ranch. Later, an unoccupied tent house on the ranch was broken into, furnishings were broken and scattered, and bloodstains were found.

A harsh, coughing sound made Ralph "Bud" Chambers of Elfers, Florida look around as he was walking in some woods near the Anclote River in the summer of 1966. He saw a giant hairy thing standing in the trees. "The thing had a rancid, putrid odor like stale urine," Chambers said.

He hurried away and brought back a friend. They followed the creature's tracks into a swampy area. Chambers' dogs refused to follow the scent. They whined and could not be coaxed into going near the creature's trail. Later, Chambers had another sighting. He said the thing was over seven feet tall, and "at least four feet wide" at the chest.

There were several hairy monster reports around Brooksville in 1966-67. In May 1967, Joan Whritenour was invited to a ranch near New Port Richey, where strange three-toed tracks had been found. The county sheriff revealed that cattle were disappearing. No truck tracks or other evidence had been found to lead to the rustlers. "Just where does a rustler put a full-grown cow?" A sheriff's deputy asked Mrs. Whritenour. "Sure as hell not in his back pocket!"

Kentucky

Trimble County, Kentucky, was plagued with "monster mania" in June 1962. A farmer named Owen Pike said he saw the thing when it attacked and mauled his dogs, one a Collie, the other a German shepherd. He described it as black, six feet tall, with hanging arms that reached to its knees. One June 8, Silas McKinney claimed the creature killed one of his calves. The calf's carcass was found fifteen feet outside of its enclosure, yet the gate was still shut.

Claw marks were found around the barn, and traces of black hair were also discovered. Examination of the calf indicated it had been killed by a blow on the head. Other animals in the area disappeared or were found mutilated.

Sheriff Curtis Clem took the matter very seriously. Seven police dogs, a helicopter, and a posse scoured the area. Large footprints were found, like those of a giant dog. But various eyewitnesses attested that it was a large ape or gorilla with reddish hair.

Michigan

Beginning around 1962, folks living in the vicinity of Sister Lakes, Michigan, started seeing something nine feet tall that made a whimpering sound. Then, in May 1964, "monster mania" hit the region full force. A man named Gordon Brown told how he and his brother had seen the creature one night and followed its tracks. "We came to a tree," Brown said, "but knew there hadn't been a tree there before. So, we hightailed it right out of there."

Three teen-aged girls met the creature in broad daylight while walking along a side road in Silver Creek Township. Joyce Smith fainted on the spot. Patsy and Gail Clayton stood motionless, paralyzed with fear, as the thing charged off into the underbrush.

"It didn't look like a man," Joyce said. Patsy described it as being about seven feet tall with "a black face."

John Ultrup told the Cass County sheriff that he had seen the monster several times. One night, as he was driving into his yard, he saw it standing behind a bush. "It had big, bright shining eyes," he said. Mrs. Ultrup told of how one of her shepherd dogs chased the monster one night and came back with the pupil of one eye turned a pale blue color. Weeks later, the eye returned to normal.

Many other witnesses came forward and were named in the extensive newspaper accounts. Hundreds of people flocked to Sister Lakes and the usual futile monster hunt took place. Local drive-ins did a big business selling "monster burgers," and station WSJM sponsored a program of new monster reports and special "monster music."

In August 1965, the monster returned to Michigan, this time to the placid little community of Monroe, due east of Sister Lakes in Cass County. Sixteen people reportedly encounter the monster in June and July 1965. Things really got serious when two attacks occurred in a single week. One Wednesday, August 11, David Thomas was driving a group of women home from a neighborhood baby shower when the thing jumped in front of their car.

Thinking that it was a neighborhood prankster, Thomas got out of the car to take a swing at it. When he discovered that it towered above his six-foot frame, he prudently decided to return to the car.

It struck him in the back, he said, throwing him against the auto. He leaped back into it and drove of as the hairy arms thumped on the roof and fenders. Other people in the immediate area saw the creature that same night. Keith Mercure said he fired his shotgun at it. Some witnesses described it as "smelling moldy." Most agreed that it was at least seven feet tall, hairy, and had very long arms. It "grunted and growled like a mad dog."

Mississippi

Two truckers, William and James Cagle, were headed for Marietta, Georgia, on Tuesday night, November 8, 1966. As they rounded a curve near Winona, Mississippi, a strange creature ran down a slope towards their vehicle.

"When my headlights picked him up, he was on our left side," James Cagle explained. "He was aggressive, angry, and ready to attack. The face looked like a mixture of a gorilla and a human. The arms and legs were very large. The chest was at least three feet thick. His eyes glowed in the dark, and did not seem to have pupils. It looked us over, and then slowly raised an arm like the Indians do when they greet someone. I had seen all that I wanted. I floor-boarded the accelerator."

Montana

Harold E. Nelson pulled his camper off the highway to settle down for the night outside of Billings, Montana on Wednesday, September 11, 1968. As he was gulping down a can of beans, he heard a noise outside the camper, so he picked up a flashlight to take a look. When he opened the door, he found a huge thing staring straight at him.

"It had an apelike face, but it was definitely not a gorilla," Nelson said later. "The head was slightly pointed, sloping down like the sketches of cavemen. The whole body was covered with reddish-brown hair. There were a few spots of white hair along the edge of the enormous shoulders. It stood erect, like a man, and must have weighed six hundred to eight hundred pounds. He was big – real big."

After a long moment of total immobility, Nelson scrambled back into his camper to find his gun. The creature peered in the door curiously, and then turned and shuffled off into the darkness.

New Jersey

Towards dusk on the evening of May 21, 1966, Raymond Todd and three friends were parked in an automobile in the Morristown National Historical Park, Morristown, New Jersey, when they saw a very tall ("at least seven feet tall") entity ambling across the lawn. They described it as being faceless, covered with long black hair, and with scaly skin. What impressed them most was the breadth of the creature. It had huge shoulders, they said, and walked erect with a stiff, rocking movement. They were absolutely certain that it was not a bear or other known creature.

The quartet became hysterical and drove to the entrance of the park, where they stopped cars and warned people that there was a "monster" on the loose. Todd stopped a car driven by a young lady and had her rush him to the Morristown Municipal Hall, where he reported the encounter to the police. The police said that his fear and hysteria were genuine.

Oregon

In the fall of 1957, Gary Joanis and Jim Newall reportedly saw a giant, humanlike figure while hunting near Wanoga Butte, Oregon. Mr. Joanis had just shot a deer, and the tall being came out of the bushes suddenly, picked the dead animal up with one arm, and walked off quickly with tremendous strides. The creature was "not less than nine feet tall," with very long hair on its arms. It made a noise like "a very strange whistling scream."

Two boys from Roseburg, Oregon, told state police that they had seen a fourteen-foot-tall manlike creature in a nearby wood on Wednesday, July 29, 1959. They said it was covered with hair, walked upright, and had human characteristics. They saw it first on the previous Friday, but did not tell their parents because "we didn't think anyone would believe us." They returned to the spot again, armed with a rifle. The monster reappeared, and one of the boys fired five shots at it from a range of about fifty yards.

"It ran off screaming like a cat, but louder," he said. Police found humanlike tracks, 14 inches long, showing five toes. The boys were certain it was not a bear.

Pennsylvania

A six-foot-tall "person or thing" was seen by seven persons on the shore of Edinboro Lake, Pennsylvania, Wednesday night, August 17, 1966. "The witnesses fired at the figure on two occasions with weapons they had taken along. Apparently the creature was not hit," said *The Erie Times* (August 19, 1966).

A heavy UFO "flap" was taking place in the area at the time. Another tall, unidentified creature had been seen on Presque Isle, on July 31, some eighteen miles from Edinboro. One report claimed that a man had come face to face with the Edinboro monster near the lake, and had been so badly frightened that he was unable to speak for three days.

Tennessee

Brenda Ann Adkins reported meeting a hairy creature on Monteagle Mountain, north of Chattanooga, Tennessee, in the spring of 1968. She had stopped near the edge of a cliff to take some pictures, when she became aware of a nauseating odor and heard a noise in the woods behind her. Turning, she saw the thing lumbering towards her.

"I was absolutely frozen with fear," she said. "This thing was at least seven feet tall and must have weighed several hundred pounds. I'll never forget his enormous chest and those huge arms and legs. His body was completely covered with blackish-red hair. The face was a mixture of ape and human. I will have nightmares about that afternoon.

He seemed to be angry and was growling. I thought he would push me off the cliff or something. Then, he stopped about six feet from where I stood, cocked his head in a quizzical way, and just stared at me. He studied me for a few moments, then seemed to smile, made a little blubbering noise, and walked back into the brush."

Washington

At 4 a.m. on Wednesday, March 5, 1969, Don Cox drove around a bend on Highway 14, near Beacon Rock State Park in Skamania County, Washington, when a monstrous creature appeared on the road in front of his headlights. It was, he said, eight to ten feet tall, with a "face like an ape."

"It ran like a man and was covered with fuzzy fur," Cox stated. "I had just come out of a fog bank that had caused me to slow my car, when I first saw what I thought to be a tree leaning toward the middle of the road. I slowed my car further, and turned my headlights to high beam. It was then that I saw this fur-covered human form with the face of an ape. He ran across the road in front of the car, leaped up a forty degree slope, and disappeared into the woods."

Deputy John Mason investigated, and found smears that indicated the creature had made an eight-foot jump up the embankment – a feat beyond the capabilities of any bear.

In April 1969, the Skamania County Board of Commissioners passed an ordinance making it illegal to kill a Sasquatch, providing a ten-thousand-dollar fine and up to five years imprisonment.

At 2:30 a.m., Sunday, July 27, 1969, Deputy Floyd Sund was driving along a deserted wooded road north of Hoquiam, Washington, when he had to slam on his brakes to avoid colliding with an animal standing directly in front of him. He got out of his car and pointed his spotlight at the animal. It was, he said, eight feet tall, with a humanlike face, but was covered with hair (except for the feet and the hands). He estimated that it must have weighed about three hundred pounds. Somewhat dismayed, he drew his pistol, but the animal ran off into the woods.

Police searched the area for footprints the next morning, but it was "too gravelly." Sheriff Pat Gallagher said he thought it could have been a bear. Deputy Sund grumbled, "It sure didn't look like one."

West Virginia

In the summer of 1960, a group of young men were camping in the woods near Davis, West Virginia. One night, one of them was cutting wood for the fire, when he heard a noise and felt someone poking him in the ribs. He thought one of his friends was trying to scare him. He turned around, annoyed, only to find himself confronted with a "horrible monster."

He described it: "It had two high eyes that shone like big balls of fire. It stood every bit of eight feet tall, and had shaggy, long hair all over its body. It just stood and stared at us."

By the time the boys had recovered from their shock, the creature had shuffled off into the darkness. They broke camp early the next morning. Gigantic footprints were found where the creature had been, but the witnesses didn't feel like following them.

Wisconsin

A large, powerfully built "man," covered with hair, was seen by three men in the Deltox Marsh on October 17, 1968. The same men, together with nine others, encountered it again on November 30. On the first occasion, they tried to follow it, but it eluded them in the thick underbrush. On November 30, the 12 men were combing the swamp looking for it. They found it, but didn't shoot because "it was too manlike." Again, it got away.

A number of interesting comparisons can be drawn from the foregoing. Viewed cumulatively, these random sightings reveal several hitherto hidden aspects. We can now categorize these events and speculate that there are two main groups.

Group 1 consists of real animals possessing common characteristics of appearance and behavior. Group 2 are "monsters" in the true sense of the word, and seem to be part of a paranormal phenomenon, like ghosts and flying saucers. That is, they are a problem for parapsychologists rather than biologists.

Witnesses to "monsters" very rarely report to the local newspapers or police. In our travels around the country, we have uncovered many spectacular cases that had never received any publicity of any kind. Often, when the witness tells his family and friends about the incident, he is so heavily ridiculed that he shuts up. In most cases, the man or woman who does report to the police or newspaper is not taken seriously.

We have to keep repeating this vital question: If you encountered a ten-foot-tall creature covered with moss and slime, with two huge, luminous red eyes, who would *you* tell? And do you think anyone would take you seriously?

These events are being taken more seriously now by larger numbers of people. Our channels for communicating these experiences have improved greatly. The handful of well-equipped researchers involved today have more and better data to work from, and we are finally getting very close to a "solution."

CHAPTER 5

MYSTERY AEROPLANES OF THE 1930s – *FLYING SAUCER REVIEW* –
MAY/JUNE 1970

Throughout the 1930s, thousands of people in the isolated villages of
northern Scandinavia saw, and were puzzled by, the repeated appearances of large gray aeroplanes, which bore no markings or insignia. These
aeroplanes became the object of massive searches by land, sea, and air,
grimly launched by the military authorities of Norway, Sweden, and
Finland. The Scandinavian Press commented on these events at great
length and the mystery even attracted the attention of *The New York
Times*.

Recently, Mr. Ake Franzen, a researcher in Stockholm, Sweden, Mr.
B. Hogman of Gothenburg, Sweden, and others, sifted through the
newspapers of the period and located over 100 reports on the "ghostfliers"
– as the mystery planes were then known. Lucius Farish and his team
of researchers located other reports in the American press for the same
period. We have collected together all of these reports, indexed them,
charted the courses of the sightings on detailed maps, and attempted to
analyze the behavior of the objects.

Additional research has been conducted into the aviation lore of the
period, and the various historical elements have now been assembled. It
has been impossible, of course, to cover all the material in this article, but
the data is on file. As usual, it can be viewed by serious researchers interested in this particular phase of the UFO mystery.

Mystery aeroplanes are an important, but grossly neglected, aspect of
the overall phenomenon. After we published an article on the subject in
a popular magazine, we were inundated with new, valid reports, many
of which were identical in description and behavior to those reported in
the early Scandinavian wave. Both *Flying Saucer Review* and APRO have
independently published mystery aeroplane reports in the recent past.

Before we attempt to outline some of the more interesting Scandinavian
reports, we must review a few of the reports that came from elsewhere
during that period. On the surface, these reports seem easily explainable
and irrelevant to the flying saucer mystery, but in actuality, these mysterious aeroplanes were able to out-perform any known aircraft of the
period, and could fly in inclement weather – even blinding snowstorms.
The patterns of their flights defied military analysis.

Although there were sporadic ghostflier reports in 1932-33, the subject did not create interest until Christmas week of 1933. Other great waves, such as the flap in the northeastern United States in 1909, have occurred during Christmas week. Many ufologists have already commented on the fact that innumerable important UFO events have tended to occur on the 24th of the month.

The 24th day of March, April, June, September, November, and December apparently play an important part in the UFO time cycle. Thorough researchers will find that so-called occult events follow this same pattern.

The "airship" wave of November 1896 was centered around November 24th, the week of the Thanksgiving holiday that year. But, of course, UFO events can and do occur at other times. A massive study of thousands of sightings of all types would be necessary before any true significance of this particular factor could be established. Unfortunately, practical studies of this kind have not been attempted by anyone other than the U.S. Air Force.

We attempted superficial examination of these factors in recent *Flying Saucer Review* articles, and noted that a high percentage of Type I sightings in 1966 seemed to take place on Wednesdays. In our study of the 1934 ghostflier reports we find that the majority of the known *landings* occurred on Wednesdays. However, the Scandinavian press referred to them as "Sunday fliers," because the majority of the *sightings* took place on Sundays.

Overflights of high altitude LITS (lights in the sky) are separate and distinct from low-level Type I sightings, and could represent an entirely different aspect of the phenomenon. "Hard" sightings of seemingly solid machines may, in many cases, be only tenuously related to the more numerous "soft" sightings of "diamond" lights.

During 1934, the "hard" sightings took the form of aeroplanes accompanied by engine noises, but reports of "soft" and LITS types outnumbered the "hard."

"Decoy" sightings have been widely prevalent in the U.S., particularly in areas where auto pursuits and animal mutilations have been common. It is probable, therefore, that "hard" objects – whether they be aeroplanes or discs – are less important to our understanding of the overall phenomenon than we have led ourselves to believe.

The cunning use of decoys and "hard" landings has been a mere diversion. These events have seemed to follow patterns of psychological warfare. Some of these patterns become self-evident in the 1934 material.

The operations of these mystery aeroplanes have been too blatant to be meaningful. In December 1969, the citizens of St. Louis, Missouri were upset because a mysterious aeroplane, gray and void of markings or lights, twice flew under the recently erected Gateway Arch in that city (Associated Press dispatch, December 22, 1969). The mystery plane first performed this hair-raising maneuver on Friday, December 12. It returned on Wednesday, December 17, to repeat the performance.

One of our earliest mystery aeroplanes chose to indulge in night-flying directly over New York City, in 1910. Like similar craft of later years, it performed hazardous maneuvers, at treetop level, over crowded Madison Square Park. According to *The New York Tribune* of August 31, 1910, "It was heard before it was seen. The whirring sound of a motor, high in the air, caused many necks to be craned toward the Metropolitan Tower at 8:45 p.m., when a long black object was seen flying through the air toward the tower. The vague bulk, as it came into nearer view, took on the semblance of a biplane. It swung past the tower, then turned and described one graceful circle after another, around the illuminated structure, its outlines standing out clear in the lights from the many windows."

The *Tribune* went on to describe how the object executed a "series of swooping circles, and dipped down so that it seemed to brush the tops of the trees."

The next night, Wednesday, the aeroplane returned to the very same park at 9.00 p.m., and repeated the maneuvers. In a lengthy story on September 1, 1910, the *Tribune* discussed the whereabouts of all the known pilots and planes in the vicinity, and concluded that none of them were the culprit.

Indeed, the primitive open biplanes of that day could hardly risk fighting the dangerous updraughts around Manhattan's towers. Few pilots were willing to attempt night-flying at all. "Persons who saw the mystery last night differ as to the number of lights it carried," the *Tribune* reported. "Some say it carried two red lights, others lean to the three green theory."

Apparently the phantom flier of Manhattan was never identified, despite the *Tribune's* wishful statement: "If he comes again tonight, the aviator may drop his name to Earth in an otherwise empty bottle."

Three weeks later, on Wednesday, September 21, 1910, "a fleet of balloons" passed over New York City in broad daylight. The *Tribune* noted (Sept. 22, 1910):

> Some persons said they must be at least five thousand feet

in the air, and a few thought they could discern two or three passengers in each. Others said they were just toy balloons used as advertisements. These latter proved to be right as to size, but if the balloons were used for advertising purposes, there was nothing in their appearance to show it.

The last of the balloons passed over the lower city about 5 o'clock, floating in the direction of Long Island. While the spectacle lasted, the police had their hands full in keeping the streets and sidewalks clear.

The next evening, Dr. Dennis Ready, an engineer at the Dunkirk Waterworks, reported to the police that he had seen "a large, cigar-shaped balloon hovering over the lake, about two miles from shore. The balloon appeared to be unmanageable. It gradually disappeared, and he believes it dropped into the lake." A fishing tug was sent out to search for it.

The story appeared in *The New York Tribune* on September 23, 1910. Dunkirk, New York is on the shores of Lake Erie, approximately 500 miles northwest of New York City. It is about 25 miles west of Sinclairville, New York and Cherry Creek, New York, sites of UFO landings and low-level activity in 1965-66. It is a very active "window" area.

THE SNOW PHANTOMS

On Tuesday, August 24, 1909, "an unknown controllable airship" caused great excitement in the Estonian city of Tallinn (Reval) as it circled twice before disappearing in the direction of Finland. A report published in *Dagens-Nyheter* of August 25, 1909 stated that "the population is frightened and is urging that the formation of a defensive air fleet." Newspapers speculated that the object was "probably Swedish," even though no such craft existed in Sweden at the time.

Exactly one month later, on Friday, September 24, 1909, a winged object passed over the Castle Forest near Gothenburg, Sweden at an altitude of about 100 meters. Earlier in the day, a "dirigible" of the "Percival type" flew low over the eastern part of Grason and Osthammar. It came from the northeast, and disappeared in a westerly direction.

We have a number of mystery aeroplane and unidentified dirigible reports from northern Europe throughout the 1920s and 1930s. We also have a few interesting subsidiary mysteries to research and contemplate. On Friday, December 21, 1923, the French dirigible *Dixmude* vanished forever somewhere over the Mediterranean or the Sahara desert. Extensive searches failed to locate any debris, or any sign of the 52 passengers.

One of the first ghostflier reports to appear in Stockholm's *Dagens-Nyheter* in 1933 came from Kalix, on December 24, 1933. It started simply: "A mysterious aeroplane appeared from the direction of the Bottensea at about 6.00 p.m. on Christmas Eve, passed over Kalix, and continued westward. Beams of light came from the machine, searching the area."

These "beams of light" became a familiar feature in the 1934 reports, just as they are common in modern UFO descriptions. The beams were often described as "blinding." They illuminated the ground over which they passed "like daylight." Such searchlights were also reported in the flaps of 1896-97, and 1909.

Arc lights had come into use in the 19th century, but these required heavy, powerful energy sources. Any flying craft using an arc light would have necessarily been overloaded with batteries or a large generator. We tend to forget now just how primitive the flying machines of the 1920s and 1930s were.

Night flying was still rare and daring in 1934. Conventional aeroplanes were equipped with landing lights very similar to automobile headlights. These would not have been bright enough to provide a satisfactory explanation for the brilliant UFO lights. Customarily, landing lights are not kept on while the plane is aloft.

Instrumental and navigational aids were also crude in 1934. Only a few hardy pilots dared to venture into even a mild rainstorm in those days. Most of the planes then in use were clumsy biplanes, with open cockpits. They were short-ranged and quite inefficient machines. Airborne radios were not widely employed, being heavy, expensive, and cumbersome to handle by a single pilot in a small plane.

Nevertheless, the ghostfliers were equipped with radios, and their broadcasts were intercepted throughout Scandinavia. Some of the planes described by the witnesses were obviously larger than any known aircraft of the period, with the exception of the China Clipper, which was then in the early stages of development.

Unlike conventional pilots, the ghostfliers were seemingly fond of operating in impossibly difficult weather. One even circled over New York City during a heavy snowstorm on Tuesday, December 26, 1933. *The New York Times* devoted nearly a full column to the story on December 27, naming witnesses and giving the full details.

The plane was first heard circling above Park Avenue and 122nd St. at

9.30 a.m. Numerous witnesses began to call the National Broadcasting Company. Reports continued until 2.25 p.m., meaning that the mystery plane had circled low over Manhattan in a blinding snowstorm for five full hours – an amazing endurance feat, if nothing else.

"All airports were notified," the *Times* said, "and at Newark Airport, the radio operators from the Department of Commerce and airlines joined in offering what help they could. Beacons on the field were lighted, and searchlights flashed through the white smother of snow. All airfields in the Metropolitan district reported there had been no flying during the day, and no stray plane had dropped down from the snowy skies."

There were other puzzling incidents of this type. Researcher Charles Flood found the following item in *The Portland Oregonian*, February 15, 1936:

> Mystery Plane Battles Snow – Cody, Wyoming, Feb. 14 (AP). An unidentified airplane tonight battled a raging blizzard and 20-below weather over Cody, as residents here attempted to guide it to the local airport, about three miles from town. The ship was heard roaring over the city at about 6 p.m. (Mountain Standard Time). After it circled several times, the sound of its motors faded, and it was not heard again for almost an hour.
>
> At approximately 7 p.m., it was heard over the town again, the pilot accelerating his motor as he circled for several minutes. Residents of the city fought their way through heavy snows to the airport, and circled the field with flares. Before the flares could be lit, however, the sound of the unknown plane's motor had again faded.

Two days later, the *Oregonian* carried a follow-up report: "Cody residents today still had no explanation for, and no further information on, a mysterious aeroplane heard circling over the town last Friday night."

Approximately 35% of all the known sightings of the 1934 Scandinavian wave took place during severe weather conditions. Heavy snowstorms, blizzards, and dense fog were mentioned in many of the accounts. The aircraft even operated at very low level during snowstorms, hedgehopping with great skill and circling low over villages, ships, and railway stations in hazardous mountain regions remarkably similar to the rugged terrain around Cody, Wyoming.

The ghostfliers' abilities to operate in the most appalling weather remains one of the more puzzling aspects of this flap. One witness, a lighthouse-keeper named Rutkvist, claimed that he observed a mystery aeroplane during a blizzard that included winds measuring 16 meters per second. From his lighthouse at Holmogadd, Sweden, he saw the object on at least two occasions.

On Monday, January 8, 1934, he reported watching it maneuver over the nearby island of Grasundet. He said that it would hover and then slowly spiral down toward the island. When it neared the water, it would ascend again, and repeat the maneuver. It continued to do this for an hour. "I have never seen anything like it," he said in a story published in the Stockholm press on January 9. "It was a very strange action for an aeroplane."

Very strange, indeed! The governments of Sweden, Norway, and Finland took the ghostflier reports very seriously, and launched massive investigations.

In a widely published story datelined Oslo, Norway, March 10, 1934, General Henriek Johannessen of the Norwegian Air Force was quoted as saying, "Reports still trickle into the newspapers. We can't reject all of these observations as illusions."

Other officials and aviation experts were interviewed by the press, and unanimously expressed the opinion that the ghostfliers were far more expert than any pilots in northern Europe, that they were superbly equipped with advanced radio and navigational equipment, and seemed to represent "an extraordinary organization." Authorities were particularly disturbed over the mystery planes' penchant for flying over forts and "strategic areas."

On April 30, 1934, Major General Reutersward, commanding general of upper Norrland, made this statement to the press:

> Comparisons of these reports show that there can no doubt about illegal air traffic over our secret military areas. There are many reports from reliable people that describe close observations of the enigmatic flier. And in every case, the same remark can be noted: no insignia or identifying marks were visible on the machines…

> It is impossible to explain away the whole thing as mere imagination. The question is: Who or whom are they, and why have they been invading our air territory?

The first flight over the North Pole was made on May 8-9, 1926, by the then Lt. Commander Richard E. Byrd, and aviation pioneer Floyd Bennett. They took off from Kings Bay, Spitsbergen, and made the Arctic circuit in 15 ½ hours, in a Fokker trimotor. The flight made headlines worldwide, and photographs of the plane were widely published throughout Scandinavia.

Two years later, Sir Hubert Wilkins and Carl Ben Eielson made the first trans-arctic flight when they flew from Point Barrow, Alaska to Spitsbergen. That same month (April 1928), Captain Hermann Koel and Captain James Fitzmaurice attempted to fly from Dublin to New York City, but they crashed on Greely Island, Labrador, and were rescued.

The flight of Byrd and Bennett in 1926 inspired one of the most persistent myths in ufology, for a radio operator claimed to have received a message from the expedition describing a forested land beyond the pole, populated by large animals. This purported message has become a key piece of "evidence" for the popular theory that the earth is shaped like a doughnut, with a big hole at the North Pole.

Actually, anomalous "intelligent" radio signals have always been with us, and some of them have created outrageous hoaxes. In 1899, Nikola Tesla claimed to have received such signals with his apparatus in Colorado, at a time when *there were known radio stations in existence*. Marconi commented on the mysterious signals his company received during and after World War I. Such signals became common in the 1920s, and their source remained inexplicable.

In the early 1960s, Frank Edwards published the sensational details of an anomalous broadcast received at various amateur receiving stations equipped to monitor Soviet space shots. These broadcasts lasted for several days, and were supposedly from orbiting, manned satellites – at a time when the Soviet Union was simply not prepared to make such flights.

The U.S. manned space program has been plagued with these inexplicable signals. The manned lunar flights of 1969 featured several incredible inter-ruptions, with strange voices and sounds being received by the Houston Space Center, which definitely came from outer space – not from the American spacecraft.

During the search for the lost submarine *Scorpion* in 1968, radio signals were received and triangulated by the Navy, coming from a spot far from where the *Scorpion* had actually gone down. The signals employed the very low frequencies (VLF) reserved for nuclear submarines, and utilized top-secret naval codes. Rescue planes and ships rushed to the spot immediately, and found nothing.

Our unidentified radio hoaxers seem to have superb and expensive equipment of a rare type. It is highly probable that the Byrd broadcast of 1926 was really their handiwork. During the 1934 "ghostflier" wave, anomalous radio signals were received throughout northern Europe, and added greatly to the consternation created by that wave.

Diversionary tactics form a fundamental pattern in the UFO mystery. Evidence of a false and misleading nature is frequently sown in the path of the objects. Elaborate diversionary events are often staged to support various frames of reference, and to obscure the real activities and purposes of the UFOs. Since 1896, this pattern of "psychological warfare" has become apparent in every major flap. Direct contact was (and is being) established with random witnesses, to circulate new rumors and nonsense, and to lend weight to the popular theories.

I suspect that while an aerial phenomenon definitely exists, it consists mostly of camouflage and deception, and has falsely represented itself to us.

Perhaps the plan is a very long-range. Contrivances such as the 1926 Byrd broadcast can, forty years later, become "evidence" for the hollow earth believers. Acknowledged hoaxes of one year become "fact" in later years. Contactees have been told (by "them") of flying saucer crashes. These stories have been picked up and repeated until they became a "fact" to many ufologists.

The best example of this might be Frank Scully's *Behind the Flying Saucers*, in which he repeated contactee hearsay. Today, many UFO researchers still write to the Air Force and ask about Scully's "little men," supposedly pickled in bottles at the Pentagon. In his books in the 1950s, Donald E. Keyhoe, it seems, also escalated hearsay and secondhand information to the regal status of "fact."

The island of Spitsbergen, 400 miles north of the Norwegian mainland, is the site of another persistent UFO legend. In the early 1950s, a European tabloid, noted for its devotion to fictitious scandals, published a phony story about a flying saucer crash on Spitsbergen. The article named non-existent Scandinavian scientists and military officials, and went into graphic detail about the construction of the object, including such bits of intelligence as a description of a power plant that was "surrounded by a nucleus of plutonium."

A translation of the story was published in *Fate* magazine in 1954. Frank

Edwards picked it up from there, and turned this piece of fiction into a "fact" in his book, *Flying Saucers – Serious Business*. In 1966, I visited the Swedish Consulate and ran a check through the available reference books. We were unable to locate any of the names mentioned in the article. Meanwhile, Brad Steiger asked his Scandinavian researchers to try to track the story down. They came up with a blank.

More recently, a Finnish movie producer, Mr. V. Itkonen, launched a search of his own. He discovered that the newspaper generally credited with the origin of the story had not even existed at the time. We can state categorically that the celebrated "Spitsbergen flying saucer crash" was nothing more than a cheap journalistic hoax.

As near as we can reconstruct it, a writer on vacation may have heard tales of a wartime incident: this then formed the nucleus for his plutonium-loaded flying saucer. This incident was mentioned (rather pointedly) in the CIA's 1953 Robertson panel report:

> It was the opinion of Dr. Robertson that the "saucer" problem had been found to be different in nature from the detection and investigation of German VI and V2 guided missiles prior to their operational use in World War II. In this 1943-44 intelligence operation (CROSSBOW), there was material evidence of the existence of "hardware" obtained from crashed vehicles in Sweden.

Hollywood eventually produced a spy thriller, *Operation Crossbow*, based upon that intelligence operation.

Like Scully's pickled little men, the Spitsbergen UFO never existed in the first place. But this blatant hoax has been elevated to "fact" in book after book, and article after article. However, there was one other incident that is not so easily explained. It may have served as a prelude to the 1934 flap.

In 1925, the Norwegian explorer, Roald Amundsen, took off for an attempt to fly to the North Pole and back. His expedition was equipped with two twin-engined Dornier-Wal aircraft. As they neared the pole, one of the planes crashed. The other one landed nearby. The crews of both planes were missing for three weeks, until they managed to clear a runway, squeeze into the remaining plane, and fly back to Spitsbergen.

Later, Amundsen and Lincoln Ellsworth became the second team of fliers (after Byrd and Bennett) to reach the North Pole by air. (Amundsen was also the first man to reach the South Pole, overland, in 1911.)

In 1928, Amundsen organized another North Pole flight, and this one ended in a fatal disaster. His twin-engined Latham aircraft was never seen again. It went down somewhere far north of the Arctic Circle.

Three years later, the dirigible Graf Zeppelin carried a group of scientists on a photographic reconnaissance of the Arctic Circle. When the expedition returned, one of the scientists, Professor Paul Moltschanow, was surprised to find that he had photographed an object that no one had noticed. The object was shaped like an airplane, and was resting on the snow and ice on the southeastern part of the far north island of Nova Zembla (also called Novaya Zemlya).

The New York Times carried several items on this discovery in August of 1931. A confusing debate quickly arose.

"The plane was lying on a strip of snow," Professor Ludwig Weickman said (*New York Times*, August 22, 1931). "It is a monoplane with sharply rectangular wings, and can be seen clearly. It is a two-seater and undamaged. It seems impossible that it could be Roald Amundsen's plane, because he had a two-motor Latham. We have no idea so far what it might mean."

Captain Walter Bruns, founder of the Aero-Arctic Society, which sponsored the Graf Zeppelin expedition, was quoted in an Associated Press dispatch datelined Potsdam, Germany, August 20, as stating that it was "extremely unlikely" that the plane belonged to Amundsen. Amundsen's plane did not carry enough fuel to reach the remote island, he said. But, he added, "there is no record of any other plane ever having come to grief in that territory."

A dispatch from Berlin, dated August 22, 1931, stated: "The airplane photographed by Professor Paul Moltschanow from the Graf Zeppelin, lying in the snow in Nova Zembla, was identified today as a Dornier-Wal seaplane. Experts who determined this dispelled all possibility that it might have belonged to Roald Amundsen.

"It is assumed that the machine is one of two sent to the Arctic by the Russian government for exploration around Lake Cara. The other one was sighted by passengers on the Graf Zeppelin as they passed over Dickson Island.

"It is also held impossible that the plane could have been one abandoned by Amundsen near the North Pole on his first polar air expedition, because it could not have been blown so far south."

A few days later, officials at the Dornier works in Friedrichshafen, Germany, revealed that two Dornier-Wal planes had been sold to Russia in 1930, and were being used along the Siberian coast. "Dornier officials consider that the plane shown in the photograph, contrary to one theory, would not likely by the Dornier abandoned near the North Pole by Roald Amundsen, lost explorer, because the Amundsen plane was left afloat when the party moved south, and in all probability, was crushed by pack ice unless driven ashore." (*New York Times*, August 27, 1931.)

There were no further items on this incident, and we have been unable to locate a reproducible copy of the photograph. However, the few facts that are known make it unlikely, if not impossible, for the mystery plane in the photograph to have been Amundsen's or the Russians'. It remains an unidentified airplane, sitting on the snow of a very remote spot in the far north. How it got there, and to whom it belonged, will remain in the realms of mystery.

THE STATE OF THE ART OF FLYING – 1930

Aviation progressed slowly between the two world wars. In the early 1930s, the Soviet Union was still underdeveloped, and had no plane-building industry worth mentioning. As already mentioned, Russia had purchased two planes from Germany in 1930. Aeroplanes were still a rare sight in most parts of the world. Most Americans got their first glimpse of a genuine aeroplane in the 1930s, when a troop of barnstormers would pass through, carrying passengers aloft briefly in crude biplanes, most of which were frayed survivors of World War I.

Germany was forbidden by the Versailles Treaty to construct warplanes of any kind, or to establish an Air Force. After Adolph Hitler came to power in 1933, he began – secretly at first – to build the Luftwaffe. But, and this is an important point, neither Germany nor the Soviet Union had an appreciable air fleet in the early 1930s. In 1933, Germany had a reservoir of about 300 pilots, mostly veterans of World War I. Hitler would not and could not risk this meager force in a reckless and pointless adventure over Scandinavian in 1933-34.

We must also consider the fact that the Great Depression was at its worst in those years, and the problem of equipping, launching, and supporting an aerial invasion of Scandinavia would simply have been too expensive for Russia and Germany.

Great Britain and the United States were also badly hit by the Depression and, again, neither nation had the motivation for a furtive aerial survey of Norway, Sweden, and Finland. Such an operation would call for extended lines of supply, the establishment of well-hidden bases to maintain the aircraft, and vast numbers of trained personnel to keep the operation going. The distances covered by the "ghostfliers" of 1933-34 were so great that the best available planes of 1933 would have needed landing fields all over Scandinavia for refueling and maintenance.

The only alternative to land bases would be to operate from aircraft carriers. Crude experimental carriers were used in World War I, but the court-martial of General William Mitchell in 1926 had set back United States development of military aircraft and carriers. The American carriers of the early 1930s were hardly fit to sail the rough seas of the Arctic Ocean, and they were capable of launching only a few short ranged biplanes.

Many of the aircraft sighted over Norway and Sweden in 1934 were described as twin-engined machines. Even in 1942, General Jimmy Doolittle was able to launch only a few twin-engined B-25s from a carrier in his raid on Tokyo. The planes could not return and land on the carrier, but had to fly inland to China.

Only Japan was left as a possible culprit. But Japan was totally engaged in the war with China in the 1930s, and did not have the reason or the resources to perform an extensive aerial reconnaissance of Scandinavia, half a world away.

If any nation had risked such an expedition, a mistake or accident would have exposed their identity and, in all likelihood, involved the unthinkable risk of war.

Nevertheless, a large number of people throughout northern Norway, Sweden, and Finland saw large, gray aeroplanes night after night, sometimes even flying in formations of threes. They came from the north, from the general area of Spitsbergen, swooped along the coast of northern Norway, turned east into Sweden, passed over Finland, and then headed north again. Some flights can be traced southwards, along the same routes, night after night, covering all of Sweden and aimed for Denmark.

The "ghostfliers" came back, again and again, to the same areas in the years 1935 to 1937. Unlike an ordinary secret military operation, they did not attempt to maintain radio silence, but chattered back and forth across the airways for all to hear.

We hardly need mention the fact that people living in the northern latitudes are very familiar with mundane phenomena such as the Northern Lights, comets, and meteors. They were not likely to mistake a falling star for a blinding aerial searchlight. They were not likely to mistake a bolide for a twin-engined plane. There were not many weather balloons floating around that thinly populated sector of the world, and it was too cold for swamp gas.

When the various reports had been correlated, it became apparent that at least six machines of conventional airplane configuration were aloft simultaneously. These were generally of the two and three-engined type. The logistical problems of supporting an air fleet of this size in the inhospitable northern latitudes were monumental. If Japan or the United States were behind this project (they are the only two nations that could be even remotely suspect), it would have been necessary to maintain a steady supply line of ships to some hidden northern base. Such a supply line could not have remained undetected for very long.

The only other possible suspect, the Soviet Union, was in no position in those days to afford such an operation. In any case, the Soviets would have faced the same logistical problems, and they did not possess the necessary ships or planes to carry out the aerial survey.

Early in the flap, the Scandinavian press offered an alternate solution. It was suggested that the "ghostfliers" were smugglers of some kind. But official Swedish and Norwegian investigators quickly dropped this idea. If the planes represented mere smugglers, they had to be part of a tremendous, well-financed organization. No such organization was known to exist anywhere in the world.

It has been necessary for us to deal, at length, with all these factors and possibilities before we can begin to explore some of the many sightings of 1934. The first basic point that needs to be comprehended is: the 1934 mystery airplane wave was *impossible*. No known nation or organization had the facilities, resources and, most important, the motivation for carrying out an aerial survey of northern Scandinavia.

THE FIRST SIGHTINGS

The bulk of our data was located by Mr. Ake Franzen of Stockholm. Mr. B. Hogman found confirming reports of the same events in the newspapers of Gothenburg. UFO historian Lucius Farish and his American team have located other confirming items in the American press of the period.

This flap has been vaguely touched upon by other ufologists over the years. Edgar Sievers mentioned it in his book, *Saucers Uber Sudafrika*, referring to an article that appeared in the German religious journal *Christ*

& Welt in 1955. The magazine *Space Probe* carried a brief summary of a couple of the reports in September 1959.

Mr. Franzen found that many of the items were wire stories, which were repeated in several newspapers. Our main sources are the following publications: *Dagens Nyheter, Stockholmstidningen, Vasterbottenskuriren,* and *Norrbottens Allehanda.* Unfortunately, Mr. Franzen did not include specific source references for wire stories that appeared in these newspapers. But we will give the full citations for the exclusive stories that appeared during the period.

Our major source is *Dagens Nyheter.* Mr. Franzen translated this material into English. In the interests of readability, we have modified his translations, but have carefully retained the full facts and meaning of each item. This research project was launched late in 1968, and has taken over a year to complete.

Item number 44 in our catalog is of special interest, because it provides the first clue that the "ghostfliers" were active over Sweden in 1932 and the summer of 1933:

> Jan. 22, 1934. Pitea. The permanent curate in Langtrask has reported that he has been seeing mysterious airplanes in the area for the past two years. Last summer, the ghostflier passed over the community 12 times, following the same route, southwest to northeast. On four different occasions, the plane appeared at very low altitude but no marks or insignia were visible.
>
> Once the plane's altitude was only a few meters above the parsonage. For a few seconds two persons were visible in the cabin. The machine was grayish in color and single-winged. The curate had not reported this earlier, because he thought the flier had been reported by the coastal population.

This was also one of the several occupant reports. In these, the pilots were always described as apparently normal human beings, sometimes wearing hoods or cowls and, on one occasion, goggles (even though the pilot was in an enclosed cabin).

The one flight over Kalix, Sweden, on December 24 hardly seemed worthy of the fuss that followed immediately. We must assume that Swedish officials received a rash of unpublished reports that week, for on December 28, the following announcement was widely published:

> December 28, 1933. Tarnabay. The ghostflier will be hunted

by the Flying Corps Number 4 in Ostersund. Saturday, the Flying Corps received orders by telegraph to make contact with the police in the area. The flier was reported Saturday, visible over Tarnabay, and this report was very interesting because the weather was clear.

The head of the Air Force received a telephone call on Saturday from the general post government asking for help in searching for the mysterious flier in Norrland. Information and detailed descriptions will be collected about the suspicious smuggler-flier.

At 6.00 p.m. Saturday evening, the ghostflier passed over Tarnabay. People saw it cross the Norwegian border, and turn over Joesjo, the place where it disappeared Friday evening. The last sighting was eastward towards Stensele.

Across the Swedish-Norwegian border, the ghostflier was also being watched on the same day as the above sighting:

> December 28, 1933. Langmo Vefsn, Norway. An airplane was observed at high altitude over Langmo. Three lights were visible on the machine, but no other details were discernible because of the distance. This sighting is comparable to earlier observations from Hattefjallsdalen.

The mystery was now rapidly gaining momentum all over Sweden and Norway. On December 30, 1933, Norrbottenskuriren carried the report of two automobile drivers who watched a low-flying aeroplane pass over a highway at Muoijevaara, two miles north of Gallivare, Sweden. They estimated that it was at an altitude of about 150 feet. "No ambulance planes or military craft were in that area at that time, authorities said," the newspaper noted. "There is no doubt that the machine is a stranger."

SEARCH AND CENSORSHIP

On January 1, 1934, *The New York Times* carried its first report on the affair:

> Stockholm, Dec. 31, 1933. Swedish army aviators have been ordered to chase a mysterious airplane that has been sighted for many weeks over Lapland. It is believed to land among the mountains, making flights at night.
>
> The pilot was recently heard flying toward Norway in a heavy

snowstorm. It is thought he is a smuggler.

The New Year began with a bland grumble from the head of the Swedish Air Force:

> January 2, 1934. Sorsele. The head of the Air Force, Major Von Porat, refused to speculate on the phantom flier, except to confirm that he did exist. "Specific details on this affair can't be published," he said.

As late as Sunday morning, a large, gray aeroplane, bigger than any army plane, was seen in Sorsele. The machine flew in big circles over the railway station, and vanished in the direction of Arvidsjaur.

Mr. Olof Hedlund, a reliable man with a good reputation living in Vilhemina, watched the mysterious flier Sunday evening.

Mr. Hedlund was visiting in Sorsele over the weekend, and was taking a walk at 3:45 a.m., when he suddenly heard an engine roar from above. There was a full moon and visibility was very good. He saw the aeroplane come in over Sorsele from the west, flying on a course that took it directly over the railway station.

The machine turned three times over the area, in big circles, and then took off towards the north, following the railway tracks. Mr. Hedlund said the machine was about 400 meters up, and was in sight for about 15 minutes. It was single-winged and enclosed, like a passenger plane, and was equipped with pontoons or some sort of skis.

No marks or insignia were visible to the naked eye. The engine stopped during the turns over the village. The noise seemed to emanate from the propeller. The machine was similar to a one-engined Junkers. Mr. Hedlund was absolutely positive of what he had seen.

Sievers mentions another New Year's sighting by a policeman in Stensele, Ture Gustaffson, who reported "nine sharp balls of lights" in the sky. We have no further information.

The Hedlund report contains a number of interesting elements. There were fewer enclosed, single-engined monoplanes in use in 1933-34 than there were open biplanes of the World War I type. The maneuvers described by Hedlund indicate that the pilot could have been trying to get his bearings, indulging in the then common practice of navigating by following railroad lines.

However – and we must emphasize this point – It was almost suicidal to cut the engine and circle at such a low altitude. Yet in case after case, our mystery airplanes have done this; not only in the 1934 sightings, but also in many of the modern ones. We have commented on this puzzling aspect in other articles.

Swedish and Norwegian authorities took a sober view of the situation, because the low-flying planes were obviously locating and circling forts, military, and railway installations, and were boldly buzzing restricted areas of strategic importance. This pattern alone suggested that the ghost-fliers were engaged in a hostile military operation. Standard operating procedure demanded that the authorities clamp down on the release of information while they tried to figure out what was going on.

The major newspapers were also taking the flap seriously, and reporters were being rushed into the isolated northern regions. But after a flurry of stories in January 1934, the published accounts suddenly diminished sharply. Follow-up stories appeared throughout 1934, however, and indicated that although press coverage had lessened, the sightings were continuing at a high rate.

Major Von Porat reported to General Virgin on January 3, 1934:

> Many people of good reputation have seen the mysterious aeroplane with searchlight rays playing over the ground. Among the witnesses are two military men from the 4th Flying Corps. The "Flying X," one of the many names for the ghostflier, has been coming over Norway, crossing the Swedish border, and following a course over the lakes, particularly over the villages of Storuman, Tarna, Sorsele, and Stensele.

The newspaper *Vasterbottenskuriren* commented on January 4: "Hundreds of reports are circulating in Vasterbotten about mysterious aeroplanes, ghostlights, and swooping searchlights over villages, lakes, and wooded areas." The paper discussed assorted theories, including mass hysteria, stars, and moonbeams, but noted that "there were also reports of aeroplanes with low-powered engines, which sent beams of light into the sky. There are so many contradictions we don't know what we shall think about this."

It is amusing to find that these 1934 newspaper articles indulged in all the wearisome debates of witness reliability and alternate theories that would be repeated over a decade later, in both the "ghostrocket" flap of 1946 and the "flying saucer scare" of 1947. It is also plain that official behavior and reactions were identical in all these flaps, though widely separated by time. "Aviation experts" also appeared in 1934 to pontificate for the press, and offer a variety of solutions to the mystery, ranging from the ludicrous to pure warmongering. *The New York Times* led the pack in the latter:

> January 11, 1934. Alvakarleby. The ghostflier is still mocking his pursuers and seems to be growing bolder. At the moment, there are reports about a grayish aircraft from Alvakarleby.
>
> An observation of the ghostflier over the fort of Boden caused a sensation. A military guard also saw him over other nearby forts. The Minister of Defense, Vennerstrom, was informed about the incident, but after a telephone conference with the military commander in Boden, he denied the rumor.
>
> "We are dealing with more than one machine," General Virgin said. "There's no doubt about it." Military headquarters refused to say anything further on the matter.

The weather in the northern regions was severe, and the flimsy biplanes of the 4th Flying Corps had a difficult time operating at all in the windy, snowy mountains. Two of the planes crashed early in January. Fortunately, there was no loss of life. The anonymous "experts" were telling the press about Russian and Japanese "spies," but the Scandinavian papers were not taking them seriously. *The New York Times* was giving these theories a bigger play than the Swedish press.

According to the *Times*, February 4, 1934:

> The newspapers have interviewed aviation experts who state the mystery fliers show exceptional skill, undoubtedly superior to that of the northern European aviators. According to one expert's theory, the first of the "ghost" aviators was a Japanese scouting the Arctic regions, whose activities caused the Soviet to dispatch airplanes to watch the Japanese. The Soviet authorities, however, refute this theory...
>
> The appearance of a mysterious airplane over London has strengthened belief that the flights constitute an extensive scheme to explore aviation possibilities for a future war.

On February 2, 1934, *The London Times* had reported:

> Much attention was attracted last night by an aeroplane that flew continuously for two hours over the city and Central London. From the heavy note of the engines, the machine was a large one, and its altitude was sufficiently low for its course to be clearly traced by its lights. At the Air Ministry, it was stated that nothing was known of the reason of the

flight. In reply to inquiries at a number of civil aerodromes around London, it was stated that no civil machine had been chartered for a flight over the metropolis.

Four days later, Sir Philip Sasson, Under-Secretary of State for Air, offered this explanation: "The aircraft to which my honorable friend evidently refers was a Royal Air Force aircraft, carrying out a training exercise in cooperation with ground forces. Such training flights are arranged in the Royal Air Force, without reference to the Air Ministry."

Training exercises in the heart of London?

Despite this illogical explanation, that seemed to settle that. But on Monday, June 11, 1934, two more mystery aeroplanes appeared over London, according to *The London Times*, June 12, 1934:

> The sound and sight of two aeroplanes circling above the city late last night aroused interest and some curiosity. The machines were low enough for their outlines, as well as their navigation lights, to be clearly visible against the sky. At the Air Ministry, it was stated that although night-flying was frequently practiced by RAF machines, and several were up last night, service pilots were forbidden by regulations to fly over London at less than 5,000 feet. The identity of the machines in question was not officially known.

Returning to the puzzling Scandinavian search, the 4th Flying Corps gave up officially on January 18, 1934 and withdrew. Captain Zackrisson, the squadron commander, told the press that he was unfamiliar with the theory that Russian military planes had established a route over the mountains of northern Sweden.

Army search parties continued to wade through the mountains on skis and snowshoes, and military investigators swarmed over the areas, interviewing witnesses in depth. The ghostflier spread his activities to Finland, and the Finnish authorities were also launching searches and investigations:

> January 27, 1934. Helsingfors, Finland. According to official sources, a very important message about the ghostflier has arrived at headquarters.

> The situation is such that the people in authority cannot reveal the information at this time without jeopardizing a solution to the mystery.

Large, three-engined planes were sighted over Finland, and two army planes were stationed at Kemi, prepared to track them down – if possible. Eventually, the Swedes turned out two land-based planes, two seaplanes, and a number of ships in a massive search. Norwegian ships and planes were also scouring the Arctic waters and remote islands for some clue.

The ghostflier continued to ply regular routes, usually choosing periods of snowstorms, when the military searchers couldn't even get their planes off the ground.

A bailiff in Uppsala, Sweden, Ake Ponten, investigated many of the reports in Uppland, and passed them on to Stockholm. "So far as I can determine, some kind of aeroplane has passed over specific areas in our province," he said in an interview with a reporter from *Dagens Nyheter* on February 14, 1934.

Early in February, the lid began to come down. While some high officials confirmed the mystery, others began to issue denials:

> February 10, 1934. Helsingfors, Finland. The majority of the reports of the unknown aircraft that have been published in the newspapers are explained as follows: These objects have no connection with airplanes.

> Although there are many reports of flying strangers over Finnish territory, there is no assurance of their existence until the reports are compared with each other.

On March 3, 1934, *Dagens Nyheter* announced: "There had never been any ghostflier at all! The search for the mysterious aeroplanes and other strange objects has been terminated, since the investigations proved futile."

What did he mean by "*other* strange objects?"

A week later, a dispatch from Oslo, Norway said, "Both the Swedish and Finnish Air Forces have stopped searching for the mysterious ghostflier, but the Norwegian General Staff is still looking for him. In Troms Fylke, a mysterious plane has been seen at high altitude, and the Air Force has been informed."

Irrefutable military logic had been applied to the problem. No bases, secret landing fields, or lines of supply had been discovered. The planes were operating under impossible conditions, carrying out dangerous, low-level maneuvers beyond the capabilities of known machines and pilots. Therefore, the thousands of witnesses were obviously wrong. The ghostflier could not possibly exist.

But, like the bumblebee that doesn't know that his wings can't support his body, the ghostflier continued to fly anyway.

THE LANDINGS

On Wednesday, January 10, 1934, the Scandinavian "ghostfliers" reportedly landed in several isolated areas in northern Norway and Sweden, according to *Dagens-Nyheter* (Stockholm) and the other newspapers that were closely following the wave of mystery aeroplane sightings.

Item 20 in our catalogue is datelined January 11, 1934, from Skelleftea, Sweden:

> A report was received from the village of Norsjo, Monday evening, describing a bright light that was visible over the entire area. It was exceptionally strong, and moved over the southern horizon. A man employed by the Royal Telegraph Service in Norsjo watched the mysterious light over the swamp at Kvammer. He saw it from his car on the highroad. The police searched the swamp during a violent snowstorm but found nothing...
>
> An unconfirmed rumor from Anderstjarn, south of Norsjo, tells of a landing by the ghostflier on the ice. Some traces were found after the machine was seen.

The "unconfirmed rumors" were quickly replaced by substantial eyewitness reports, which prompted the Norwegian government to dispatch the cruiser *Eagle* to the landing sites:

> January 11, 1934. Trondheim, Norway. Two landings of ghostfliers were reported from northern Norway, Wednesday evening. One machine landed near the island of Gjeslingen, outside Rorvik, and the other at a place called Kvaloj, in the Namndal area. The report from Gjeslingen says that the people there saw a great beam of light, and heard the sound of a strong engine. The machine landed, and remained on the water quietly for an hour and a half. Its light went out after it landed, but the general opinion of the witnesses was that the object was still there. The second ghostflier took off 15 minutes after landing at Kvaloj, and vanished southwards.
>
> January 13, 1934. Oslo, Norway. An attempt to catch the

mysterious flier ended in failure on Friday. One mysterious
flier was seen to alight near the island of Sleipskar on Friday
evening. The island is only a few kilometers south of Gjeslin-
gen, where one of the machines was seen to land the day before.

Earlier in the evening, beams of light and engine roars were
reported in the same area. When the aeroplane was seen to
land on the water, a message was sent immediately to Rorvik.
The cruiser *Eagle* was docked there. Unfortunately, a pilot
was not available when the message was received. These
waters are too dangerous, because of the many reefs, for a ship
to sail them without a pilot.

People all over Rorvik saw the mysterious aeroplane between
two and three in the morning. It seemed to be heading
towards Sweden. Around 10:00 p.m., the plane flew over
Isfjorden, near Adalsnas. It was a biplane, equipped with
pontoons, and vanished over Romsdaksfjorden. Five persons
witnessed its flight. It was at high altitude.

January 14, 1934. Rorvik, Norway. Two aeroplanes have
landed near Rorvik, reported the police of the state. One
landing place is situated near Vikna, Kvalpsundet, and the
other at Oksbosen in Flatanger.

The duty-cruiser *Eagle* left the harbor at high speed for a close
investigation, but an accident occurred as the ship neared the
landing site. The cruiser ran aground. A salvage vessel was
sent from Rorvik, but the *Eagle* disentangled itself under its
own power.

The search for the aeroplane was futile, but people on the
nearby islands still seriously assert that an aeroplane landed at
Vikna.

The ill-fated *Eagle* never did catch up with the ghostflier, nor did the
Swedish Air Force squadron that was sent to northern Sweden to track
the planes down. Police and army units turned out repeatedly in the flap
areas, in futile attempts to locate the planes and their possible bases. Some
of the eyewitnesses said the planes were equipped with pontoons or skis,
and several reports described formations of two or three planes:

January 15, 1934. Skelleftea. For the past two months, a
person in Skelleftea has been watching three aeroplanes flying
in formation over the area. One plane usually flies in front
of the other two, and at a slightly higher altitude. It looks,

says the observer, as if the lead plane directs the others with light signals. The witness asserted that this has been going on for a couple of months, and the aeroplanes' routes follow the railways in the area.

Classic UFO-style "searchlights" were a common feature in many of the reports, and like modern UFOs, the objects frequently visited rugged mountainous regions. The lights, accompanied by engine noises, were widely seen over the Nedelpad (Sweden) area on Thursday, January 11. One group of witnesses said a phantom plane circled over Bykullen Mountain that night, and that the mountaintop was "bathed in light." Approximately thirty minutes later, it appeared over Tyndero on the seacoast.

There was a brief lull in the sightings in mid-January of 1934. Then, on Sunday, January 22, the planes returned with a vengeance, and were widely seen throughout northern Norway and Sweden. At 10.00 a.m., there were daylight sightings over Vindeln and Viriajarn. "The plane flew over at low altitude on a course towards Norway. No marks or insignia of any kind were visible," according to one report.

At 6.00 p.m., the busy pilot entertained the people of Bengtsforsen, Jamtland, and Indal, circling as he splayed his bright lights about the countryside. At midnight, a group of 30 soldiers near the fort of Boden reported seeing the object. Authorities were upset over the repeated appearances of the ghostflier over the "restricted" Boden area. That same night, the residents of Repvag, Norway "saw an aeroplane flying in circles at very low altitude."

The next day, January 23, 1934, Finland received its first visit from the ghostflier, when he roared over the village of Kemi at 6.00 p.m.

> January 25, 1934. Vasa, Finland. Two workmen saw a myste-rious aeroplane in Laitakaro, near Kemi. It came from the north of Finland, following the Kemi-Rowanjemi railway. The workmen had no ideas about the identity of the craft.
>
> On Tuesday, two aeroplanes were observed. One of them was visible above Kemi, and the other appeared over the little village of Kuivakangas. A blinding light swooped over Kuiva-kangas for a brief moment, and when the machine veered to the right, a green light was visible. The plane then flew over Tornealv, to Boden on the Swedish side.

The Finnish Air Force dispatched two planes to the Kemi area to search for the ghostflier. Meanwhile, some Finnish witnesses were reporting huge three-engined planes, and the crew of a Norwegian freighter claimed a rare *occupant* sighting.

GHOSTFLIER PILOT OBSERVED

The following report comes from Tromso, on the Norwegian seacoast:

> January 28, 1934. Oslo, Norway. The freighter *Tordenskiold* returned to Tromso from Kabelvag on Saturday. The Captain, Sigvard Olsen, and a sailor, Olsen, left Tromso last Tuesday, and were on their way home, when a plane appeared suddenly in front of the vessel. He was following a course straight towards the ship. When he reached only a few meters from the ship, the plane turned to the right and flew directly over it. A beam of light swooped over the deck, turning darkness into broad daylight for 15 to 20 seconds."

The plane was a great grayish machine, exactly like the French plane, *Latham*, which Roald Amundsen used on his last expedition. In the cabin of the craft, Captain Olsen saw a person, probably the pilot, dressed in some sort of "anorak" (hooded jacket). He wore big glasses, and had a hood over his head. The machine had no marks or insignia. It circled once around the vessel, and then vanished.

Despite the fact that the combined armed services of Norway, Sweden, and Finland had been mobilized to track them down, the ghostfliers continued to ply regular courses – and indulge in blatant maneuvers – at low level, directly over the towns and villages of northern Scandinavia. They were, in fact, *too* deliberate. It was apparent that the planes were meant to be seen. And they flew in the most severe weather, when all conventional planes were grounded.

> January 28, 1934. Haparanda. The personnel of the Haparanda newspaper watched for several minutes, around midnight Saturday, as an aeroplane flew back and forth several times over the city. Because of the foggy weather, no light could be seen, but the sound of a very powerful engine was heard by everyone on the editorial staff. The aeroplane looked like a giant shadow in the air. One hour earlier, ten persons observed a plane over Haparanda, flying back and forth.

One favorite, though suicidal, stunt of the ghostflier was to cut his engines as he circled low above the witnesses. Among the rash of sightings around Umea, Sweden on January 11, is this example: "Roartrask, northeast Norsjo, saw the machine... People there observed the engine stop three times as it passed directly over them. The machine was flying so low that the whole forest was bathed in its light. It seems that the plane wished to land, but suddenly increased his speed and followed the Skelleftea River instead."

On January 31, 1934, Lieutenant Colonel Snellman, chief of the Finnish Air Force, told the press, "There is no longer any reason to doubt the existence of the ghostflier."

One of the best reported incidents of the ghostflier wave was the apparent crash of a plane on top of the "nearly inaccessible" Fager Mountain, about ten miles from Tromso, Norway, on Monday, February 5, 1934.

> February 7, 1934. Oslo, Norway (*Dagens-Nyheter*). An unknown aeroplane has crashed or made an emergency landing on Fager Mountain in Malselv, on Monday evening. People in the valley watched the machine as it went down on the mountain. The next morning, the plane was still there, and two men were visible beside it, apparently clearing away the snow. Moments later, the machine made two attempts to take off, but without success...

> The head of the county constabulary in Malselv, Valderhaug, said he felt the report was reliable. The accident, or the landing, had been seen from both sides of the mountain, he said. Very reliable people had witnessed and reported the occurrence.

> When the plane landed on Monday evening, no engine sounds were heard, but a raging snowstorm at the time may have smothered the sounds. On the other hand, an engine sound was heard from the mountain today. A woman on Martensson's Farm heard the engine this morning, as she fed the animals... Later, other people heard the same sound, and that kind of noise is very uncommon up there. That was probably when the plane tried to take off and failed.

Eight men struggled up the mountainside that day, and failed to find any trace of the craft. That night, at 10.00 p.m., four persons reported seeing an aeroplane passing over Malselv on a south-west course "straight from the area of Fager Mountain."

Three more search parties climbed the mountain the next day, and the Norwegian newspaper *Tidens Tegn* reported: "Farmer Martensson of

Fugleli said that one of the patrols discovered two parallel traces in the snow, 300-400 meters northwest of the point where the aeroplane had been seen. The traces were about 75 meters in length and 80 centimeters wide... The patrol also found footprints of people around the traces. The search will begin again tomorrow, at dawn. Lt. Kjaer, a specialist from the Defense Department, will command the operation."

The ghostflier appeared again, at midnight on Thursday, February 8, over nearby Sigurfjord, according to the paper *Norlands-Nytt.* "It was approximately 500 meters high, and projected a very powerful searchlight on both sides of the nearby hilltops. Observers noted a red lantern on the machine before it vanished in a southwesterly direction."

Meanwhile, a lighthouse keeper named Bjornsen was watching a "mysterious vessel" near the Makkauer Lighthouse, Vardo, Norway. The ship first appeared on Tuesday afternoon, February 6, pursuing an easterly course. Then it changed directions and moved out of sight toward the west.

It reappeared on Wednesday. Bjornsen said it reminded him of the inspection ship *Frithof Nansen*, and was approximately the same size. "No foreign ship has requested permission to call at Norwegian harbors," the newspapers noted.

While the stalwart *Eagle* charged up and down the Norwegian seas, searching for phantom ships and ghostfliers, the rugged climbers on Fager Mountain threw up their hands in disgust. It was impossible, they said, for any plane to land or take off from the high, snowbound plateau.

Norway's *Adress-Avisen* had the last word on the incident, when it reported on February 10 that "one of the men who took part in the search of Fager Mountain said, in a telephone interview, that the mysterious aeroplane on the plateau was a stone!" Had the longtime residents of the valley mistaken a stone, twenty feet long by twelve feet high, for an aeroplane?

The ghostflier reports began to trickle out by the middle of February, even though the planes seemed to be getting larger:

> February 15, 1934. Melbo, Nordland, Norway. Several persons reported watching an aeroplane near Boroy-sund in Melbo at noon on Thursday. The machine was flying so close to the water that the witnesses thought it was going to land. But it did not... This machine was much bigger than the other planes seen over the community earlier. It was two-winged, and followed a course southward... The sound of an engine was reported at several places along its route.

Reports became sporadic during the remainder of 1934. But the ghostflier never really went away. The mystery aeroplanes were sighted infrequently throughout the 1930s.

> April 1, 1934. Oslo, Norway. Five persons have reported seeing a very large aeroplane over Sandnessjoen, according to *Tidens-Tegn*. One witness, a sixteen-year-old boy, said he saw the machine in the brilliant moonlight over Altenfjord. It was a very large aeroplane, he said, and the engines stopped when it suddenly descended towards the water. Eight propellers were observed. Instead of landing, the craft started to move in wide circles, so the boy was able to view it from all sides. He noticed that the cabin windows were all lighted.

An eight-propeller aircraft would be a remarkable sight, even today.

GEOGRAPHIC DISTRIBUTION

One of Dr. Jacques Valle's important contributions to ufology is his discovery that the phenomenon tends to concentrate itself in thinly populated areas. Although there were a number of mass sightings in southern Sweden (the most heavily populated section of the country), the greatest percentage of reports came from the sparsely populated lake country, and the mountainous regions of the north (where the average population density is three persons per square mile).

Jamtland, Vasterbotten, and Norrbotten were most often named in the Swedish reports. The Norwegian reports were mainly concentrated in Troms and Nordland, while the Finnish accounts were centered in the states of Oulu and Lappi.

We can assume that communications were fragile in some of these areas in 1934, and that a great many sightings went unreported. But we do have enough detailed reports to trace the routes pursued by the planes, and have been able to lay out some flights from point to point on specific days. However, on some of the flap dates, ghostfliers appeared simultaneously over many points in the south, as well as the north, indicating that either many planes were in the air at that time, or that the whole of Scandinavia was witnessing some rare form of atmospheric phenomenon.

Many of the reports do describe nothing but lights in the sky (LITS). During that period, every LITS was obviously regarded as the ghostflier. This does not explain, of course, the many low altitude, gray, unmarked aeroplanes accompanied by engine sounds. As we have already stated, the deployment of these planes and their deliberate maneuvers seems to suggest that they were designed to provide a frame of reference – or explanation – for the more mysterious wavering searchlights and multicolored, high-altitude lights.

If we disregard the LITS altogether and concentrate on the movements of the definite aircraft, we find that their flights seemed to originate above the Arctic Circle, somewhere north of Norway, perhaps in the vicinity of Spitzbergen. Reports would be understandably scanty from the northernmost state of Finnmark (population density 1-4 persons per square kilometer). As they moved down the coast of Norway, towards the more densely populated areas, the reports would increase – and they did. There were some reports as far south as Trondheim.

But in most flaps, the craft turned inland around Tromso, Norway, crossed into Sweden, and moved to Gallivare, which is in the center of Norrbotten. Gallivare appears to have served as a key landmark to the ghostfliers. From here, some flights proceeded southeast to Lulea, Haparanda, and Kemi, in Finland. Then they moved on down the coast of the Gulf of Bothnia, to Skelleftea, Umea, Sundsvall, and Uppsala, just north of Stockholm. Other flights pursued inland courses from Gallivare to Sorsele and Ostersund.

If these were conventional planes operated by smugglers or by some foreign power, this was an enterprise of unprecedented boldness and risk. The terrain was mountainous and dangerous. The ghostfliers chose to fly in the worst kind of weather, so they had to be extraordinarily good navigators. They could rarely see the stars, so they had to rely on instruments. But the known navigational instruments of the period were unreliable and primitive, at least for this kind of flying. Small wonder that the Scandinavian press commented with wonder on their navigational skills.

Assuming that they represented a foreign power, it is possible that they could have been launched from a ship in the Arctic Ocean, and could have flown the 300-400 miles to another ship in the Gulf of Bothnia. But why would they find it necessary to make such a hazardous trip, daily, for months on end? And why would they risk exposing their whole clandestine operation by clowning above the villages and towns along the way? What was the real purpose behind their seemingly insane missions?

The Finnish reports indicate that some flights returned to their mysterious home base by flying northwards over Lappland, on a course that might have taken them to Novaya Zemlya, the islands where a mysterious aircraft was photographed in 1931.

There are numerous other phantom aeroplane reports from the 1920s and 1930s emanating from other parts of the world, and this suggests that the Scandinavian style operation could have been repeated in Europe and North America.

Ivan T. Sanderson recently attempted to tie together the various reports of phantom ships and submarines over the years, to support a speculation that some form of super-civilization exists under the seas. Ray Palmer has for years advocated the concept that there is a hole in the North Pole and that some UFOs originate there. The 1934 Scandinavian wave can be used as new "proof" for any of these theories, and probably will be.

It cannot, however, be easily accepted by those who believe in the extraterrestrial hypothesis. Those believers will undoubtedly dismiss the whole affair as the work of Germany or the Soviet Union, even though anyone who is willing to spend an hour in a public library can learn that neither of those countries had the capability of launching and sustaining the Scandinavian overflights in 1933-34.

Only one basic fact can really be established from these reports: the ghostfliers originated from the Arctic Circle, and returned to that region.

OTHER GHOSTFLIERS OF THE 1930s

In his article "Over the Borderline," published in *Unknown* magazine, September 1939, Fortean Eric Frank Russell cited many of the UFO events recorded in 1938. "In July 1938," he wrote, "an 'unknown aeroplane' flew over Croydon, London (*Daily Herald*), its noise fading eastward. Note that what passed over in the night was not necessarily an aeroplane, but definitely was a noise resembling that of a plane. Exactly one year earlier (*Daily Telegraph*), 'unknown planes' made strange mechanical noises in the darkness over Hendon, London."

Scandinavia was plagued by a long succession of UFO-type manifestations throughout the 1930s. Consider this item from the *Vastermanland Lans News*, October 10, 1936:

> A strange light phenomenon has been observed over a meadowland in the area of Kanikebo, near the community of Moklinta. Several times in recent weeks, people have observed a reddish light, sometimes almost dazzling, on dark evenings between the hours of 8 and 9 p.m. The light rises slowly, and increases little by little in size and strength, until finally, a clear glowing ball the size of a coffee-saucer is visible.

Sometimes it dies out slowly, expiring completely, only to rise again in nearby places. A scientist will investigate the area by aeroplane.

A month later, the same newspaper carried this follow-up report: "November 10, 1936. Vasteras. No cause has been found for the mysterious 'light bodies' in Moklinta. Some of the residents are convinced the phenomenon is caused by the bones buried in the immediate vicinity, which are said to be thousands of years old."

Norway also shared the flap of 1936:

> November 21, 1936. Harstad, Norway. Reports of a mysterious light have arrived from several different places. The Norwegian Telegraphic Agency correspondent learned of the sightings during an interview with the Sixth Division. An inquiry into the reports is being conducted by the county constabulary. The division has also received a message about mysterious lights seen Tuesday evening outside Tromso. There is every reason to believe that the observations are real. During the last sighting in upper Norway, many people received mysterious radio signals. Earlier speculations that these signals were a Russian military code are disputed.

Mysterious radio signals had accompanied the 1933-34 ghostflier activity. *The Hudiksvalls News* reported on January 1, 1934:

> Radio listeners in Umea have been receiving conversations on their loudspeakers containing information about the ghostfliers, indicating their intelligence service is modern. The conversations are on the wavelength of a Gramophone program in Umea, and discussed meeting at a special point.

These "pirate" radio broadcasts were heard by others in Norrbyskar, Hedesunda, Nordmaling, and Halsinguna that month, on the 230-275 and 900 bands. In some cases, the phantom broadcasters spoke in broken Swedish.

In the early 1930s, the haughty *New York Times* was already rattling its saber for war, particularly against Japan. It repeatedly cited "rumors" that were never mentioned in the Scandinavian press. On November 20, 1934, *The New York Times* carried a dispatch datelined Helsingfors, Finland, claiming that the ghostflier had "revived rumors of Soviet naval armaments on the Arctic coast." It also commented on the "equally deep mystery surrounding wireless signals, supposedly of a military nature, in the Arctic."

These signals were "solved by Finnish radio experts," the newspaper said. "They located the sending stations on the German Baltic coast, near Koenigsberg. The signals are believed here to have been in connection with German experiments to perfect military aviation." Then this brief item was tagged onto the ghostflier story:

> Berlevaag, Finnmark, Norway, November 19 (AP). The mystery of "ghost" airplanes and ships at sea deepened tonight when it was reported two warships, not Norwegian, were observed last night from the outermost islands in the Arctic Ocean to the north.

Time – and the historical record – vindicated both Germany and the Soviet Union as possible sources of the ghostflier phenomenon. Years earlier, on March 19, 1921, *The New York Times* fussed over the appearance of a "Bolshevist aeroplane" that circled Paris.

> For some obscure reason, the French meteorological office issued a notice to the press stating that an aeroplane, flying at a great height, passed over Paris about 9:45 on March 5, making a semicircular tour of the city, from the southwest to the west-northwest side. As it went, the plane left behind it a trail of smoke, which at times resembled a ribbon, and at others a featherlike cloud.

> A mystery is being made as to why meteorological experts should wish to know about this airplane, but they are apparently very anxious to learn its type and characteristics, its exact trajectory, its height and speed between 9:45 and 10 o'clock and, lastly, the direction and speed of the wind at the altitude of the flight.

The German press rattled their swords on November 24, 1936, when the newspaper *Der Angriff* published a front page story, complete with maps, claiming that the Soviet Union was building 16 military airfields on the Kola Peninsula, far north of the Arctic Circle, in a desolate, thinly populated wasteland with virtually no military value.

The Germans warned that 300 military planes would be based there, and might be used to invade Scandinavia. Where the Russians would get 300 planes, in 1936, to a base in that part of the world was not explained. Perhaps the Russians were also seeing ghostfliers, and had become alarmed over the possibility that some foreign power was invading their territory from the north.

Early in 1937, our friendly ghostfliers were busy from northern Norway to Vienna, Austria. On Thursday, February 11, 1937, the crew of the fishing boat *Fram* started out from Kvalsvik, Norway, at 9:00 p.m. Just outside of Kvalsvik, there is a cape with high hills separating it from the mainland. As the *Fram* circled this cape, they discovered a large aeroplane resting on the water. Thinking the plane was in trouble, the captain changed his course and headed for it. Red and green lights were glowing on the machine, but as the boat approached, the lights were suddenly extinguished. Then, the plane was quickly enveloped in a cloud of smoke, and it vanished!

At noon the next day, according to *The Berliner Borzen Zeitung* and *The National Zeitung*, a mysterious aeroplane circled over Vienna, Austria, at high altitude, exciting speculations that it was of Czechoslovakian or Russian origin. A few days later, the phantom pilot revisited the fort at Boden, Sweden. It returned, still again, that April.

In May, a government hearing on the status of the ghostflier was held in Umea, Sweden. A representative named Lindbergs demanded that a new investigation should be held. But the Minister of Defense pointed out that extensive investigations had already been held, that special search-lights and listening apparatus had been mounted in the sighting areas, and that all the results had been negative.

It all sounded depressingly familiar.

In September 1937, "unfamiliar aeroplanes" repeatedly buzzed the Swedish naval installation at Karlskrona. The Minister of Defense explained at an inquiry that he had no answer to the mystery, but could only confirm that "a foreign machine had flown over the restricted military area." As usual, the plane carried no insignia or identifying marks.

On October 24, 1937, the six-man crew of an unnamed fishing boat near Mylingslykten outside of Hammerfest, Norway reported seeing a very large aeroplane resting on the water. As they neared it, it suddenly turned on bright lights and took off, passing so close to their vessel that they feared a crash.

In February 1969, Mr. Ake Franzen, the Stockholm researcher who uncovered and translated many of the reports used in this study, telephoned Dr. Tage O. Eriksson of the Research Institute for National Defense (named on page 554 of the Condon Report) to discuss the 1934 wave. Dr. Eriksson cordially invited Mr. Franzen to drop by his office.

"The conversation was not as fruitful as I expected," Mr. Franzen reported.

He said that all the articles in the newspapers at the time

[1934] were only imagination and mass hysteria. Dr. Eriksson's own explanation of the phenomenon was hot air balloons!

I told him about Major Porat and General Virgin [two of the officials named in the 1934 accounts] and he said the newspapers had distorted their statements. I asked him if there exists any official files on these 1934 reports, and he denied it. He agreed with Dr. Condon and his report on UFOs, and said he had met two of the Condon committee in the United States last summer, and that they were very reliable people.

I regret that I must disagree with Dr. Eriksson. I believe that the 1930s reports form an important body of evidence in the UFO puzzle, and that the ghostfliers' gray, unmarked aeroplanes were "hard" objects of a most extraordinary nature. I have spent many long, tiresome hours in the Library of Congress and the New York Public Library trying to uncover historical evidence to support the "obvious" answer – that the planes were of mundane origin. But such evidence does not seem to exist.

In recent months, there have been new UFO waves in the same areas of Scandinavia, and new reports of phantom ships and submarines off the coasts of Norway and Sweden. Apparently, whoever visited the Arctic Circle so mysteriously, forty years ago, is still there.

Perhaps Ivan T. Sanderson is correct when he suggests that the navies of the world have been far more involved in UFO research than our Air Forces. It was well known that the U.S. Office of Naval Research has been interested in UFOs for years and maintains huge, expensive, and mysterious installations in the Pacific. I wouldn't be at all surprised if the Navy found that the ghostfliers were flying around all at once, all over the globe, and that their sightings coincided with the many fireball and meteor reports that turned up in our material.

CHAPTER 6

When the massive UFO publicity flap of 1966 began, interested journalists and scientists discovered that the available UFO data consisted almost entirely of random anecdotes that were uncorrelated, and had not even been indexed. No valid statistical studies were available, and NICAP's *UFO Evidence* was the only existing source of information.

While it was a notable effort, it was a one-man (Richard Hall) compilation, and was biased and filled with flaws. Despite twenty years of controversy and alleged "research," this serious lack of effective research materials discouraged many of the professionals who were briefly attract to the subject. This enabled cranks and "skeptics" to run amok and exploit the field.

In Hollywood and on Madison Avenue, they speak of a "generation cycle." Generally, it has been found that a new "generation" (market) appears every seven years. For this reason, motion pictures such as *Gone With The Wind* are re-released every seven years, ostensibly to an entirely new audience. Most movie stars are signed to seven-year contracts.

With a few notable exceptions such as Cary Grant, John Wayne, etc., the average movie star is no longer "box office" at the end of his or her seven-year term.

There is a "generation cycle" in ufology, also. The average ufologist remains actively interested for from 3 to 5 years. We have made a thorough study of the UFO magazines covering the past twenty years, and estimate that the average journal has a life expectancy of about 18 months. Many of the publications that blossomed in 1966 have now faded from the scene, and their once-enthusiastic editors have abandoned the subject.

The same was true in 1950s. A very few, such as APRO, NICAP, and *Flying Saucer Review*, have struggled on for years and have provided what continuity there is to UFO research. Several of the journals now publishing are suffering from the growing decline in interest and may soon fold; all express hope that a new "flap" will revive interest and enable them to continue.

Unfortunately, publicity flaps are not actually related to UFO activity. They are based upon a series of delicate subjective factors. Public interest in any subject is most fickle. It is impossible to hold the public's interest for very long. Yesterday's sensation becomes today's bore. The press is influenced by the trends in public interest, and editors also become bored. When the magic words "flying saucers" on the covers of their magazines and newspapers no longer produce added sales, they move onto other subjects that do.

After 5 to 7 years, a new "generation cycle" occurs. New attention is paid to something that has been here all along. A new UFO book lands on the bestseller list, or a new Michigan-type flap wins the attention of a wire service. A new group of young people is intrigued, and they begin to churn out newsletters.

Instead of bemoaning the current "lull," we should be taking advantage of this quiet moment in UFO history. We should be studying the flap material of the recent past, compiling the desperately needed statistical studies, and preparing a valid body of well-documented material. Then, when the next big publicity flap finally does happen, the scientific community will have more than just a ragged collection of mushy quotes asserting that "where there's smoke, there must be fire."

Judging from past trends, we cannot really expect a new explosion of interest in the phenomenon until about 1972. We should gear our present efforts to that date. Teamwork is essential. Too much energy has been spent on intramural feuds and emotional side-issues. There has been too much nonsense and not enough hard, tedious research.

In *Anomaly* and *Flying Saucer Review*, we have outlined the problems and suggested new avenues of approach. Several American UFO magazines have accepted our challenge, and are now working to compile and publish data using the Data Reduction System.

The Aerial Phenomena Research Organization (APRO) recently announced plans to issue biannual statistical studies of the reports they receive. These efforts must be encouraged, and every researcher should try to participate. A responsible, objective methodology must replace the immature, ego-ridden, subjective approach of the past.

The year 1972 is not very far off. When it comes, what will we have to offer? Tirades about governmental conspiracies? Reams of semantics and opinions? Or will we be able to present well-documented studies of the hard data to a skeptical press and the general public. Endless anecdotes are not evidence.

We must extract the correlative facts from these anecdotes and present them in an objective, unemotional manner. The angry and often paranoid "causes" of the past can be, and must be, replaced by sensible, down-to-Earth research. We can – and will – prove our case.

A great number of UFO sightings are entirely subjective. That is, the objects are seen only by specific individuals under very specific conditions, while non-specific persons in the same areas see nothing. RAF Air Marshal Sir Victor Goddard has suggested that such sightings are made by persons with latent or active psychic abilities.

When non-psychics stand within the aura of the psychic percipients, they are also able to see objects that would normally be invisible to them. Our own field experiments indicate that this incredible hypothesis may actually be valid.

When a specific individual with the proper qualifications is located in a specific "window" area, at a time when specific electromagnetic conditions exist (a "flap" period), then that individual is able to perceive beyond the visible spectrum, intercepting a "signal" that plants an image in his or her mind. While the image may be very vivid and detailed, it is usually non-real, subjective, and "hallucinatory."

The big problem with this type of sighting is that it takes a highly trained investigator to determine whether or not the reported observation was real or subjective. None of the published UFO cases contain the information necessary to make a definite determination. However, in those cases in which the witness reported an unusually intense emotional reaction, it is probable that a subjective event occurred.

We term these cases "non-events." They are quite real to the percipient, and can rarely be distinguished from objective sighting reports of possibly solid, physical objects – except by a very thorough, in-depth investigation using objective professional methods. Many close (nearby, low-level) LITS (lights-in-the-sky) sightings have proven to be subjective rather than real.

CHAPTER 7

ANCIENT ASTRONAUTS, MODERN MYSTERIES: THE MOONSTONE
MYSTERY – *SAGA* MAGAZINE – DECEMBER 1974

Thousands of years before the Native Americans settled in North America, another culture thrived here. They were primitive by modern standards but, like the early Egyptians, they were fine craftsmen and very industrious people. They mined copper, iron, lead, gold, and coal. They even drilled for oil.

They were also great builders, and dug canals and irrigation systems all over the continent. Remnants of their efforts still survive, including massive stone walls, roads, and earthen pyramids. They measured the seasons and the movement of the stars by erecting circular stone astronomical calculators similar to England's Stonehenge.

In those far-off days, huge mastodons still roamed North America. Our unknown predecessors carved artifacts from mastodon tusks and scratched pictures of the animals in cliff faces. They even left depictions of dinosaur-like creatures, resembling the fabled dragons of China and Great Britain. And, in the tradition of the Chinese and British dragon carvings, they usually drew a circle or disk in front of the creatures.

The disk was, in fact, a very significant part of that culture. Thousands upon thousands of tiny stone disks, carefully and laboriously carved by human hands, have been found at archaeological sites through out the country. Most of them are less than 6 inches in diameter. Many look like miniature cogwheels, notched with such precision that they almost seem machine-made.

A large quantity of these cogged stones have been found in Bolsa Chica (Orange County) area of Southern California, in a strata of earth that has been calculated as 8,000 years old. Other disks have been found in the lower levels of the huge, manmade mounds of the Ohio and Mississippi Valleys.

Scientists have failed to come up with a satisfactory explanation for these curious artifacts. Some have suggested they were used in games, like modern checkers. Others think they might have been used as money. They must have had some important purpose, for the task of carving them was certainly arduous and time-consuming.

Lacking a better term, archaeologists call them "moonstones." They are a constant embarrassment to scientific theorists, so most of these moonstones are stored in museum basements.

One set of moonstones found in New York State was doubly embarrassing. The disks are rimmed with a series of carefully spaced holes and were found in the lower layer of a mound – which dated them as having been carved long before the first Europeans arrived.

When scientists studied the holes, they were surprised to discover they had been made with a steel drill. Of course, the Indians didn't have steel drills.

The North American moonstones are dwarfed by the hundreds of stone spheres scattered in Central American jungles, especially in Costa Rica. Some are as big as 8 feet in diameter and weigh more than 16 tons. Others are only a few inches in diameter. All are perfectly formed spheres. No one knows who carved them, when, or why. Were they the bowling balls of giants? Did they have some religious significance?

One thing is certain. It would take an enormous amount of effort to carve just one of these balls and grind it down to a perfect sphere. To do the job, the ball would have to be constantly rotated, and rotating a 16-ton block of stone would be no easy task. Some of these spheres have been found laid out in a measured geometric pattern on the jungle floor. How were they transported and moved into place?

One group of large spheres is laid out in a neat row aligned with magnetic north. Did the carvers have a magnetic compass?

Colonel Fawcett, the explorer who vanished while searching for a legendary lost city in the jungles of Brazil, studied native stories about stone spheres that glowed so brightly at night that they were used as streetlights.

Some of the spheres in Costa Rica are mounted on stone pedestals. If some magnetic anomaly caused them to glow at night, they would probably light up a large area.

But can stones glow?

East Haddam, Connecticut, was the site of a very strange luminous rock story in the late 1700s, according to an article published in *The American Journal of Science* in 1840:

> About 50 years ago, a European by the name of Steele came into the place and boarded with the family of a Mr. Knowlton for a short period. He told Mr. Knowlton, in confidence,

that he had discovered the location a fossil which he called a "carbuncle," and that he should be able to procure it in a few days.

Accordingly, he soon brought home a white round substance resembling a stone in the light, but which became remarkably luminous in the dark. The night on which he procured it, he secreted it in Mr. Knowlton's cellar, which was without windows, yet its illuminating power was so great that the house appeared to be on fire, and was seen at a great distance. The next morning he enclosed it in sheet lead, and departed for Europe. He has never since been heard of.

If the story is true, we can conjecture that the Americas may have once contained luminous stones, and that Colonel Fawcett's South American accounts may have contained some truth.

The Indians called the East Haddam, Connecticut, area "Morehe-moodus," meaning "place of noises." Strange explosions, like heavy cannon shots, have always haunted the place, and are still heard there occasionally. Fortean researcher William R. Corliss has located a number of modern reports of this phenomenon, known locally as the "Moodus Sounds." Scientists are at a loss to explain the noises.

While the natives of Costa Rica were grinding stone spheres, and the "Indians" were carving thousands of tiny stone disks, other mysterious stonemasons were hard at work all over the world. The "Plain of Jars" in Cambodia is a high plateau surrounded by mountains, and gets its name from the huge stone jars strewn all around: over 1,000 of them.

Some of these jars are six feet high, and some are big enough to hold six men. They are carved of limestone and granite, and they have always been there. The Cambodian people don't even have any myths to explain their existence. Why would anyone devote so much labor to carving such useless artifacts in such a remote and inaccessible place?

Our ancestors often engaged in seemingly pointless exercises. The Barren Islands off the cost of Scotland are covered with menhirs (standing stones), dolmens, and Stonehenge-like constructions. Similar structures can also be found in Portugal, deep in the Sahara Desert in Africa, and high in the Andes Mountains of South America. They are even scattered among isolated Pacific Islands, built of a kind of stone that cannot even be found on those islands.

When the first Europeans arrived in North America, they found numerous manmade mounds, carefully built stone walls, and even stone towers. The Indians disavowed any knowledge of the builders.

Some of these structures were clearly patterned after similar structures in the Middle East. Many were laid out with geometric precision so exact that they seem to be beyond the abilities of the Indians. The mounds were often surrounded by a low (two or three-foot-high) wall built in a perfect circle. Obviously, such walls were worthless as "fortifications" – but that's what modern archaeologists still call them.

As the Europeans drove the Indians back, they also wantonly destroyed most of these ancient structures. Treasure hunters chopped up the great mounds, usually finding nothing but a few bones, pots, and beads. Settlers broke up the stone walls and buildings to use the stones for their own houses. Only a few hundred of the largest mounds were preserved, largely in the Ohio and Mississippi areas.

The mounds of Mexico met a similar fate. A Christian church was built on top of one of the largest ones. The largest of all, larger and older than the Great Pyramid of Egypt, is the step-pyramid at Cuicuilco, Mexico. Archaeologists have found that the lower layers were covered with volcanic ash, which could be dated.

They estimate that the pyramid was constructed at least 8,500 years ago! In other words, an advanced pyramid culture was hard at work in the Americas thousands of years before the Egyptian civilization supposedly began.

We know shamefully little about that culture, because archaeologists can't fit it into their theories. They still maintain the myth that the Indians migrated to this continent from Asia, across the Bering Straits. The Indians themselves have other explanations for their origin. The Cherokees claim they came from the east, across the Atlantic Ocean. The Hopis and other southwestern tribes believe they migrated north from Central and South America.

Scientists digging in New York State have unearthed artifacts that were obviously made by Eskimos. Eskimos in New York? How did they wander so far from their Arctic tundra? Or did they start from here, being driven northwards by the invading moundbuilders?

The Indians were latecomers, probably migrating to North America a few thousand years ago, long after they pyramid builders and irrigation-ditch diggers had faded from the scene.

The men who flourished here after the Ice Age were another breed. They fought the mighty mastodons and slowly built a great culture in the wilderness, patterning it after ancient Chaldea and Babylonia, bringing with them the Druidic practices of Northern Europe as well.

When the Egyptian civilization began to bloom, occasional travelers visited it and wove tales of a fabulous continent far across the sea. Intrigued, the Egyptians sent out ships to find it. But after traveling for weeks across empty ocean, they turned back in dismay, and reported that the great continent had obviously been swallowed up by the sea.

So the remains of fabled Atlantis sit in the basements of a thousand museums: boxes of fragments that don't fit accepted theories, such as tiny stone disks with holes bored into them with steel drills.

THE AMBROSIA FACTOR

According to mythology, when mortal men were ushered into the presence of the gods in ancient times, they were invariably handed a goblet containing a thick, syrupy liquid, and were told to drink it. If they were suffering any ill effects from their visits to the palaces of gods (usually on top of some mountain), their symptoms vanished as soon as they drank the concoction. So, the first legend to spring up around this "ambrosia" claimed that it had medicinal powers – that it was a great magical cure-all.

Later, this was greatly embellished. Ambrosia was supposed to make the drinker immortal, and it rendered divine powers – the ability to communicate directly with the gods. Even though belief in the gods of the Romans and Greeks gradually faded away, the "ambrosia factor" remained an integral part of supernatural manifestations.

During the Middle Ages, most of Europe was engulfed in an epidemic of little people and faeries. Thousands swore they saw the diminutive creatures, and some even claimed to have been kidnapped and taken into their underground palaces. Some men even returned with bizarre tales of having been forced to mate with the Fairy Queen, presumably to introduce a human strain into the fairy world.

As in ancient times, those selected for these palace visits were plied with food and drink – especially a thick, sweet substance identical (apparently) to the ambrosia of the ancient gods of the mountaintops.

Scholars, historians, and priests who investigated the fairy manifestations decided that the little people did not really exist. The witnesses, they speculated, had been "enchanted" by some mysterious force. Little was known about hypnotism in those days, and even less was known about hallucinogenic drugs, but the voluminous descriptions of these fairy episodes clearly indicate that the victims were exposed to one or both.

The fluids forced down their throats may have been a forerunner of LSD, opening their minds to complex hallucinations and clouding their memories of what really happened. It was not uncommon for an "enchanted" man to stagger home like Rip van Winkle, thinking only a few hours had passed but finding that several days – even weeks – had elapsed since he had entered the fairy domain.

This compression of time is a sure sign that the victims had been hypno-tized in some way, and had a completely false memory introduced into their minds, to account for the period in which their bodies had somehow been used by the enchanting force. This could be a form of possession – the occupation of the human body by an outside intelligence.

The fairy faith died out after 1848, with the introduction of spiritualism. Spirit mediums lapse into an unconscious state and willingly turn their bodies over to forces professing to be the spirits of the dead. The rapid spread of spiritualism made the old fairy game unnecessary. The enchanting force now had a growing army of willing victims.

During the 1930s, a Polish émigré named George Adamski began teaching universal truths and mysticism in California. He served as the guru to a small following of a few hundred people, and would have remained totally obscure (in a state filled with countless obscure cults) if flying saucers had not suddenly appeared in 1947.

Soon, strange aerial objects were appearing nightly over Adamski's home on the slopes of Mount Palomar.

Adamski was already steeped in the lore and practices of self-hypnosis, spiritualism, and the esoteric religions of the Far East. His mind was already trained to accept cosmic interlopers. He embraced the UFO mystery with enthusiasm. Within a few years, huge cigar-shaped objects were landing on the desert near Mr. Palomar and tall, longhaired "Venusians" were holding face-to-face meetings with the aging guru. Modesty not being one of Adamski's virtues, he gleefully told his followers about his experiences, and soon his story was appearing in newspapers and magazines.

Adamski's new friends were quite obliging. They invited him aboard their craft and flew him to the moon. But, of course, before they whisked him into outer space, they offered him a drink. One of the beautiful Venusian women on the spacecraft handed him "a small glass of colorless liquid." It tasted like water, he later wrote, but was "a little denser, with a consistency something like very thin oil."

Since he was one of the first UFO contactees to publicize his alleged experiences, Adamski quickly became the center of controversy. The self-styled "scientific ufologists" (who were then few in number) frothed at the mouth each time his named appeared in print. He was denounced as a liar and a fraud, despite the fact that he produced photographs to back up his story and, on a number of occasions, other witnesses were present when he met with the saucer pilots.

He was taken more seriously in Europe, where he traveled in the late 1950s, and was accorded meetings with kings and queens, and even a *private audience with the Pope*. In 1965, however, he was stricken with a heart attack and died.

Throughout the 1950s, the flying saucer phenomenon paralleled the well-known fairy games of old, with the ufonauts frequently pausing to draw water from streams and wells in front of astonished witnesses (an old fairy practice), and indulging in the kind of mischievous pranks that led the American Indians to label the little people "tricksters." (Indians were seeing the "wee folk" long before the Europeans arrived on this continent.)

More and more UFO contactees bravely followed Adamski's example and revealed their experiences publicly, often to their everlasting regret, because they were usually ridiculed and harassed into silence.

A sign painter in New Jersey, Howard Menger, claimed that UFOs were landing on his farm. On one occasion, he met a tall entity in a suit of shining armor, which sounds exactly like one of the ancient Greek or Roman gods.

In another age, Adamski and Menger would have probably been elevated to the rank of High Priest, and their tales of these encounters would have been carved into stone. But in these "unenlightened" times, the general public views the contactees as clowns and lunatics.

As time progressed, the contactees were increasingly embraced by saucer buffs and ET believers, leading (naturally) to an increase in publicity-seeking charlatans and profiteering hoaxers.

As more and more contactee stories surfaced, a number of interesting facts and similarities developed. It was especially common for the contact experience to begin with a sudden, almost blinding flash of light; then the object or entity would materialize in front of the startled witness. (This same factor was present in many of the fairy stories, and in many religious miracles.)

Often the witness would find himself rooted to the spot, unable to move. This is a clear indication that he or she went into a trance state after the light flashed. After the object departed, the witness would cease to be paralyzed, and would discover that several hours had passed, even though it had seemed like only a few minutes.

Serious students of the phenomenon now advocate an interesting hypothesis: that the same force that generated the myths of the gods in ancient times is still active, and is now propagating the worldwide belief in flying saucers from outer space. Whatever the witnesses see is not nearly as important as *what made them see it.*

Adamski and Menger both sincerely believed they had been aboard a spaceship, and had even flown to the moon. But were the memories of their experiences any more reliable than the memories of the men who had been seduced by the Fairy Queen in her underground palace?

Contactees the world over have enjoyed liquid refreshment aboard spacecraft. Some have described the liquid as tasteless, like thick water. Others found it heavy and sweet. A few have claimed it was brackish and unpleasant.

Some of the scholarly investigators of the Middle Ages warned that if you were taken underground by the fairy people, you should refuse whatever food and drink they might offer you. This is still good advice, but UFO passengers apparently don't often have that option.

The story of Antonio Villas Boas of Brazil is now very well known. In 1957, he was allegedly taken aboard a UFO and introduced to a blonde space woman with whom he had sexual intercourse. Before his X-rated adventure began, the little men onboard the craft took off his clothes and bathed him with a wet sponge.

"The liquid was as clear as water," he later told Dr. Olavo T. Fontes, "but quite thick, and without smell. I thought it was some sort of oil, but was wrong, for my skin did not become greasy or oily."

The Greeks and Romans believed that the gods used ambrosia as an ointment when they bathed. In many ancient cultures, human sacrifices were anointed with oil before they were killed. This practice overlapped into Christianity. Christ's followers rubbed him with an expensive oil before he was crucified, and, in fact, the very name Christ comes from the Greek "Khristos," which means "the anointed one."

It is intriguing that Boas underwent the ancient anointing ceremony aboard that spaceship in Brazil.

Larry Foreman of California didn't receive a cosmic bath, but during a series of UFO contacts near Socorro, New Mexico in the 1960s, he claims to have tasted ambrosia. To him it was "some kind of punch – a berry of some kind, I think." Foreman's story includes a variety of obvious hallucinations common to the victims of enchantment.

More recently, in May 1969, a Brazilian soldier named Jose Antonio underwent a remarkable experience when he was kidnapped by a group of tiny humanoids and transported to a cavern-like room of stone. There his captors offered him a drink from a stone cube with a pyramidal-shaped cavity in the center. It was a dark-green liquid with a bitter taste. But he said he felt better after drinking it.

Woodrow Derenberger, a contactee in West Virginia, also felt better after he drank a liquid given to him by an alleged ufonaut in 1967. Derenberger had been suffering from a stomach ailment, and he claimed the outer space potion cured it.

Those who drank ambrosia on Mount Olympus were supposed to have enjoyed increased intelligence and heightened perceptions afterwards. In modern UFO cases, many of the contactees have undergone dramatic changes after their initial experience. Their IQ increases, they develop psychic abilities, and they suddenly acquire new knowledge of science, astronomy, and ontology.

Others, unfortunately, undergo reverse changes. They become nervous wrecks, get divorces, lose their jobs, go bankrupt, and have a very hard time in all personal relations. The ancient gods had a nasty reputation for causing the same kind of havoc in the lives of those who were privileged to meet them.

Could it be that the modern UFO phenomenon is nothing more than an updated version of these ancient games? The gods of old were accepted as residents of this planet. It is unnecessary to assume they were visitors from some far-off galaxy. They have always been right here, manipulating us, muddling our lives, fostering our beliefs in spiritual and supernatural matters.

The rites of many modern religions are nothing more than slightly modified versions of the rites of the ancient Druids, and other cults that dealt directly with the gods. The fairies of the Middle Ages were also regarded as residents of Earth. One popular belief was that they lived under the seas. And, as these columns have pointed out before, there is a considerable amount of evidence suggesting that modern UFOs come from the world's oceans, not from outer space.

We are trapped into basing our speculations about the phenomenon on the testimony of scattered witnesses who, no matter how sincere and truthful they might be, are seeing only what they are supposed to see, and remembering only what they are supposed to remember. Their trips to other worlds may be trips of another kind altogether, produced by sips of ambrosia rather than the roaring rockets of some advanced extraterrestrial civilization.

CHAPTER 8

VLF: MARCONI'S SPACE AGE WEAPON – *UFO INTELLIGENCE DIGEST* – 1975

After years of controversy, "Project Sanguine" recently died a quiet death. The Defense Department finally canceled its dramatic plan to convert a huge portion of the state of Wisconsin into a massive radio transmitter. Millions of tax dollars had been spent on the engineering aspects of the plan, while the citizens of Wisconsin organized and fought it vehemently. It may well have been a blessing that the project failed.

Essentially, Project Sanguine called for building the world's biggest radio antenna by burying cables in the form of a giant grid throughout Wisconsin. The cover story for the undertaking was that it would serve a system designed to communicate with atomic submarines anywhere in the world. Like "Project Mohole," the ill-fated scheme to dig a hole to the center of the earth (which cost the taxpayers over $50 million before it was abandoned), it looked pretty good on paper, but was both impractical and irresponsible in actuality.

Atomic submarines communicate via very low frequency (VLF) radio-waves, which can travel a great distance and penetrate underwater. Since VLF transmitters and receivers require inordinately long aerials, the technique for mounting such antenna on submarines is a closely guarded secret. There are now more than 200 VLF broadcasting stations around the world, operated by various governments.

But VLF receivers are not sold on the open market. Very few amateur radio operators have ever seen one. Sets made during WWI, when VLF experimentation began, command extremely high prices – when you can find one. Even if you do have a VLF receiver, there's nothing to listen to except for the time signals broadcast on some VLF channels.

Since voice transmissions do not carry well on VLF at all, these lower frequencies are primarily used for telegraphy and teletypes. VLF broad-casts are so rare that the Federal Communication Commission sends out postcards to owners of VLF receivers when it plans any kind of transmission.

The huge naval setup at Cutler, Maine, has an antenna that covers many acres. Other VLF stations are located in Norway, the Middle East, Washington State, West Virginia, and various isolated islands around the world. Project Sanguine, planted in the heart of Wisconsin, far from the world's oceans, would have augmented these other transmitters, but couldn't have replaced them.

What exactly is VLF? When an electric current passes through a wire steadily, you might rate it as "0" on the electromagnetic scale. Turn this current on and off 60 times in a second, and you have 60 cycles – like normal house current. Fluctuate the flow 1,000 times per second, and you have one kilocycle (kc). When the current "vibrates" that fast, electrical energy escapes from the wire; it becomes a radiowave and enters the atmosphere.

The AM dial of your home radio is built to tune in signals from 540kc to 1600kc. The greater the number of cycles, the shorter the wave becomes. Theoretically, the shorter the wave, the shorter the antenna needed. Microwaves, very short waves, become narrow beams that can actually be focused like light waves, as in radar systems.

Obviously there isn't much loss – or radiation of energy – at 60 cycles. The direct current in telephone systems is fluctuating at a low rate, oscillated by the human voice, and so there is some loss over long distances – which is why the telephone system uses amplifiers and other devices to transmit long-distance calls.

However, telephones are basically a VLF system and – this is a very important point – can be interfered with by exterior VLF systems. Innumerable other modern devices, such as the ignition systems of automobiles, also operate in the VLF range (0 to 1,000 cycles) and can also be interfered with by a VLF transmission on just the right wavelength.

During his experiments with VLF at Ostia, Italy in 1936, Guglielmo Marconi discovered these characteristics of the VLF waves. He actually caused whole lines of automobiles to stall. (These incidents were well publicized at the time.) He also found that local telephones became useless when he cranked up his transmitter, because his VLF waves interfered with the telephone circuitry.

Other experimenters were apparently making the same discovery. There was the mysterious mass stalling of autos in Germany in 1930, and the famous incident in Appleton, Wisconsin in 1941, when a 15-year-old boy allegedly stumbled upon the secret.

Fortunately, Marconi's discovery did not have a military application, because the long VLF waves could not be focused. You couldn't build a VLF raygun that could be aimed at a plane, a tank, or a ship. You needed a long and complex antenna for the VLF transmissions, and when you turned it on, you would knock out your own equipment as well as the enemy's.

The advent of UFOs after World War II stirred renewed interest in the so-called "electromagnetic effect" (or "EM effect"). Motorists everywhere reported the mysterious stalling of their auto engines when UFOs were present. Only diesel engines seemed immune, for they do not rely on ignition systems. Telephones also went crazy when the mysterious objects were around. Countless witnesses reported leaving their porches while watching UFOs to answer their ringing phones, only to find there was no one calling – a classic VLF effect.

Whatever the UFOs are, it is obvious that a powerful VLF field often surrounds them. Is this field a byproduct of their propulsion system, or are the UFOs using VLF for their own communications?

In 1967, I sat in the home of a radio amateur in West Virginia during a UFO flap, listening to his homemade VLF set. Strange voices were chattering back and forth on frequencies that supposedly cannot carry voice transmission. They spoke in a rapid-fire, guttural language we could not identify. At first, I thought it might be ordinary people speaking through a "scrambler," but later I sought out and listened to samples of voice transmissions through different kinds of scramblers, and there was no similarity.

Other strange sounds are common on the VLF frequencies. Sunspots, rocket launchings, and even the aurora borealis can cause eerie whistles, beeps, and birdlike, chirping noises on VLF. The teletypes used by the Defense Department sound like bagpipes.

People who live near VLF stations often complain about trouble with their telephones. A powerful VLF output can cause electric meters to run wild (you can find yourself getting bills for hundreds of dollars from your local utility). The good people of Wisconsin had valid reasons for objecting to Project Sanguine.

Now that the Sanguine scheme is dead, we can wonder about its real purpose. Was it really just a plan to communicate with far-flung submarines? The code name "Sanguine" has a double meaning. It could be interpreted as meaning either "optimistic," or "bloody." If we built a VLF antenna covering hundreds of square miles, it would take enormous energy to power a transmitter big enough to handle it. Every time it was turned on, everything from hearing aids to TV stations would blow out. The whole state could be blacked-out.

More sinister, perhaps, is the possibility that an antenna that big could be focused to a certain degree by a circuit that would use only certain elements. It might be possible to focus enormous amounts of VLF energy in a beam across Canada and over the North Pole, to the industrial valleys of the Soviet Union on the other side of the world. In the advent of war, Sanguine could have blown all the fuses in Russia!

The technology involved has been known since 1936, and is hardly a secret. When we reflect on the many power outages of the 1960s, we have to wonder if maybe some other country, or another civilization, hasn't built and tested a "Project Sanguine" of its own.

But did Project Sanguine really die as claimed? More than likely, it be reconfigured, or moved to a more remote location (Canada, Alaska, etc.). While it will drive the local wildlife crazy, its effect on humans may be minimized if it is placed far away from population centers.

BOOK REVIEW – *THE EDGE OF REALITY* BY JACQUES VALLEE AND J. ALLEN HYNEK – 1975

This greatly overpriced book consists of the transcripts of a series of discussions between Dr. Vallee, Dr. Hynek, and a few others, and is presented as "a progress report on unidentified flying objects." Highly readable and often entertaining, it appears to be intended as an introduction to the subject for those who are just entering the UFO arena.

Unfortunately, the conversations are often marred by the surprising naiveté of the participants, even though Vallee and Hynek have been deeply involved in the UFO studies since the early 1960s. At one point, Dr. Hynek declares that the works of Charles Fort make him "nauseous," yet both he and Vallee adhere to the "Fortean line" throughout, expressing annoyance, even contempt, for the general attitude of most scientists towards the unexplained.

Dr. Vallee describes for the first time publicly his own UFO sightings, and Dr. Hynek reveals that he once photographed a UFO from an airliner (the photos are included). A chapter titled "The Night an Occupant Was Shot" summarizes a case from the early 1960s, when a group of hunters fired at, and apparently hit, a being near a grounded UFO. The next day, one of the men was visited by two strangers who seemed to be fully informed about the incident. They never bothered to identify themselves.

Other chapters deal with the use of hypnosis in UFO investigations, the intrusion of psychical elements in many cases, the general UFO literature, and a "brainstorming" session in which all of the prevalent theories and explanations are touched upon.

Most of it will be very familiar to the avid flying saucer fan. The book will probably become more of a curio than an actual contribution to the subject.

-John A. Keel

BOOK REVIEW – *THE MYSTERY OF ATLANTIS* BY CHARLES BERLITZ – 1975

Just as Bigfoot, Nessie, and flying saucers have captured the public's imagination in this century, the subjects of pyramidology and Lost Atlantis enthralled millions one hundred years ago. Both have since declined, overshadowed by the seemingly more provable speculations on monsters and extraterrestrials.

But small bands of scholars, intermingled with the inevitable crackpots and con artists, still pursue the futile game of guessing at the hidden meanings in the pyramids and romantically searching for a long-lost supercivilization. The literature on both these matters is now both voluminous and wearisome.

Charles Berlitz's exhaustive examination of the Atlantis myth is as refreshing as an open window in a smoke-filled room. Originally published in 1969, *The Mystery of Atlantis* has been updated by its author for the paperback edition, and contains a succinct review of some of the new discoveries of the past few years.

Are the peculiar stone constructions in the waters off the Bahamas remnants of Atlantis? Or was it in the Mediterranean, as some modern scientists now claim? Did the massive pillars discovered under 6,000 feet of Pacific Ocean, off the coast of Peru, belong to Atlantis? Or was it near the Azores, as some others believe?

Mr. Berlitz examines all the lore and evidence, carefully weighs the complaints of the skeptics and beliefs of the advocates, and then chooses sides. Atlantis is really out there somewhere, he has decided, and he spends part of his busy life exploring the mysterious underwater world of the Bahamas.

Thus far, his efforts have produced little more than a suntan and this highly readable book. If you have room on your crowded bookshelves for only one Atlantis tome this year, this should be your choice.

-John A. Keel

CHAPTER 9

In the slang of the intelligence community, a "sleeper" is a spy who is deliberately kept inactive for years while living under "deep cover." He or she remains a loyal agent, but doesn't do any actual espionage work until – sometimes decades after being "planted" – the intelligence organization has a special need.

For example, it was recently revealed that an East German spy was sent to live in West Germany and carry out one specific mission. His job was to train his own five-year-old daughter and promote her into a job, after she had grown up, as a secretary in a West German government office. It sounds incredible, but this kind of long-range planning and manipulation is common in the shadowy, "James Bond" world of international espionage.

Sleepers are planted throughout our society. Some live and work in a community for 20 years or more, accepted by everyone as teachers, journalists or businessmen, drawing a monthly check from some agency in addition to their regular income, and waiting for the day when they might suddenly be called upon to break open a safe, take furtive photographs, or even – in extreme cases – shoot somebody between the eyes.

Since the intelligence community is also notoriously ruthless, sleepers are often sacrificed, against their will, to further some larger scheme. There is evidence that Lee Harvey Oswald may have been a sleeper who was being set up as the patsy for a complicated plot to kill Cuba's Fidel Castro.

Instead, someone knowledgeable in intelligence maneuvers manipulated Oswald into the role of patsy in President Kennedy's assassination. The agency, or agencies, that were retaining Oswald had to scramble to cover up their own plots. The thing snowballed until there were cover-ups *within cover-ups*. Assassination investigators remain confused and thwarted to this day.

Candy Jones, the famous model and wife of Long John Nebel, the New York radio talk-show star, was a slightly different kind of "sleeper." Through hypnosis and drugs, the CIA turned her into a deep-cover spy. She was sent on missions in a trance state, using a false name and even, believe it or not, a false *personality* given to her through brainwashing techniques.

When she returned from these missions, she resumed her own life and personality, and had no memory whatsoever of her escapades as a spy. She was a victim of an intelligence practice that has been in use for many decades.

In the 1960s, I discovered – to my astonishment – that "sleepers" are common in the UFO field. Like Candy Jones, ordinary people are pressed into service for the UFOs. They are used to carry out all kinds of missions, but have no conscious memory of those missions when they return to their normal lives.

In contactee terminology, they are said to have been "used."

Like all contactees, such sleepers have two important characteristics: they have latent or active psychic abilities; and they are very suggestible (that is, they are easily hypnotized). Quite often, as I have pointed out in various articles and books, a contrived memory or fraudulent experience is planted into their minds to account for the period during which they were being used. A person who has no memory of, say, one week, returns with the vivid impression that he or she has been taken to another planet.

The human psyche is such that layers can be laid upon layers in the unconscious mind. The phony experience fills the uppermost layer, while sensory memories of the actual experience are hidden in a deeper layer.

An unskilled investigator using hypnosis reaches only the surface impressions, and does not even attempt to reach the layers below. Once the amateur has brought the initial impression to the surface, the hidden layer is buried deeper than ever, and becomes almost impossible to reach.

In a conventional intelligence procedure, like the one inflicted on Candy Jones, the sleeper must first be hypnotized or drugged into a deep trance. Subsequent trances are easily induced by a "trigger." Triggers can take many forms. A sound at a specific pitch can cause the victim to lapse instantly into a trance. Such sounds can even be transmitted by telephone. Lights flashing in a specific pattern can do the job, or even a simple word or command can be used.

After Dr. Benjamin Simon (who ran an Army hospital that reportedly carried out CIA experiments) first hypnotized Betty and Barney Hill, he was later able to put them into a hypnotic state by simply saying, "Trance, Barney." Mrs. Nebel often went into a spontaneous trance when she looked at herself in a mirror.

I have examined contactees who were programmed to fall into a trance when they saw a certain written symbol – usually a Greek letter, or combination of Greek letters. They believed they had seen these letters painted on the side of a spacecraft.

It is more probable that the letter were merely shown to them. A post-hypnotic suggestion was then linked to these symbols, along with a surface impression of a spacecraft; their minds blended the two.

Ordinarily, a post-hypnotic suggestion will wear off in a few months or at, most, a few years. Therefore, once a person has undergone a contact experience, the hypnotic episodes must be repeated periodically. This is why eyewitnesses claiming a close encounter with a UFO often have repeated experiences spaced no more than three years apart.

Unfortunately, the subsequent experiences are usually well buried in the unconscious mind. The witness may have no conscious memory of them. Only the initial experience, with its vivid surface impression, can be recalled.

"Silent" contactees who experienced some form of UFO contact years ago, even as children, can become sleepers. They experience periods of temporary amnesia throughout their lives without ever relating these lapses to their first UFO contact.

The minds of some eyewitnesses cannot adjust to this kind of overt tampering. In some cases, a classic conflict develops between the conscious and unconscious minds. The impressions hidden below the surface work their way through, and there is an overlap that leads to confusion, anxiety, or even partial insanity. Betty and Barney Hill sought out psychiatric help because they were bothered by horrible nightmares, a standard result of such overlapping.

As the impressions in the lower layers infiltrate the surface layers of the conscious mind, the subsequent blend causes many contactees to become fanatical UFO evangelists. In innumerable cases in UFO annals, we find that the hidden impressions actually took over the conscious mind, causing the contactee to assume an entirely new personality. In extreme instances, the contactee has declared themselves to be a space person! And many, like Candy Jones, find themselves battling dual personalities.

But people who adjust to the "alien presence" without these problems can serve as sleepers in all kinds of ways, too. A mysterious phone call of beeping sounds can send them into a trance, during which they may write and mail a "crank" letter, or carry out some other activity that they normally would not do under any circumstances. After they have performed this action, they return to normal and have no memory whatsoever of what they did.

In one case in New England a few years ago, a young man who was – without his conscious knowledge – a sleeper got into all kinds of trouble for taking a potshot at a "Man in Black in a black Cadillac." Actually, the "MIB" was an ordinary citizen in a hunting outfit, and the "Cadillac" was really an old Ford. The young UFO investigator was hallucinating while in a semi-trance triggered by a sound on his car radio! His unconscious mind was projecting material overtly to his conscious mind.

The frightening thing about all this is that each new UFO wave may bring more people under the hidden control of this phenomenon. We have no way of estimating how many sleepers there may be after 30 years of UFO sightings, and we have no way of finding all the triggers in use. We can, however, theorize – with some certainty – that almost every person who develops an obsession with UFOs has been subjected to some form of mental programming at some time in his life.

Who or what is doing this? Is some sinister organization plucking us off highways to hypnotize or drug us? Are invaders from space embarking on a worldwide campaign to brainwash us before landing and taking over our world? This doesn't seem too likely. This phenomenon has always existed, and lies at the root of all our religious beliefs, our myths and superstitions, the ancient arts of witchcraft and black magic, and the fundamental philosophies that have given us most of our social and political ideas.

From the medical symptoms of the contactees we can deduce that the phenomenon consists of an energy form rather than a solid physical state. This energy, like a type of radiowave, is sometimes visible to us as glowing shapes or beams of bright light.

Years ago, the intelligence community discovered ways to produce the same effects through hypnosis, drugs, and brainwashing techniques. But it is unlikely, if not altogether impossible, that any nation could, or would, attempt to use these methods on entire populations.

The individual experiencer is still at risk, however. Perhaps it was the CIA's studies of UFO contactees that gave them the idea of creating sleepers like Candy Jones.

CHAPTER 10

When Sir Martin Ryle and his team of radio astronomers first detected radio signals from pulsars in 1967, they held an excited debate among themselves. Initially, they speculated they had intercepted "a navigational beacon, fashioned by an extraterrestrial race," and they worried about what course to take. Should they tell the press or the government, or send a note to *Nature* magazine?

"No, the news might seep out and create a public panic, of a War-of-the-Worlds type," a professor said. Fortunately, they decided to keep their discovery a secret, and soon found that the signals were natural in origin, rather than technological.

But the lesson from this episode is clear. If any scientist anywhere should ever actually stumble upon genuine evidence of an extraterrestrial civilization, he would, in all likelihood, keep his finding a secret. Ufologists would be among the last to know.

The scientist would check and recheck his discovery, perhaps for years, and eventually enlist the aid of a few trusted colleagues. In time, he might publish an obscure and obtuse paper, reducing the event to a few mathematical formulae. Then, he would become the center of a controversy, thus risking whatever reputation he might have; for science is dominated by egotistical administrators, and, alas, outright crackpots.

Science is more an application of the known than a pursuit of the unknown. Charles Fort's barbed criticisms of the scientific establishment of his day still hold true – so true we can seriously question the usefulness of scientists in a study of the UFO phenomenon. Chances are that if a large number of established scientists became embroiled in UFO research, they would generate more controversy and personality conflicts than any of our hardcore amateur UFO groups. We already have some outstanding examples.

The scientists and scholars organized by Colorado University into the Condon Committee very quickly polarized into two conflicting groups. Within a year, they had lost sight of their contractual goal, and were engaged in hopeless infighting, which ultimately destroyed the whole purpose and worth of the Colorado UFO project.

Two outside scientists, the late Dr. James McDonald and Dr. J. Allen Hynek, later devoted incredible effort to discredit the Condon project. Others, notably Philip Klass, an aerospace writer, labored unduly to attack and discredit McDonald and Hynek. Dr. McDonald spent his last days painstakingly re-investigating cases listed in the Condon Report, while Dr. Hynek used a large part of his long-awaited book to rehash the whole Colorado mess.

Dr. Condon, whose scientific reputation far outweighed that of Hynek and McDonald combined, got in a few licks of his own, in his speeches and public statements. The whole affair developed into a bitter and largely pointless conflict, comparable to Major Keyhoe's campaign against George Adamski in the 1950s.

Similar discord had occurred in the U.S. Air Force in the 1947-55 period, just as the various amateur UFO organizations and publications splintered into dozens of factions, all antagonistic to one another. These battles have kept UFO research in the U.S. in a state of paralysis.

My first encounter with the scientific community came in the mid-1950s, when archaeology was one of my chief interests. I met, interviewed and befriended a number of prominent archaeologists and Egyptologists, and was soon concerned over their conflicting interpretations of basic facts, and the rather silly feuds and controversies in which they were entangled. Later, I discovered these same problems permeated every scientific discipline.

As a science editor for Funk & Wagnalls, a large publisher of encyclo-pedias, one of my tasks was to edit the contributions of scientists. The company called upon leaders in every field to contribute to their books. Only top-ranking physicists, chemists, astronomers, etc. were asked to submit articles.

I was frequently appalled and frustrated by the overall quality of the papers submitted by these distinguished savants. Many bordered on illiteracy. When I tried to find a genuine expert on meteors, I found that astronomers were just as weird, confused and egocentric as archaeolo-gists. After a go-round with nuclear physicists from the Atomic Energy Commission, I began to question their maturity, too. (Indeed, the history of the development of the atomic bomb graphically illustrates the naiveté and philosophical confusion of the men who engineered that feat.)

More recently, I spent a year in Washington, D.C. as a special consultant to a large government agency primarily concerned with medical and psychological problems (the Department of Health, Education, and

Welfare). There I had daily encounters with all kinds of doctors, psychiatrists, radiologists, and other assorted scientists. So, my personal experiences with science and scientists are both broad and detailed.

Early in my UFO research, I openly questioned the government's practice of calling upon astronomers such as Dr. Carl Sagan for UFO consultations, when the problem seemed to be largely a military and legal one, rather than an astronomical one. If the UFOs were, in fact, manufactured vehicles, they were openly violating our air space (a military problem), landing illegally in farm fields (a problem for the Federal Aeronautic Administration), and openly harassing citizens by pursuing automobiles, etc. (a problem of law violation – the province of the Federal Bureau of Investigation).

Obviously, none of these agencies were really concerned with the subject, and the Air Force effort was largely a public relations ploy. Apparently, the government decided in the early 1950s not to take UFOs seriously on a public level. Instead of building a small task force of qualified investigators intelligence personnel, psychologists, and scientists trained to interview people in depth, the government established ad hoc committees of astronomers and interested laymen – an approach that could only lead to negative results. And even then, no UFO event was investigated as thoroughly and as systematically as a routine meteor shower, or the discovery of a bit of bone in an old tar pit.

Dr. Hynek was clearly aware of this problem, and frequently stated in interviews that UFO events should be given the "FBI treatment." The FBI was, in fact, peripherally involved in a few UFO investigations, but when I asked to review the FBI's UFO files in 1967, 1 was told that no such files existed.

Of course, the UFO buffs had speculated for years that the government was hiding some "truth" from the public, assuming that if any real proof was ever found, the Air Force would keep it as secret as Sir Martin's pulsar signals. Yet, knowing how the government operates, and being on intimate terms with many top officials, I found it puzzling that there wasn't even any real rumor of such a discovery (outside the wild ramblings of the ufological press).

The big question is: if we enlist the aid of modern science in UFO research, what kind of scientists do we approach? Dr. Hynek has been talking about his "Invisible College" of scientists for many years now. Very few members of this body have surfaced. We have had more than our share of astronomers and "exobiologists" pontificating on the probabilities of life existing elsewhere in the universe. But that has little, if anything, to do with the real UFO problem.

The real problem, as Dr. Hynek himself keeps stating, is to study the witnesses who have these experiences; that is the logical first step to a real UFO investigation. Once we have established that our major UFO events are caused by an outside stimulus, we can proceed to the second step: the study and interpretation of that stimulus.

The problem thus becomes identical to the problem faced by parapsychologists and psychic investigators. Ufology becomes a behavioral study. When I first pointed this out in Britain's *Flying Saucer Review*, I was subjected to the animosity of many UFO groups, because it was a radical departure from the unproven and unprovable, yet always popular, extraterrestrial hypothesis.

If ufology succeeds in attracting larger numbers of scientists to the fold, what can we really expect?

First of all, the subject offers no profit, and not even an opportunity to win a large government grant. Few, if any, major scientists will be interested. More than any other group, scientists are very concerned with publicity. The right kind of publicity can lead to fame, fortune, and the Nobel Prize. But being associated with any fringe subject can be very detrimental to a scientific career. (Even my own career as a professional writer has suffered greatly because of my connection with UFOs.)

Ironically, Dr. Condon was the most prominent scientist to enter the UFO fray in these 25 years. But he was an exception in many ways, since he had also lent his name to many unpopular causes. He became the subject of so much abuse and ridicule that he was forced to become very negative and defensive soon after the Condon Committee got underway. Other leading scientists will see him as an example and will avoid the subject, not wishing to repeat his experience.

This will leave ufology with a cadre of scientific second-stringers for some time to come. Some of them will see ufology as a means for gaining publicity and promoting a flagging career (although such publicity will have an opposite effect – as they will soon discover). Others, those with the fewest qualifications for dealing with the many hidden problems in UFO events, will blunder into the field and serve only to add to the confusion and controversy.

The petty arguments of the UFO journals are already spreading to some of the scientific journals. Phil Klass denounced the Socorro, New Mexico landing as a stunt to promote tourism. Dr. Hynek found Socorro so baffling (after 17 years as a UFO consultant!) that he asked the Air Force if the object wasn't really a secret test vehicle.

New scientists lured into ufology will have to start from scratch, since even at this late date, very little scientific data has been published on the subject. They will have to go through all the bewilderment and theorizing of the amateur newcomers. They will have to learn to separate obvious psychic phenomena from possible UFO phenomena, and often the line is so fine it is almost indiscernible.

Every scientist who dares to enter the UFO field will have enemies who will delightedly attack him and his new interest at every opportunity. If he does come up with some important new piece of evidence, he may feel that he has to sit on it for years – or forever.

The pitfalls far outweigh the slender advantages in becoming a scientific ufologist. And what would be the point? The scientific community is already capable of generating more controversy, nonsense, and vituperation than any of the UFO organizations.

RANDOM NOTES, SITUATIONS, AND DEVELOPMENTS – *PURSUIT* MAGAZINE – 1977

Bigfoot, an apparent pal of the ufonauts, has received something of an endorsement from the U.S. Army Corps of Engineers! The latest issue of *The Washington Environmental Atlas*, a compilation of a variety of data concerning the environment of the State of Washington, mentions Bigfoot as one of the ecological features of the state. The report may be ordered from the U.S. Government Printing Office, but it costs $48.00, and contains only the following remarks about Bigfoot:

> The very existence of Sasquatch, or "Big Foot" as it is sometimes known, is hotly disputed. Some profess to be open-minded about the matter, although stating that not one piece of evidence will withstand serious scientific scrutiny. Others, because of a particular incident or totality of reports over the years, are convinced that Sasquatch is a reality. Alleged Sasquatch hair samples inspected by FBI laboratories resulted in the conclusion that no such hair exists on any human or presently known animal for which such data are available.
>
> Information from alleged sightings, tracks, and other experiences conjures up the picture of an apelike creature standing between 8 and 12 feet tall, weighing in excess of 1000

pounds, and taking strides of up to 6 feet. Plaster casts have been made of tracks showing a large, squarish foot, 14 to 24 inches in length and 5 to 10 inches in breadth.

Reported to feed on vegetation and some meat, the Sasquatch is covered with long hair, except for the face and hands, and has a distinctly humanlike form. Sasquatch is very agile and powerful, with the endurance to cover a vast range in search of food, shelter, and others of its kind. It is apparently able to see at night and is extremely shy, leaving minimal evidence of its presence. Tracks are presently the best evidence of its existence. A short film of an alleged female Sasquatch was shot in northern California, which, although scoffed at, shows no indication of fabrication.

The Pacific Northwest is generally considered to be the hotbed of Sasquatch activity, with Washington leading in number of reports of tracks or sightings since 1968. However, reports of Sasquatch-like creatures are known from as far away as the Parmir Mountains in the USSR and South America.

If Sasquatch is purely legendary, the legend is likely to be a long time dying. On the other hand, if Sasquatch does exist, then with the Sasquatch hunts being mounted, and the increasing human population, it seems likely that some hard evidence may be soon in hand. Legendary or actual, Sasquatch excites a great popular interest in Washington.

This year has brought us news of phantom (wild) cats in Ohio, wild (house) cats terrorizing a town in New Jersey, giant skunks discovered in Java, miniature kangaroos in Australia, and attacks of killer bees in South America.

As Forteans, we must realize that the continual evidence of these kinds of phenomena, on a worldwide scale, indicate ever larger overall patterns that may eventually enable us to abstract a greater understanding (by means of a more holistic, interdisciplinary approach) of the nature of Fortean phenomena.

We wonder what the weather will be like next year (1978): this year and last have brought strange weather patterns, including drought and flood conditions, to many parts of the country. Two Pacific hurricanes, one this year and one last year, have hit the southwestern part of the U.S. (the norm is supposed to be about one every hundred years); and prevailing upper air winds dipped further south in winter (there was snow in Miami), and further north in summer (in July of this year, prolonged record highs were sustained hundreds of miles further north than usual).

There are those who would suggest that weather modification is possible on a planetary scale. During this past winter, there were even accusations and speculation that the Russians were tampering with the world's weather patterns, by utilizing certain energies explored in the past by such researchers as Nikola Tesla and Wilhelm Reich.

Next year, we will explore a historical perspective of weather modification, and the resulting attitudes developed toward those who have attempted it, from classical antiquity to modern times – from superstition in the Middle Ages to the scientific witchcraft of today.

We feel the necessity, now that another year is drawing to a close, to issue a couple of awards. The belated Quote-of-the-Year Award (for 1976) goes out to a Salt Lake City, Utah weather forecaster who stated, during the televised evening news, that an earthquake that occurred that day in Price, Utah, had no connection whatsoever with a prediction that an earthquake would occur in the area on the same date.

And the Situation-of-the-Year Award for 1977 involves a UFO hoax. It is an answer of sorts to the query put forth by a number of innocents in the past (when confronted with the question of belief concerning UFO occupants): "Why wouldn't they just land and communicate their presence if they exist?" We are not proud to present the following situation, which took place somewhere in New York City this past summer. What originally was planned as a hoax may, however, serve as a lesson to us all.

One early morning, some of those who had left their apartments, preparing to go to work, were surprised to discover a strange sight awaiting them on the sidewalk: a small, cone-shaped, metallic object emitted beeping sounds. Nearby lay a little inert humanoid. Films made of the event were shown on the evening news. Innocent bystanders stopped to stare, mute and perplexed.

By the time a small crowd had gathered to observe, the spectator attitude had changed to one of puzzled frustration, giving rise to brief exchanges of uncomfortable joking and muttering. In the dawn light, an occasional figure would dart sporadically forward, to poke tentatively at the small humanoid, which subsequently turned out to be a G.I. Joe doll covered with modeling clay.

The cone-shaped object, when eventually knocked aside, revealed only a few tape recorder components. A desperate gesture of hostility finally dispelled one man's fear of the unexplained; he viciously kicked the doll out into the street, where it was crushed under the wheels of a large truck.

CHAPTER 11

John Keel is a very hard worker. Since leaving home at 17 for New York City, he has supported himself by his writing. He is the author of many magazine articles, and has worked as a TV comedy writer for years. He is the editor of a magazine called "Pursuit" and a newsletter called "Anomaly – A Journal of Forteana." Mr. Keel is also one of the most prolific researchers and writers in the field of UFOs.

Keel estimates that he has interviewed thousands of people who claimed to have had sightings or been actually contacted by UFOs. A partial list of some of the books he has authored includes: "Operation Trojan Horse," "Our Haunted Planet," "The Mothman Prophecies," and his most recent book, published in January of 1976, "The Eighth Tower."

EXCLUSIVE INTERVIEW WITH PETER BLUM – *UFO REPORT* – NOVEMBER 1977

Do you ever get tired of running around the country, interviewing thousands of people who claim to have seen saucers or little green men?

You get very tired. Long ago, I grew weary of hearing housewives talk about lights they've seen in the sky; there's so much of it going on all the time. It's incredible; people who don't keep track don't realize how much of it there is.

Do you feel it has picked up more in the last 10 or 20 years?

Well, the reporting has improved greatly in the last 10 years, but it's been going on at the same level for 100 years or more. Only in the last few years have we begun to notice it. It's only in the last five or eight years, though, that people have begun to take it seriously.

It seems that you are trying to put "it" into a larger perspective.

Yes, you start wandering into philosophy and other things – especially psychic phenomena. I was interested in psychic phenomena long before I got into UFOs. I had always believed, as most people do, that UFOs, if they existed at all, were extraterrestrial. But when I got into it, and started investigating these things firsthand, I realized that I was investigating psychic phenomenon again – a variation of it. Of course, the people who believe in extraterrestrials got very unhappy with that conclusion.

You're a heretic amongst heretics.

I get a lot of flak from them. But, fortunately, I have a lot of experience with psychic phenomena, and was able to see the many similarities between the UFO cases. Within six months after getting into it seriously, I had to drop the whole extraterrestrial thing, and go off in another direction.

This energy spectrum you deconstruct in "The Eighth Tower" is interesting.

Well, I've been trying to find a general theory.

Sort of a unified field theory?

The more I get into all these things, the more obvious it becomes that they all have a central cause, whether it's UFOs or monsters. I'm very interested in monsters. We get a lot of monster reports.

As mentioned in your previous book, "The Mothman Prophecies."

In January of this year, they saw the equivalent of Mothman near San Antonio, Texas. Quite a few people, including police officers, saw this giant bird. Some schoolteachers who saw it described it as an ancient pterodactyl. It came down very low over their car. It made headlines all over the country, except here on the East Coast.

There are stories of this creature going way back among the Mexican-Americans living in Texas. It's an isolated community. They don't have much contact with reporters. They claim they've been seeing these things for 20 or 30 years – that they've attacked people and the like.

There's one thing that I kept wondering while I was reading this stuff, because I tend to go along with you. Both the saucers and the hairy creatures are forms that human minds help to create, out of various energies that already exist.

A lot of it is basic demonology. In demonology, of course, almost any kind of creature can appear, if you believe in it enough. Or – if you're in the kind of atmosphere where these things can easily be produced – even if you *don't* believe.

That's getting to the heart of what I was going to ask next. It seems that some people are more susceptible to creating or perceiving these things.

Well, in the beginning of my UFO research, I was astonished to find that most of the close-up UFO witnesses were people with a very high degree of psychic ability. I could spot them a mile away. And then later, I discovered that people without psychic ability couldn't see these damn things.

So, two people could be standing next to each other and see different things…

Well, if they're fairly close, then the person without ability can see it. They can graft off of the psychic's aura, so to speak. I've been with groups of people, and some of us would see this thing going over, very low. Yet other people would say, "Where, where… I don't see a damn thing."

So, this psychic quotient is terribly important. I've had a lot of dealings with UFO contactees – probably more than anyone else in the U.S. – and all of these UFO contactees were people with either latent or active psychic abilities. When I'd sit down and go over their whole life story, they'd tell me incident after incident of psychism. The UFO experience is just another psychic experience. Of course, the hardcore believers in extraterrestrials just don't get this at all. In addition, there seems to be a selection process going on.

People don't accidentally see these things; certain people seem to be selected.

Yes, and I've tried to figure out the system by which they're being chosen, and it's not easy. I've tried to do rough statistical studies. For example, Catholics and Jewish people rarely see these things, but a fallen Catholic – someone who's given up Catholicism – is more apt to see it. People with Indian and Gypsy blood in their background are more apt to see it than people with no Indian or Gypsy blood.

Those are two very important factors that I've found. If you have a great grandfather who married an Indian girl, the chances are that you're more apt to see a UFO than somebody who hasn't got that in his background. Of course, this is very controversial, and a lot of the UFO "believers" are screaming about it. But when they go out and try to check out my figures, they always find that I'm right.

Then, we've found many other factors. The UFOs appear

at certain times of the year, and even on certain days. I got something in the mail the other day from some researchers in Ohio. In 1897, there was an enormous UFO wave in the U.S., and the newspapers carried all kinds of stories about landings, asking what were these strange things.

They took 49 of these basic sightings and worked it out by the days of the week. They found out that Wednesday was the big day. So out of 49, you should get an average of seven for each day of the week. But Wednesday got twice as many. And going through old occult books, we found that in ancient times, when people made references to strange things in the sky, it would happen particularly on Wednesdays and Saturdays. So it's been going on forever. Why it would work out to Wednesday, I don't have any inkling.

The only thing that immediately strikes my mind is that it's the middle of the week.

Yes, well any study of that kind has to have a peak. There's a man at Colorado University, Dr. David Saunders, who has now fed over 50,000 sightings into a computer, to test this out. At the beginning, he thought I was full of baloney – I'd used only 700 sightings in my sampling. And now, with his 50,000 sightings, he's come up with the same thing. And we don't know why.

Also, the period from the 21st to the 24th any month has more sightings. There are researchers now trying to work it out with the cycles of the moon. Of course, in different years, and in different months, you have different phases of the moon at different times, so it's a difficult puzzle.

We also have, on the summer and winter solstice, enormous waves. The UFO wave of 1896, when it really started, took place around the Boston area around Christmas time. And we've had, in June, around the summer solstice, these enormous waves of UFO sightings.

Any theories?

None at all, unless they're related in some way to sunspot activity. There are people trying to check that out, too. And of course, that also makes the ET believers unhappy, because we keep finding explanations for some sightings. And "mundane" explanations don't sit very well with true believers.

Would you categorize most ufologists as wasting their time?

Yes, I think so. I think it's becoming a terribly sophisticated study; it's not a study for amateurs at all.

I think it's becoming evident that no matter what these things are, they've produced a lot of changes in our way of thinking, directly and indirectly. A lot of people certainly have been thinking about "cosmic questions" that they never thought of before. And so, in that way, the extraterrestrial idea is not a bad thing.

But there are a number of people that are sort of "evangelists" for it, and they stomp the country giving lectures, saying, "The brothers are coming from outer space to save us." I don't agree with that at all. NASA's great search for extraterrestrial life may have started because some of the people at NASA, in the 1950s, were very big UFO buffs.

Another story is that the aliens have been contacting our major world governments with offers of peace, but have been ignored or turned down.

If that were really to happen, I think we would know about it. I think they'd probably contact us as a civilization. They wouldn't contact individuals, or even individual governments. If we found there were life on Venus, I don't think we'd single out somebody and talk with them. We would first make our presence known, and then go from there.

We would send in the real estate developers.

Yes, or drop the atom bomb. But it's been going on too long, and there are too many subtleties involved. A lot of the UFO phenomenon appears to be a cover-up for something else, just as many of the things that happen in demonology are cover-ups for something else. For centuries, this has led religious people to believe that we're being manipulated – by the devil, by god, or by something else. There are similar beliefs in ufology – that we're being manipulated by the flying saucer people. There's a big belief that some of the leaders in government are actually spacemen.

Aliens. Well they are "spacemen," but they're from Earth.

The entities that contact the contactees give them prophecies of their own future, and even help them out in various ways, until they believe absolutely that these entities are from wherever they say they're from. Then they'll accept anything that the entities tell them. Then, the entities start feeding them propaganda: "Oh well, you know the Secretary of Defense is one of us," and this type of thing. Naturally, the contactee believes it, because everything else prior to that has come true. So they start circulating these stories for the entities.

That implies a purpose behind the playfulness.

It's a mischievous purpose. A good analogy is that the Bible warns you to beware of pretenders and angels in disguise (i.e., "false angels"). In a way, these entities are the same thing. Usually, when a contactee swallows the whole lie, they end up in deep trouble. Very often, he or she is completely ruined by the whole experience. Their husband or wife leaves them, they lose their job, and very often, they go insane. There are many cases of that.

Have you been in touch with any people who've gone through such a "psychotic episode" touched off by contact, and then come out of it with some perspective?

A few have. One is a man who became very famous in the 1950s. His name is Howard Menger, and he was a sign painter in New Jersey. He claimed these things were landing on his farm in New Jersey. He started getting publicity on radio and television, and he was written up in all the newspapers. And after a few years of horrendous difficulties, including the breakup of his marriage, he began to piece everything together.

He figured out that he had been lied to, and that the whole thing was some kind of a colossal hoax. So he retracted everything. But it's unusual for someone to do that. Usually, they go off the deep end, and stay off the deep end. There've been a number of suicides, too. It's a very bad business. I know that a lot of people cherish a secret ambition to be contacted by flying saucers, but it's nothing to fool with.

I would suspect that those people who have been contacted did cherish that kind of ambition, but weren't consciously in touch with it.

Well, you have an almost identical situation in religion, where the budding fanatic wants to be contacted directly by God. Usually, at some point, he thinks he *has* been contacted. He hears a voice, sees an apparition, and then he becomes a total fanatic. It usually ruins his life. He dedicates his life totally to it. You see them in the subways of New York – the men walking the streets with signs. They do this because they've received messages and heard voices; many of them believe this totally. They literally sacrifice themselves, and throw their lives away for the cause – whatever the cause is.

And some of the UFO contactees have done the same thing. They believe totally in their own senses; they think that they've seen these space people, when they probably have just seen some kind of entity. But they've received communications that they feel are terribly important.

Whether it's that the Secretary of Defense is an evil space-man, or some politician is working with the Serpent Race, these flying saucer entities always pick on whatever is the current fear. In the 1950s, it was the atomic bomb, and then the hydrogen bomb; they were always giving messages about atomic energy. And then they gave messages about Vietnam, because we were in a war there.

We find, going back to 1897, that there were many landings. At that time, the big issue was Cuba; we eventually went to war over Cuba against Spain. These entities were delivering a lot of messages about Cuba. So, it's just an old game that's played over and over again, like a skipping phonograph record.

During the period where there were a lot of cases of demonic possession, one theory proposed that this was very often sublimated sexual activity. In mixing sexual energy with psychic energy, a lot of repressed stuff comes out, or is manifested.

Well, there are a number of psychiatrists that are interested in UFOs and contactees, and that is one of the things they've been looking for. But they've found no real evidence of it, beyond the tendency for poltergeists to manifest around teenage girls. We do have a number of interesting sexual cases, where people claim they were taken aboard flying saucers. If they were women, they were raped by the spacemen, and if they were men, they were forced to submit to a spacewoman's advances. Quite a few of these cases haven't been published.

There's a new book that just came out, written by Hans Holzer, who stumbled across a few cases of this. It's called

The Ufonauts. Hans believes totally in the extraterrestrial idea. He gives a number of sexual cases in here. So they're stirring that up, which I hate to see, because when people read those stories, they'll start having the experiences, just like when people went to the movies and saw *The Exorcist,* they started thinking they were possessed.

It makes one cautious about introducing anything into the mass media.

You have to examine these people carefully to find these influences. Find out what they've been reading, and what movies they've seen. A lot of the things they think happened to them have really just lapsed up from their subconscious.

Have you come across cases where the witness actually received profound or significant teachings?

Usually it's just a sophomoric philosophy. There are cases that seem a little more profound, but these have generally happened in South America, Spain, or France. There has been a case going on in France for some time now. After his initial experience, a simple, elderly peasant began spouting Einstein-type ideas.

He's coming up with the kind of things he never could have come up with himself. He doesn't read or anything, so where is he getting these ideas? They are certainly more refined than the ideas the American contactees have come up with. In my search, I am always looking for the perfect case – and that one comes close.

In the beginning, I figured, if the flying saucers are really real, then you don't need 10,000 cases. You just need one case with enough evidence in it, and you can prove the whole thing. I've traveled in 20 states and talked to thousands, and I've yet to come across that one case that is substantial enough to say, "This proves it."

I think the Air Force went through that in the beginning, too. I know in the early days, in the late 1940s and early 1950s, many of the officers connected with "Project Bluebook," their investigative unit, were strong believers in the extraterrestrial idea. But, after all their experiences and searches and investigations, one by one, they turned negative.

There's an Air Force man with NASA now, named Al Chopp, who was a big extraterrestrial believer in those days. But by 1966, he told me, "Well, I used to believe in Santa Claus, too." He's gotten so disheartened by it all.

What's the nature of the reception that you get from the government when you come into contact with them?

I get total cooperation from them. You hear so much about government conspiracies and all that, but I've never run into any flak of any kind. You'd think that if they were going to shut anybody up, then I would be one of those they would shut up. I've been waiting for them to buy me off or something. But I haven't had a single offer. I can go into the Pentagon, and ask for anything, and I'll generally get it. They've taken me on tours of secret radar installations – anything that I've wanted.

So the UFOs aren't a conspiracy of the government?

No. In fact, years ago, I worked in the government. I know how the government works. I can't really give them credit for being able to carry off that kind of conspiracy over a 20-25 year period. Maybe for four or five years, they could get away with it, but eventually, people start talking – people retire from the program and write a book.

Look at what the CIA is going through now. You can't keep a secret. Look at how Nixon tried to keep his secrets. UFOs are too big a secret to keep. If the UFOs were real and wanted to contact us, and got a cold reception from Washington, they'd simply land in Paris or London. Can we accuse every government in the world of being in on this enormous conspiracy? If so, it would be the *only* thing they've ever worked together on, ever, in history.

One area that you concentrated on are these "quasi-official" contacts that happen, other than the sightings in the air.

Yes, we call these the "Men in Black," because they're most often dressed in black suits. In the beginning, I started coming across these cases, and I thought they were government officials. But then, when I started investigating cases in depth, it seemed impossible for them to be government officials.

For example, a farmer in Ohio told me he had seen a thing land in his farmyard one night. He didn't call up the police or his neighbors or anybody. Early the next morning, this black Cadillac pulled up – they usually prefer black Cadillacs – and a man in an Air Force uniform got out and told him not to tell anybody about what he'd seen the night before. The farmer was enraged by the whole idea that somebody would tell him to shut up, so he ordered the guy off his property.

When I got the description of the Air Force officer from him and from others, they describe them as looking Oriental, and being slight in stature; which is the same way that many people have described the UFO pilots. When they saw a UFO land and somebody get out of it, it was usually somebody 5 or 5 ½ feet tall and looking like an Oriental. And so it became obvious to me that, well, maybe these fellows are riding around in Cadillacs too, as well as flying saucers.

Step by step, I put it together. Two men ran around Long Island in 1966-67 posing as Air Force officers, and talking with quite a few people. I went directly to the Air Force. I had the names of these men and everything. We ran a complete check on the names and the license numbers of the cars, but we could never identify these men. They were not in the Air Force.

In "The Eighth Tower," you talk about trying, very seriously, to meet up with them, or track them down.

Yes, sometimes I missed them by 10 minutes. I arrived 10 minutes after they had left.

Would you say that this is a manifestation of the same phenomenon?

Well, it's hard to say. Some of these men seem very, very real. Dr. Hynek came across several cases in his travels investigating UFOs. Some seem like very real people, but others seem like apparitions, so it's hard to separate the two. If they're real people, I'd like to know who the hell they're working for. Because I'm convinced they're not working for the CIA, the Air Force, or any of them. It's got too long a history for it to be the CIA.

But, as I say, once I gave up on the extraterrestrial idea, I kept turning up these Men in Black cases. I said, "Well, I'm never going to catch a flying saucer, but maybe I can catch one of these guys."

I have a lot of friends in the different police departments around the country, and my plan was just to whisk one of these guys into a jail somewhere, and find out who the hell he was. But they seemed to anticipate my moves. It was baffling. One time, I checked into a motel on Long Island that I had chosen at random, and they had a flock of messages for me! Somebody had left a lot of nonsensical messages for John Keel. This has happened to other researchers, like Brad Steiger.

I guess if you had in your own psyche, in your own psychological make-up, an inclination toward any kind of paranoia, that kind of stuff could push you over the edge.

This kind of paranoia has destroyed different amateur UFO groups around the country. After every wave, groups of people get together and say, "Let's start a UFO club," and really investigate these things. Before you know it, they're really at each other's throats. They're getting mysterious phone calls, and they think, "Well, Charlie's playing a trick on me."

And of course, it isn't Charlie. Charlie's getting the same phone calls, and he's saying, "My God, George is trying to put me on!" So Charlie and George aren't talking. And then other terrible things happen, and finally the whole group not only breaks up, but everyone in the group hates each other from then on.

The same identical things are going on with the groups of "assassination buffs" – the people who are privately investigating the assassinations of John F. Kennedy, Bobby Kennedy, and Martin Luther King. It's really weird that so many different groups have the same problems. That's why, for a long time, it seemed to me the CIA was the answer, but now that we learn more about the CIA, I really doubt it.

The CIA might be responsible for some of this stuff, but it wouldn't make such sense to tap the telephones of teenagers and little old ladies, and harass citizens who certainly have never done anything in their lives to deserve it. The FBI has taken an interest in a number of UFO cases, but it seems baffled, too. One a few occasions, the FBI and I have crossed paths on these cases, and they seem troubled by it all.

Do you hear anything about UFO sightings from the Oriental countries? Do they see six-foot Caucasians in their saucers?

Yes, there's a very active group in Japan, and my books have been published in Japanese. I have corresponded with them a number of times. They tend to see the "little people" more, just as they do in South America.

Howard Menger saw people who were the equivalent of Greek gods, even in armored plates. The door on the space-ship opened, and this Greek god got out, with golden hair – sort of like the Michael Rennie character in the movie *The Day the Earth Stood Still*. However, generally, the descriptions do hold true. There is only one similarity across the board, and that is the Oriental features.

Even in the orient?

Yes, be it in the Orient, or in Africa. When the devil appeared in ancient times, and of course he appeared quite often, he usually had an Oriental cast to his features, and was wearing a black suit. He would ride a black horse in those days. Later, he had a black carriage. Now he's got a black Cadillac. It's just the Devil updated, catching up with us.

There are a lot of curious things about the Men in Black entities. They very often are out of step with the times. They'll be wearing suits that are now out of fashion, maybe by 10 or 20 years. They would turn up with double-breasted suits in 1960, when double-breasted suits were really "out." Also, their vehicles tend to be old, like maybe a 1955 Cadillac that looks brand new. How did they keep it so brand new, even down to the "new" smell inside?

In 1949, a rumor circulated that a flying saucer had crashed somewhere in New Mexico, and that the Air Force had rushed people in, scientists and all, and had found bodies in the flying saucer, of little men. Supposedly the little men were dressed like people in the "gay 90s."

The flying saucer was supposedly loaded onto a truck and whisked off to an Air Force base somewhere. The little men were put into little bottles of alcohol and preserved. To this day, the Air Force gets letters asking, "Is it true that you have little men preserved in alcohol?"

It's a rumor that will live on forever. There probably is no truth to it at all. I'm certain there isn't, but there are a lot of people who believe there is truth to it. Of course, when a rumor like that comes up and the Air Force denies it, then the believers say, "Ah, a cover-up." And there's no use in denying it, because it only adds fuel to the fire of conspiracy. There have been many absurd rumors throughout the history of this business.

In Vallee's "The Invisible College," he talked about "Ummo" artifacts that were exchanged.

Yes, that is still going on. There was a saucer landing in Spain, where they found tubes afterwards, made of pure nickel. The tube, when opened, contained a piece of plastic. They were able to trace the manufacturer of the plastic. DuPont, in the good ol' USA, made them specifically for our space program. About the only use for them is in the nose cones of our space shuttles.

Now, how this would turn up in Spain, in a nickel tube, is anybody's guess. But what added to the mystery was that several of these tubes were found. The local people just collected them at the landing site, and walked off with them.

A few days later, handbills were passed out in this little town, saying, "We will pay you 18,000 pesetas for the return of these tubes." The local investigators tried to track down who passed out the handbills, but they were never able to find out anything. That's either another act of our mysterious Men in Black, or it was a very good practical joke.

Some of these practical jokes seem to be very expensive and very sophisticated. There have been some very elaborate humdingers, which have kept the UFO believers in great turmoil. It is baffling, unless you consider it may be some intelligence, experimenting in some way, to find out how humans will react. There was a scientist who worked on the atomic bomb project, Dr. Leon Davidson, who came up with that theory in 1960.

Davidson decided the CIA was behind the whole thing, and that it was an experiment to find out how people would react to an actual visit by extraterrestrials. To this day, he believes the CIA is behind the whole thing. But as I say, the history of it goes too far back. In fact, there were Men in Black in the 1940s, before the CIA was even formed, so it's hard to explain it as a CIA venture. I think the CIA is into bigger stuff than playing around with UFO believers.

There are a number of cases in South America and Europe where Americans have turned up immediately after a UFO sighting. In other words, they had an American accent and looked American, and behaved the same way as our Men in Black behave here. But if that was the CIA, again, they were pretty clumsy. If they were going to send someone around to harass UFO witnesses overseas, they should have sent someone with an undetectable accent.

Could you summarize the idea of this other, "extra-dimensional reality" that intertwines with our own?

Well, again, that's a very old, basic idea in religion, and in the occult. It seems as if there is another state of energy that can co-exist with us, in the space we're occupying now.

The entities in that other dimension are able to move into our dimension rather freely, and cause some our ghost reports, and a lot of the other strange things that have happened. If that is true – if that's where these things are coming from – then they are beyond our reach, probably forever. They can toy with us whenever they want to.

But I envision this "fourth dimension" not as a world, but as a state of energy. These energy forms can take any form they want to in our world. Again, that's a very old religious idea. You know, I talked with people who have been visited by important historical figures, like Abraham Lincoln and Jesus Christ – who swore that that "Abe" and "Jesus" were physical.

And whether they're spacemen or Christ or Abraham Lincoln, they all give essentially the same message, the same kind of philosophy. Whatever your particular frame of reference is, they'll appear in that frame of reference. For instance, I've been a magic buff all my life, so if I meet one, it should be "Harry Houdini." I won't accept a Venusian or Abraham Lincoln, but if Harry Houdini walked in, I'd love to talk with him for a few hours. If they wanted to reach me, that would be the way to reach me.

It seems like the electromagnetic spectrum is an important link.

Yes, we now know a lot of these physical manifestations in terms of the electromagnetic spectrum. Many of the witnesses suffer sunburn – at night – from these objects. There are many effects. They stall automobiles. We know that this happens with very low frequency (VLF) waves. When you get up to the very high frequency waves, gamma rays and things like that, they can kill you.

We have a number of cases where people have died almost immediately after being exposed to a flying saucer. Some people have been badly burned, and some have simply died of leukemia two or three days later. Normally, leukemia takes weeks, months, or even years to kill you. But in these cases, people who were perfectly healthy came down with leukemia the day after seeing a UFO, and they were dead three days later. It baffles the doctors.

So, we know that these objects are giving off all these energies from the different levels of the electromagnetic spectrum. They've often been observed going through certain changes of color, which indicate they are crossing the visible spectrum, going from ultraviolet to infrared.

Energy is always coming both down from the skies, and up from the earth's crust.

Yes. Astrology is based on this. We're surrounded by – bathed in – energy from space, and we're getting all kinds of energy from the earth.

I came across a fascinating thing when I did a lot of investigating in West Virginia. Before the white man arrived here, the Indians avoided West Virginia. West Virginia has all kinds of monsters and things, but it's a very fertile area – wooded, and great hunting grounds and everything. The Indians lived in Ohio, and they settled all around West Virginia, but they stayed the hell out of West Virginia. They thought it was a cursed place. They had tall, hairy monsters, all kinds of UFO landings, the Mothman, and winged creatures. Crazy things happen down there all the time.

You know, Delphi in Greece was one of these highly charged places – whatever the charge is. I tend to think that it's some kind of magnetic field in these areas.

Shouldn't we, as our technology advances, be able to duplicate these effects?

We're now starting to look into magnetic anomalies. The magnetic conditions of the earth keep changing. When they change in one particular way, you start to have a UFO wave, and people start seeing things. Maybe they were there all the time, but remained invisible to us. And when the vibes change, we can't see them anymore.

Woodstock, New York had a big UFO wave in 1966. A friend of mine, Dr. Berthold Schwarz, came up and interviewed quite a few of the witnesses and contactees. Most contactees prefer to remain anonymous; we call them "silent contactees." They never write books, and you never hear about them.

They view it almost as a religious experience. Other people, of course, can experience complete terror; their only desire is to get as far away from the object as possible. Other people, of course, have a euphoric experience. It's almost a sexual experience. They go out every night afterwards, hoping to have another such experience.

Dr. Wilhelm Reich is being re-canonized, by the way. There's a big movement now. A lot of scientists have suddenly begun to think he's right.

A lot of the research with Kirlian photography tends to verify that these magical, mysterious auras are verifiable. They're just an extension of energies we already understand.

I think the aura plays an important part in the witness-selection process. Whoever or whatever these forces are, they are able to pick people out by their auras. Some people may have a specific kind of aura that they can zero in on. There are a number of interesting sightings where the "ufonauts" or entities apparently couldn't see the people who were watching them.

That's a switch.

It was if they were looking at something else – another landscape or something. Maybe they weren't even aware that they were in our dimension. And maybe, if a person with the right aura were standing at that site, they would be able to see their aura; that may be the secret of their mysterious selectivity. They clearly do not choose people at random. If you do a study of the names of witnesses, they are not evenly distributed. There is no way that a Jankowski should be more apt to see a UFO than a Smith.

There are many unconnected "quirks," like the name game thing, which don't fit into any neat theory.

They all seem to be little clues. It takes an enormous amount of work to collect enough of these clues to get somewhere. And for the past 25 years, the ET believers have been looking for the wrong clues. It's only in recent years that we've started trying to do the statistical studies and the other, very basic kind of work, which really needs to be done before you can even ask the right questions.

At this point we don't even know what the right questions are. The question is not, "Are these things from outer space?" Or "Are they real?" Too many people have seen them and had experiences. The question really is: "What is causing all of this, and does it have any real meaning to us, collectively?"

We know that to the individual, it all has great meaning. To certain individuals, it changes their whole lives to have one of these experiences. But does it have any meaning to us as a society? People have been seeing ghosts for thousands of years, but what meaning has it really had for us? I've been looking for the answers for years, and I just find more questions.

CHAPTER 12

GENERAL DOUGLAS MACARTHUR: UFOLOGIST – *UFO REPORT* – JANUARY 1978

An elite group of scientists and military officers gathered for a very private meeting in New York City in 1958. Their purpose was to discuss UFOs. The principle speaker at the meeting was none other than General Douglas MacArthur, perhaps the greatest military leader of modern times. His record as the Supreme Commander in the Pacific theater during World War II, and his conflict with President Harry Truman during the Korean War, have been the subjects of several books, television dramas, and a recent motion picture.

Less well known is the fact that the General was an avid student of the UFO phenomenon. He was actually obsessed with the subject, for he feared that UFOs were hostile invaders from some other planet.

In the wake of the massive UFO wave of 1957, there were many quiet meetings all across the country. The U.S. Air Force, which had tried to get out of the flying saucer business in 1955 with the release of *Project Blue Book Report Number 14*, a debunking attempt, found itself once more embroiled in controversy.

The CIA's Project Windfall, a covert investigation of UFO contactees, was enmeshed in bureaucratic bumbling and confusion. Major Donald Keyhoe's new organization, NICAP, was tilting at governmental windmills, trying to force the issue and alert an apathetic Congress. The news media and the general public regarded the whole UFO affair as a carnival.

But General MacArthur knew better. In his deep, articulate voice, he told the 1958 meeting that he believed an extraterrestrial military force was scouting this planet, preparatory to a massive invasion. He felt that we should be working to develop weapons and plans to combat the invaders.

As an initial first step, he suggested that we set up a crash-program to perfect rockets and space travel ourselves. (In 1958, our space program was a feeble effort, far outclassed by the Russians, who had successfully sent a satellite into orbit the previous year.) The men who attended that meeting left tight-lipped and grim-faced, impressed and alarmed by the brilliant general's careful analysis of the situation. Details of the meeting were kept secret for years, until after MacArthur's death in 1964.

In an interview with columnist Henry Taylor in 1955, MacArthur had already publicly revealed his concern over unidentified flying objects and their possible impact on our civilization. He was then living in retirement at the Waldorf Towers in Manhattan, and felt free to express his conclusions that UFOs were real and posed a horrible threat.

A self-assured man, MacArthur was not afraid to speak his mind. He had crossed swords with Truman when he had blatantly ignored presidential orders during the Korean War. He had graduated at the top of his class at West Point, and had worked his way up to the post of Army Chief of Staff in 1930, at the age of 50. He was not at all reluctant to assume responsibility, and he didn't hesitate to stomp on the less competent people around him. During World War II, he built a military empire in the Pacific, and after the war, he directed the conversion of Japan to a democracy.

So it didn't bother him that the official U.S. Air Force position was that UFOs were weather balloons, hoaxes, swamp gas, and falling stars. He thought the public should know the truth – at least the truth as he saw it.

What were his conclusions based upon? Military men, particularly generals, are pragmatists. They act on facts, not theories. General MacArthur began to collect facts about UFOs during World War II. The mysterious "foo fighters" appeared in the European theater in 1943, but reports of their appearances were at first suppressed by military intelligence, because they were thought to be secret German devices. German pilots were also seeing the strange objects, and thought they were some Allied secret weapon.

By 1944, the phenomenon had spread to the Pacific. American ships and planes saw the objects, and even shot at them. Incredible "flying submarines" – huge cylindrical objects – rose up from the water, and flew away in full view of the entire crews of ships. As in Europe, reports of these incidents were stamped "Top Secret" and shuffled all the way to MacArthur's headquarters.

MacArthur took a personal interest in these puzzling reports and, thinking they could relate to some Japanese development, he set up a small group of intelligence officers to collect and study them. As the pile of reports grew, the team realized they were dealing with a totally unknown technology.

In some cases, American radar had detected gigantic objects, larger than any known aircraft, flitting about the Pacific. Several military planes sent up in pursuit of these things either crashed inexplicably, or disappeared altogether. Radio transmissions and radar were frequently jammed in areas where the UFOs were active. By 1945, the intelligence men were convinced – and they convinced MacArthur – that the mysterious aerial objects were of extraterrestrial origin, and were hostile.

Paradoxically, other unrelated intelligence teams operating in Europe came to a different conclusion. The Royal Air Force's "foo fighter" investigation, launched by General Massey in 1943, decided the objects were harmless – probably a natural phenomenon of some sort. The director of the RAF's intelligence branch, R.V. Jones, became steadfastly anti-UFO. American intelligence in Europe fared even worse.

The reports of American pilots were never centralized and studied, but were simply scattered throughout the massive files. Only General MacArthur and his men in the Pacific had undertaken a systematic investigation, and their findings were jealously isolated from their European counterparts, and even from the Pentagon.

When the war ended in 1945, the European foo fighters were all but forgotten, but the phantom fliers continued to be seen around the Pacific, particularly around Okinawa and the islands where the United States was installing its first air bases. And those Top Secret reports continued to pile up on General MacArthur's desk.

A five-star general has considerable power. MacArthur not only ruled his empire with an iron hand, but the tentacles of his intelligence service spread around the world. This was proven by a curious incident in Britain in the fall of 1946.

That summer, northern Europe was inundated with "ghost rockets," unidentified cigar-shaped objects that appeared over Norway, Sweden, Finland, and even as far south as Greece and Morocco. The Scandinavian countries launched full-scale investigations, fearing the "rockets" were of Russian origin. (The Russians had no rockets at that time, and most of the top German rocket scientists had been captured by the Americans.)

Soon after the "ghost rocket" wave subsided, RAF Intelligence received a report that a rocket had crashed outside of London. It proved to be a complete hoax, and was never revealed to the press, or anyone else. The intelligence officers who had investigated it were so embarrassed that they tried to keep the whole thing secret. But within a few days, a telegram reached the RAF Commander. It was from Gen. Douglas MacArthur in Japan, asking for details on the unidentified rocket that had crashed in England!

Obviously, General MacArthur was tuned in to everything happening everywhere, and he was particularly interested in reports about unidentified flying objects. (During the war, he had made special efforts to protect Standard Oil facilities, and probably benefited from their far-flung intelligence network, which was set up long before the FBI, OSS, or CIA.)

Twenty years later, R.V. Jones revealed the story of MacArthur's telegram in a public speech. Wartime witnesses of UFOs in the Pacific and Europe eventually told their stories to civilian UFO organizations, and to professional writers compiling books on the subject.

The Korean War brought a new surge of UFO sightings in the Pacific, and many of these reports found their way into print. Even *Life* magazine devoted considerable space to them. The great American UFO wave of June-July 1947 had stirred public and press interest in flying saucers. They had become a salable "human interest" subject, like sea serpents and Abominable Snowmen.

But to Douglas MacArthur, who had been collecting reports since 1944, there was nothing amusing to the endless sightings.

When he retired into civilian life, MacArthur maintained his interest in UFOs. He collected books and magazines about them and, according to a person close to him in the last years of his life, talked for hours about the "threat from outer space" to anyone who would listen.

In 1962, President John F. Kennedy invited the aging general to the White House, and they spent two hours together in private discussion. We don't know if UFOs were ever mentioned in that talk. Kennedy later said they had talked about Vietnam, and that MacArthur had outlined why we should never get into a land war in the Orient. (Whatever happened to that excellent piece of advice?)

Soon afterwards, President Kennedy announced that he was going to pour billions of dollars into a space program designed to put a man on the moon by the end of the decade.

One of General MacArthur's final public appearances was a speech he delivered at West Point, in which he told the young cadets that "the next war" would be fought in space, when a united mankind would battle "evil beings" from some other planet. The speech was widely quoted in the press at the time, but there was no real discussion of its implications, and it had no impact. To some, it was just the harmless babbling of an old man. (He was 84 when he died.)

To others, it was sober warning from a man who had access to information denied ordinary ufologists – a man not given to uttering casual, unsubstantiated admonishments.

We ignored MacArthur's advice about Vietnam. Can we afford to ignore this?

CHAPTER 13

MYSTERY EXPLOSIONS AND UFOS – *UFO REPORT* – MAY 1978

Tremendous "skyquakes" startled the East Coast of the United States last winter and scientists are completely at a loss to explain them. Now someone may have the answer.

In October 1976, I was pecking away at a typewriter in the Foreign Press office in Stockholm, Sweden when a mammoth explosion suddenly shook the entire city. Windows rattled and objects rolled off tables. Local newspapermen besieged the airports and military with queries.

Strangely, nothing had exploded in the area, and the authorities had no idea what had happened. Various rumors circulated, the most popular being that a Soviet submarine base had suffered a disaster hundreds of miles away, on the other side of the Baltic. A few days later, another violent blast shook Oslo, Norway and, like the Stockholm explosion, seemed to occur somewhere in the upper atmosphere, without leaving a trace.

Skyquakes are a relatively common phenomenon, and remained the exclusive province of a handful of Forteans until December 1977, when a series of mysterious aerial blasts shook the Atlantic seaboard.

Overnight, a wide variety of scientists and self-styled experts embraced the subject, and President Carter ordered the U.S. Air Force to investigate. One scientist, widely quoted in the press, actually proposed that the explosions were caused by bubbles of methane gas coming up through fissures in the ocean's bottom (i.e., methane gas). That's "swamp gas," folks – an explanation even more unlikely than the phenomenon itself!

Actually, these mysterious blasts have been occurring in the northeast for many years, and there are legends of "phantom artillery" going back several centuries. The most famous of these are the "Barisal Guns" of India. British colonists frequently heard the inexplicable booms around Bengal. Others reported similar aerial blasts in the West Indies, around Haiti, and in far-off Central Australia. Lake Bosumtwi, Africa, and Lough Neagh, in Ireland, were also frequently visited by the mysterious cannons.

The Indians in the Black Hills of South Dakota have legends about the explosions. The Lewis and Clark expedition is supposed to have heard the phenomenon in the Rocky Mountains. Lake Seneca, one of the Finger Lakes in New York State, has a long history of "airquakes," as the

146 CHAPTER 13: MYSTERY EXPLOSIONS AND UFOS – *UFO REPORT* – MAY 1978

newspapers of 1977 dubbed the sounds.

The gas-bubble theory was already old hat in 1897, and was generally discredited by witnesses who reported that the lake was frozen over at the times of the blasts.

East Haddam, Connecticut is another spot that has been haunted by the explosions for generations. Before Europeans settled there, the Native Americans called East Haddam "Morehemoodus," or "the place of noises."

On December 2, 1977, a skyquake jarred the residents of New Canaan, Connecticut and was accompanied by strange lights in the sky. The aerial sounds followed a course that led southward over New Jersey to the Carolinas, suggesting that some object had passed along that route into the famous Bermuda Triangle. Military authorities and aviation officials staunchly denied that any supersonic aircraft were operating in those areas at the time.

Back in 1952, when supersonic aircraft were still limited to a few experimental models, officialdom carried out the same exercise in futility. Residents of Long Island, just east of New York City, were plagued that year by skyquakes, yet the only newspaper reporter to take an interest was the late Dorothy Kilgallen. She tried to find out if any military authorities knew the cause, and was given the royal runaround. Like flying saucers, skyquakes were a non-subject. The authorities reasoned that if we didn't pay any attention to them, they would just go away.

The sobering truth is that skyquakes are on the increase. They tend to occur when UFO sightings increase, and they follow the general patterns of the UFO phenomenon. It is possible that skyquakes are produced by the rapid transit of unidentified flying objects. There is no known atmospheric condition that could cause them, and the hundred-year-old scientific speculation that bubbles of gas are the culprits is insupportable.

There are two major UFO channels or belts on this planet. One lies at 60 degrees north, indicating that a great deal of unobserved UFO activity has been taking place north of the Arctic Circle since 1840. The second channel stretches north to south, at approximately 70 degrees west, from Canada to Argentina. This belt includes some of the busiest and most mysterious places on Earth, such as the Bermuda Triangle in the Atlantic, and the baffling area around Bahia Blanca, Argentina – site of some of the strangest UFO cases.

We could list scores of peculiar events along this belt, from New England to the Carolinas. For example, at 8:15 p.m. on the night of April 25, 1966, a spectacular "meteor" passed along the channel. The brilliantly illuminated object was seen by thousands of people in several states. A number of amateur photographers managed to snap pictures of it. In Pennsylvania, witnesses claimed their automobile engines stalled inexplicably as the object passed over. After cruising over South Carolina, the thing disappeared southward over the Atlantic – towards the "Devil's Triangle."

At exactly the same time, exactly on the opposite side of the Earth, in the Tashkent region of the Soviet Union, a violent earthquake struck, killing ten and leaving 200,000 people homeless! How strange that a major disaster would strike on one side of the world, while thousands of people on the other side were viewing an awesome "meteor." Could the two events have been somehow related?

Eerie lights and aerial phenomena have been observed before and during major earthquakes in many parts of the world. But the strange lights and skyquakes of December 1977 were not accompanied by earthquakes. However, the path of the skyquakes did follow the same route as the meteor of 1966 – the 70-degree west channel. The "meteor" traveled in silence, indicating it was high above the atmosphere.

A natural object entering the atmosphere over New England would make a noise, but it would be in a retrograde orbit, and would probably burn up or hit the ground before it traveled as far south as the Carolinas. Any object traveling at the supersonic speed and thus leaving a stream of sonic booms in its wake would have to be under some kind of control to cover such a great distance. If the skyquakes were caused by an object, we can conclude it was a controlled object, one which was *flying* rather than falling.

There is nothing in nature that we know of which would be capable of producing a series of sonic booms over an area of 1,000 miles or more. The aviation authorities have assured us that no manmade aircraft was responsible for the noises.

So, we are left with an unidentified, a phantom aircraft that presumably entered the 70-degree west channel over New England, and soared southward into the Bermuda Triangle. It must have been very special, because many UFOs have been clocked traveling at supersonic speeds *without* creating sonic booms. Indeed, most UFOs travel in total silence. A UFO that leaves sonic booms in its wake is unique, and perhaps *not* a "flying saucer."

The correlation between the "meteor" of 1966 and the Tashkent earthquake suggests that some other force is at work here. It could be geological – some environmental force that is affected by geological changes. The lights seen during earthquakes could be a product of that force – a form of static electricity generated by the movements of the Earth's crust.

Skyquakes could be *implosions* rather than explosions, caused by the rush of air into holes or empty pockets in the atmosphere. Such holes might be caused by geophysical changes, or they could be created when a solid object suddenly disappears, and the air rushes into the space it had occupied. There are countless stories of UFOs disappearing suddenly, often accompanied by a loud report.

There are reliable estimates placing the force of some skyquakes as equal to several tons of TNT. Blasts of such magnitude are plainly more severe than the force generated by some of the above explanations.

A bubble of gas might, if there was anything around to ignite it, produce a pop roughly equal to the bursting of a small balloon. A meteorite crashing through the atmosphere would produce a low, steady rumble, not a sharp bang.

So what causes our skyquakes? They seem to be somehow related to UFO phenomena, yet the observational evidence precludes a UFO explanation. What they are, what causes them, and what they mean all remain mysteries.

Ironically, the skyquakes of December 1977 led the media to rediscover them, and to give them a new credibility. They suddenly became an "item," even though they have been shattering the peace and quiet of the countryside for hundreds of years.

Now that President Carter has recognized their existence, the boondoggling will begin. Government agencies will dole out fat contracts to universities to investigate. After several years of such expensive investigations, we will probably be offered new variations on the tired old Swamp Gas theory. And whatever – or whoever – is behind the "airquakes" will continue to rattle our windows with impunity.

CHAPTER 14

At precisely 9:18 on the morning of February 19, a large kitchen sink of gleaming porcelain and shining chrome came crashing out of a cloudless sky, into tding Fortean, had this to say in his book, *Investigating the Unexplained*:

> An extraordinary man named Charles Hoy Fort set wheels in motion that have now brought all of us, from scientists to bumpkins, back to reality. Fort did this single-handedly by the use of two weapons – a spear and a shield. The spear was nothing less than the amazing truth itself, with which he jabbed and stabbed at orthodoxy and unorthodoxy alike, whenever he spotted a chink in their armor. And these were not just chinks, but gaping holes. His shield was a rather fiendish sense of humor, which he also used as an offensive weapon. There is nothing more deadly than satire for puncturing stuffed shirts.
>
> However, contrary to popular opinion, Fort never denigrated true science. He went after every type of pontificator or other idiot claiming superiority. In doing so, he always chose first to quote from the pontificator himself before inserting his spear. Meanwhile, he spent his life collecting every type of "leftover" that he could find in the tangible world of reality. Most prominent among these were Fafrotskies and Oopths.

Born in Albany, New York, on August 9, 1874, Charles Fort led a rather mundane, even dull, life. He passed his days in the New York Public Library, sifting through old scientific journals at the expense of his eyesight. His eyes had always been weak, and by the time he died, he was almost totally blind. Every single night, Fort and his wife, Anna, would go to the silent movies. That probably didn't help his waning eyesight either.

It was Fort's misfortune to live in an age when writers were cheated and conned, ignored and abused, and expected to starve – a period not too unlike the 1980s. At the age of 18, he became editor of a newspaper published in Queens, New York, *The Independent*, which died after a few issues.

So, in 1893, at the age of 19, he set out to hitchhike around the world.

Already he was an imposing young man, nearly six feet tall, somewhat overweight (he would be "portly" all his life), with a fashionable moustache and a pair of thick-lensed glasses perched on his nose. His grandfather, John Hoy, financed his adventures by supplying him with the lordly sum of $25 per month – more than enough needed to survive in those days.

In the grand tradition of all young adventurers, he slept under the stars beside the railroad tracks, went hungry, and dreamed of the glorious days ahead, when his travels would inspire immortal short stories and novels.

Instead, he contracted a fever in South Africa. It was a mysterious malady, probably malaria, and it would hound him for the rest of his days. He returned a shuddering wreck to New York City, where an English girl, Anna Filing, nursed him back to health.

They were married on October 26, 1896. They did not live happily ever after. Obsessed with the business of writing, Charles Fort was doomed to spend many years on the periphery of society, barely able to meet the rent for a succession of dingy furnished rooms. He held a number of temporary jobs, working as a hotel clerk, watchman, and dishwasher. During the cold winters, he and his wife broke up the furniture to keep the fire going.

By the time he was 30, he had written ten novels. Only one, *The Outcast Manufacturers*, was ever published. And it laid a large egg.

However, Fort's sense of humor enabled him to write salable short stories. Theodore Dreiser, a young editor at *Smith's Magazine* in 1905, later recalled: "Fort came to me with the best humorous short stories that I have ever seen produced in America. I purchased some of them, and other editors did the same. And among ourselves – Richard Duffy of *Tom Watson's*, Charles Agnew MacLean of *Popular Magazine*, and others – we loved to talk of him, and his future as a new and rare literary star."

Despite the growing demand for his stories, Fort found it difficult to keep bread on the table. "I have not been paid for one story since May," he wrote in his diary in December 1907. "Have two dollars left. *Watson's* has cheated me out of $155. Dreiser has sent back two stories he told me he would buy – one even advertised to appear in his next number. Everything is pawned. I am unable to write. I can do nothing else for a living. My mind is filled with pictures of myself cutting my throat or leaping out the window, head first."

In his early diaries, notes, and letters (now preserved at the New York Public Library), Fort complained of frequent spells of depression and dark, suicidal moods. These would be followed by frenzied fits of writing, when he would churn out novels and short stories by the pound. He was obviously a manic-depressive type personality. It is even possible that his malaria-like malady was actually one form of the mysterious physical ailments that plague such personalities.

Somehow, Fort and Anna managed to stay alive through those bad years. Around the age of 32, he began to spend more and more time in the New York Public Library. While browsing through some old scientific journals, he had come across some odd, unexplained items, and he discovered that the journals, newspapers, and magazines of the 18th Century were crammed with such items.

There were strange objects seen in the sky, weird creatures and machines rising out of the world's oceans, peculiar foreign objects falling from the sky – everything ranging from great quantities of raw meat and blood to hand-carved stone pillars. People and things were often disappearing suddenly, only to reappear halfway around the world. Human footprints and manmade objects were constantly turning up in coalmines and geological strata dating back millions of years.

Fort recorded these reports on tiny scraps of brown paper, writing his notes in his own special code. Day by day, month by month, year by year, the notes accumulated, until he had thousands of them. In 1915, at the age of 41, he started to organize these notes into a book he planned to call *X and Y*. He never finished it, discarding it for another idea – a book that would eventually appear as *The Book of the Damned*.

In May 1916, his uncle, Frank Fort, died, leaving him a small inheritance – small, but sufficient in those days to support him and Anna for the rest of their lives. The long struggle was over. The Forts moved to a little apartment in the Bronx.

When *The Book of the Damned* was completed, wary editors read the opening lines and held their noses: "A procession of the damned. And by the damned, I mean the excluded. We shall have a procession of data that science has excluded. Battalions of the accursed, captained by pallid data that I have exhumed, will march – some of them livid, and some of them fiery, and some of them rotten."

By this time, Theodore Dreiser had become one of America's most famous and most influential novelists. He was also Fort's leading advocate. He took the manuscript of *The Book of the Damned* to his own publisher, Horace Liveright, and dumped it on his desk.

Liveright reluctantly read it and then complained, "I can't publish this."

It'll lose money." Dreiser told him flatly, "If you don't publish it, you'll lose me." So, Liveright contacted an amazed and delighted Charles Fort. Today, 60 years later, Dreiser is almost forgotten except for a few college classes, and Liveright has been reduced to a footnote in books about the 1920s. But the works of Charles Fort remain in print, in paperback editions, in every drugstore.

Fort's response to the publication of his first book since his ill-fated novel a decade earlier was to sink into a deep depression. He gathered up his notes – an estimated 40,000 of them – and burned them all. Then, he and Anna packed their bags and sailed for England. Fort believed that his book was a flop (sales were very sluggish), and that he had wasted his life. He was 46 years old.

American dollars stretched much further in Europe in those days, so the Forts settled in London for eight years. We don't know how Anna spent her days while her husband went off to the British Museum, to pour over old books and crumbling magazines. In the evenings, he often joined the loafers at the Speaker's Corner in Hyde Park, to amuse himself in debates. His second book, *New Lands*, was written in London. It dealt chiefly with "sky quakes," the thunderous explosions that have emanated from the sky for hundreds of years throughout the world.

In recent years, these sky quakes have occurred every January and February in the northeastern United States. The "authorities" (who are these idiot "authorities?") have repeatedly assured reporters that they are caused by airplanes, especially the Concorde supersonic jet. They neglect to mention the long history of the phenomenon. Sky quakes were with us long before jets, or even airplanes, had been invented. In 1952, columnist Dorothy Kilgallen was complaining about the sky quakes that were shaking Long Island and Connecticut – areas that have suffered from these explosions for at least 300 years.

Fort envisioned, tongue in cheek, a land in the sky that served as home base for all the debris that keeps falling on us. Huge blocks of ice, for example, have been crashing through rooftops for hundreds of years, occasionally killing people and livestock. Today, when a 50-pound hunk of ice hurtles into someone's living room, our learned "authorities" announce that it fell from a passing airplane. They have the audacity to claim that it is refuse from the plane's bathroom.

Of course, any pilot will tell you there is no way for the bathrooms to discharge water while in flight, but our "explainers" never bother to check such details. Fort chuckled a bit about these ice falls, and facetiously suggested there might be great aerial ice fields up there. A silly notion, but a few years ago NASA suggested the same thing. Somewhere hundreds of miles overhead, there might be "new lands" of ice.

Critics of Fort, most of whom are members of the scientific establishment and have never even read his books, complain that his main sources were newspapers. This is not so. He carefully cited all of his sources in his books, and they are mostly scientific journals – particularly journals of astronomy. Fort took great glee in pointing out the stupidity of astronomers, usually damning them with their own words. "I don't know what the mind of an astronomer looks like, but I think of a fizzle with excuses revolving around it," he wrote in *New Lands*.

Each new generation of astronomers discards all the theories of the previous generation, and creates some whoppers of their own. Our space probes have disproved many of the most cherished myths of modern astronomy. It's too bad Fort wasn't around to view the intellectual acrobatics of the 1960s.

Astronomers were proven wrong about many of the basics of our solar system (e.g., the temperature of Venus, the age of the moon, the rotation of Mercury, the topography of Mars, etc.). Until 1960, all leading astronomers flatly denied the possibility of extraterrestrial life. Then NASA and the space program began flashing big bucks – tax dollars – for investigations into life on other worlds. And, of course, everyone immediately jumped on the bandwagon. Suddenly, we were being told that there must be billions of inhabited planets out there.

Some scientists even created "exobiology," the supposed study of extraterrestrial life. Since we have no samples of such life, and since all of our efforts with radio telescopes and such have failed to find evidence of even a single planet outside our solar system, it is mighty difficult to investigate such life. But we still poured many millions of dollars down that exobiology rat-hole. Now that the gravy train has ended, the astronomers are quietly retreating to their pre-1960 positions.

Fort was not against the astronomers. They amused him. But the other sciences are just as amusing. Archaeologists have been busy burying more things than they dig up, because everything *must* fit into their theories. For example, they tell us that North America was unsettled by anyone except Indians before the Europeans arrived. They overlook all the stone towers and structures found all over this continent (including miles of paved roads) when the pilgrims arrived.

Fort catalogued all kinds of metal objects (the Indians didn't work metals), from swords and axes to coins that have been found and dated as pre-Columbian. Somebody was mining ore and coal in this country, and pumping oil in Pennsylvania before Columbus set sail. Rather than tussle with the problem of identifying those mysterious North Americans, the archaeologists have chosen to ignore the artifacts they left behind.

Intellectual cowardice is only one of the problems of the academic community. Fort rubbed their noses in the swill generated by their gibberish and illiteracy. It was no secret then – or now – that academic publications follow a style designed to protect the inept, and to conceal total ignorance. People with nothing to say, and lacking even the ability to say nothing, can hide behind the academic method for a lifetime.

"I shall be scientific about it," Fort noted. "Said Sir Isaac Newton – or virtually said he – 'If there is no change in the direction of a moving body, the direction of a moving body is not changed.' But, continued he, 'if something be changed, it is changed as much as it is changed…' How do geologists determine the age of rocks? By the fossils in them. And how do they determine the age of the fossils? By the rocks they're in. Having started with the logic of Euclid, I go on with the wisdom of a Newton."

Perhaps the mostly widely quoted Fortean statement is his allegation that we "are property," that somebody or some thing owns this miserable little planet, and owns us as well. Fort had reinvented religion! Like the religionists, he saw that mankind was constantly being manipulated, that some indefinable influence was controlling our individual and collective destinies.

Thus, in his way, Mr. Fort reinvented what theologians call "predestination." He knew, as our better-informed philosophers now know, that the present does not control the future, but rather that the future – and its needs – somehow controls the past.

If Adolf Hitler had been born in Bolivia, 20 million victims might still be alive. But the future needed Hitler, because it needed the atomic bomb and the accompanying hardware capable of destroying the planet. We would not have developed the doomsday machine if we hadn't launched a crash program as part of our effort to crush Mr. Hitler. We not only failed to save his 20 million victims; we built the gallows for the entire human race. Since we still do not know how to read the future, we are all Napoleons marching confidently to Waterloo.

Fort and his wife returned to New York in 1929, just in time to watch the lemmings of Wall Street pull the "flush" lever on the economy. Luckily, Fort had invested his meager inheritance in the right kind of bonds and real estate ventures, so he managed to stay afloat. They moved back to the

Bronx and he worked on his new book, titled *LO!* This one assaulted the astronomers, and listed the many strange reports of unidentified aerial objects.

Sitting in his tiny study, Fort pecked out two simple sentences that, although he probably didn't realize it fully at the time, would invent the flying saucer mystery, define it, and touch upon the only possible explanations. "Unknown, luminous things, or beings," he observed, "have often been seen, sometimes close to this earth and sometimes high in the sky. It may be that some of them were living things that occasionally come from somewhere else in our existence, but that others were lights on the vessels of explorers, or voyagers, from somewhere else."

For the first 20 years of the modern UFO epoch (1947-1967), the notion that those mysterious lights and objects belonged to "the vessels of explorers, or voyagers, from somewhere else" was the most popular theory. A handful of cranks and wishful thinkers spread the propaganda that extraterrestrial visitants were flocking to this mudball.

But the great UFO wave of 1964-68 attracted a new generation of investigators and scientists. They soon realized that the extraterrestrial hypothesis was untenable for many reasons. So, they fell back on the explanation that the objects came "from somewhere else in our existence." That "somewhere else" could be as elusive as the fabled fourth dimension, or the "other planes" of psychic lore.

Fort himself had realized, early in the game, that the events he was studying were not unusual. They happened year after year, century after century. More importantly, they tended to occur in the same geographical locations. This strongly indicates that these events – be they fish falling from the sky, or strange aircraft adorned with flashing lights – are inexorably linked with the earth. They are as much a part of our environment as clouds and bumblebees.

Another important factor, often overlooked by believers in a single type of phenomenon, is that all "Fortean" events are interrelated in some mysterious fashion. Science-fiction writer Damon Knight went through the trouble of extracting some 1,200 events from Fort's books. These were fed into a computer at Bell Laboratories in New Jersey, and some very interesting patterns were revealed.

"One salient fact about UFOs is missing from all modern accounts I have seen," Knight commented. "Fort's data show that they are not isolated phenomena. Unknown flying objects, unknown bodies seen in space, appearances and disappearances, poltergeist activity, falls of strange substances and organisms from the sky – all these things show strong positive correlations with each other. Taken together, they show evidence of rhythmic fluctuation."

Incredible though it may be, sightings of sea serpents tend to occur simultaneously with sightings of unidentified flying objects, showers of frogs and worms and kitchen sinks (actually no kitchen sinks have ever been reported – the anecdote at the beginning of this article was just a sly hoax), and mysterious disappearances.

As for the latter, they are most often grouped in the month of July – which is also a big UFO month. A man goes out to mow his lawn and is never seen again. Some 3,000 people disappear annually in the United States in this fashion; that is, 3,000 people vanish with no apparent motivation – no hint of what happened to them or how. Naturally, many hundreds of thousands of others disappear, fleeing the law, relatives, or creditors.

When a UFO wave develops (usually about once every five years), we can be sure that sightings at Loch Ness will increase sharply, that showers of stones (always warm to the touch) will start pelting isolated homes in suburbia, and that people will start to disappear everywhere. These manifestations are accompanied by magnetic storms – sharp and dramatic deviations in the earth's magnetism in certain locales – particularly in areas such as the famous Bermuda Triangle.

In the 1950s, a Canadian named Wilbur Smith devised a special instrument that could detect and measure the collapse of molecular structures during the magnetic storms. That is, all kinds of objects would literally fall apart when the conditions were just right. Volunteer airline pilots carried Smith's instruments around the world, and he was able to make crude charts of the phenomenon. Unfortunately, no one continued his experiments after his death.

Charles Fort intuitively understood much of this, and defined it all, in an age when very few people were willing to take any of it seriously. Those few – Dreiser, Hecht, Tiffany Thayer – made humble pilgrimages to the Bronx to visit with Fort.

He was not the most sociable man around. He and Anna remained by themselves. They didn't have a telephone. When Fort was not at the library, or sorting through his thousands of notes, he was working on his super checkers game – a game he had invented that employed hundreds of pieces, and was so complicated that he was the only one who could play it.

On January 26, 1931, a distinguished group of authors, newspapermen, and publishers held a dinner at the Savoy Plaza. Fort had spurned invitations, but was tricked into attending. Tiffany Thayer, a successful hack novelist, announced the formation of a Fortean Society, and Fort was appalled.

Meanwhile, strange things began to happen in the Fort household. Pictures fell off the walls. Books slid off shelves. Glassware went crashing to the floor without visible cause. Fort kept careful notes on these curious events.

In 1932, he completed *Wild Talents*, his fourth and final book, in which he discussed mysterious animal mutilations (which are still going on worldwide) and teleportations of people and objects. In fact, he coined the word "teleportation."

By the end of April, Fort was very weak – barely able to walk. On May 3, 1932, Charles Hoy Fort died. He was 58 years old. He left behind some 60,000 scraps of paper covered with almost indecipherable notes about the damned. Anna Fort lived another five years, and was haunted by mysterious rappings and noises, according to Dreiser.

Tiffany Thayer ran the Fortean Society until his death in 1959. The society died with him.

Charles Fort perceived a truth that had been ignored by all the scientists and all the historians. Our world has two sets of natural laws. One set tells us stupidly simple things about gravity and nature. The other tells us that space and time are constantly distorted in our reality, and that we are all subject to the still undefined laws of this second set.

We never know when we might step through that magic door that will take us suddenly 10,000 miles away. We never know when we might suddenly encounter a beast or a being from "somewhere else in our existence." Fish might rain on us anytime, or red snow, or clouds of insects that no scientist can identify. Flying saucers will continue to buzz our farms and swamps, just as they have done for 2,000 years.

Science attempts to work with the first set of laws, and they come up with black holes. Magicians, occultists, and psychics strive to manipulate the second group of laws. In the closing years of this century, science and magic are merging. We are entering a new Dark Age when, as in an ancient time, the bizarre events of the superspectrum (a spectrum of energy beyond the known and the visible) dazzle and terrify.

Charles Fort anticipated the decline and fall of our civilization. He sought to understand the owners, controllers, and manipulators of our pitiful world. When he studied their many manifestations, he was obliged to ask, "If there is a universal mind, must it be sane?"

CHAPTER 15

THE ENDLESS PROCESSION – *PURSUIT #15* – SEPTEMBER 1982

On a warm June evening in 1430 A.D., four peasants in the village of Jaen, Spain, witnessed a remarkable procession. From four separate locations, they watched an estimated 500 people parade along the dusty roads, led by a tall, beautiful woman in a white robe, carrying an infant in her arms.

She wore a glowing mantle, ablaze with iridescent colors casting so much that it nearly blinded the witnesses. The procession was headed by seven youngsters dressed in white and bearing white crosses, followed by twenty priests marching in two rows, all chanting in an unintelligible tongue. Hundreds of people swarmed behind them, with hordes of barking dogs bringing up the rear.

The procession wound its way through the deserted streets to the church at San Ildefonso, where the glowing lady ascended a silvery throne. Suddenly, at the stroke of midnight, the entire mob vanished, inexplicably, leaving the four amazed peasants standing alone in the darkness. There was not a single footprint or trace of the procession in the dirt along their route.

When they reported their strange experience, the four witnesses were subjected to weeks of questioning and investigation by civil and religious authorities. They had all apparently seen the same identical things, and their report led to the origin of a sacred cult that flourished in Spain for several centuries.

According to the extensive records of the event, one of the witnesses had heard a voice on June 7th and 8th that whispered: "Do not sleep, and you will see good things." The procession appeared at 11:30 p.m. on the 10th of July.

Ghostly parades were not restricted to the fifteenth century. In my own investigations, I have heard many bizarre tales from sincere witnesses describing gatherings of strange beings on beaches and hilltops. There have been mysterious convoys of automobiles lacing through small towns in the wee hours, their drivers pale and seemingly entranced.

In one case on Long Island, two witnesses reportedly saw "hundreds of dogs, of all sizes and breeds," blocking roads and converging on a field where UFOs had previously been seen. Oddest of all, phantom police cars and men in police uniforms have appeared in remote places, diverted traffic, and then vanished. During one of their investigative sorties, Ivan Sanderson and his wife were detoured, on a backroad, by a mystery man in a naval uniform.

In a simpler age, the testimony of a solitary witness was sufficient to launch a legend. The thousands of religious miracles, so carefully investigated by religious authorities through the ages, were usually witnessed by one or two people, most often small children. It is probable that a large part of all mythology and folklore has a basis in fact; that a few witnesses actually saw (or thought they saw) the gods or monsters.

In the days before the printed word and electronic media, such incidents were preserved by oral tradition. When a succession of witnesses had reported essentially the same thing, often in the same geographical location, generation after generation, the existence of the god or demon became an established fact. Even the most hardnosed skeptic regarded the cumulative testimony as empirical.

The gods of ancient India and Egypt undoubtedly found life in this fashion, just as Ashtar, Indrid Cold, the MIB, and their various cronies from outer space are now becoming a part of our modern culture.

All of the manifestations of the past have served one primary purpose. They have advanced belief in some theological or philosophical concept, and supported one of the many frames of reference employed to hide the real nature of the phenomenon from us. They engage in what we now call psychological warfare, and they have always exploited our eagerness to believe.

The modern UFO scene is a sociological minefield, because it has produced a worldwide propaganda movement of willing evangelists advocating the existence of people from another planet, who altruistically intend to save us from ourselves. The leading extraterrestrial proselytizers have not had direct experience with the phenomenon themselves. Most have not even seen a funny light bobbling across the sky.

Nevertheless, they are convinced that there is someone out there, and they happily spend all of their time lecturing, appearing on radio and television, and making movies advancing their ideas about the great benign invasion from the cosmos. There are obviously many grave dangers in this kind of blind belief.

Our studies of the UFO percipients and contactees are teaching us that these encounters are more hallucinatory than real, and that some complex hypnotic process is involved. The real phenomenon is hiding behind a carefully engineered smokescreen of propaganda. Those funny lights and their hypnotic waves of energy are part of something that is related to this planet, and to us. But that something may be far beyond our meager powers of comprehension.

There are forces that can distort our reality and warp our fields of space and time. When we are caught up in these forces, we struggle to find an acceptable explanation for them, and then the manifestations begin to conform to that explanation, and so reinforce it.

Every few centuries, however, we abandon the old explanations and come up with new ones. Then the phenomenon obligingly tailors itself to those new beliefs. This factor alone indicates that part of the phenomenon, at least, is directly related to the human psyche, and these events are, in part, the work of the individual and collective unconscious.

Unfortunately, another part of the phenomenon seems to be operating outside of the human race (and often beyond time and space), manipulating us constantly, and with impunity. This is the part that we should worry about.

The gods of the ancients are returning, says Erich von Daniken. But actually they have been there all along. While many millions of people have been having casual sightings of strange things in the sky and on the ground, other millions have literally been abducted by the phenomenon and subjected to a brainwashing process.

They emerge from the experience with total amnesia, or with a vague, dreamlike memory or theory about what happened. But their lives change suddenly and remarkably. Their I.Q. is elevated. Their characters and personalities are altered. In several well-documented cases, their chronic ailments have suddenly been cured.

They divorce their wives or husbands, abandon their families, change their names, and move into new and better jobs. The process is more sophisticated now than it was in the time of the caveman, because we, ourselves, are more sophisticated. We have changed slowly, and improved slowly, over those thousands of years.

In other ages, these experiences were regarded as supernatural and mystical. Today, we try to fit them into a technological or scientific framework. Some view the contact stories with alarm, fearing that an alien race is trying to take us over. One group of ufologists is, in fact, convinced that some of these brainwashed humans have managed to attain top jobs in government and industry, and that the affairs of the world are now being controlled by extraterrestrial aliens (e.g., Reptilians, Grays, Tall Nordics, etc.).

However, the phenomenon does not really seem interested in our mundane, day-to-day affairs, except where they may influence the mysterious, long-range "plan." Darwin was partly right, perhaps, when he speculated about a process of evolution. But he did not see it as a completely controlled process. He lacked the historical perspective needed to view the development of mankind as a series of rungs on a long ladder of knowledge and *enlightenment*. The phenomenon was completely hidden from view in his day, accepted only as the exclusive province of religion or faith – the opposite of knowledge.

The flaw in the "ancient alien" theory is the absence of motive. The story goes that they arrived quietly, gave us some guidance, and then went away just as quietly. Were we just the recipients of an exercise in pure benevolence? Or were they *already* making plans for us?

If we really are biochemical robots, constructed by some mad-scientist "Nephilim" in ancient times, we were undoubtedly meant to serve some purpose. One set of Adam and Eves could not fulfill that purpose. It has taken a very long time, and required the careful conditioning of billions of people.

Today, the nature of that conditioning is slowly being revealed to us, perhaps as a first step toward revealing the entire master plan. The final revelation may not come in our generation, however, or even in the next dozen generations. The phenomenon seems to be in no hurry.

We were first controlled directly by our manufacturers. We called them gods and worshipped them. Before they departed, they set up a system of rule based on "god-kings" – human beings who had been processed and supposedly given hereditary powers not possessed by the general population. The planet was divided up among about thirty of these god-kings. Their system remained in effect for thousands of years, surviving well into the modern industrial age.

But the mode of control gradually became diluted and polluted by human greed, politics, and religion. Finally, it collapsed altogether. The legendary conflict between the "serpent race" (those who would enslave mankind) and the rulers of the biochemical robots has continued, however, and the situation is now so desperate that both sides seem willing to expose their modus operandi to us, through overt action in the framework of the UFO phenomenon.

In other ages, we accepted this conflict as a battle for the minds of men. Now, it is becoming apparent that there is more at stake. We, the biochemical robots, are the prize! The anti-human forces are now *imitating* the real UFO phenomenon, using hallucinations and distortions to confuse us. Meanwhile, the old gods are – science and fakery be damned – trying to reveal more of themselves and their purpose to us.

Millions of people are now able to "see" beyond the visible spectrum and sense the presence of these awesome forces. Our two very different worlds are beginning to overlap. The future will bring a series of small climaxes, explosions of sudden insights and information, and a gradual strengthening of the communication channels between us and "them." As our awareness increases, we may become more and more subservient to these forces, sliding back to our ancient condition – when they enslaved us.

The process of change is already underway. The UFO phenomenon is rapidly becoming a new religion – a faith based on the premise that we are inferior to some advanced race from another world, coming to rescue us from our own stupidity.

The basic theme of UFO contact has been anarchism – the promise of a marvelous new socio-religious system. It has almost been an election campaign. The promises have been dazzling, but there has been no attempt to fulfill them. The ancient gods, and their successors, the god-kings, lied to us and manipulated us, and there is no indication that the tactics of the modern ufonauts are any different.

If we are biochemical robots, helplessly controlled by forces that can scramble our brains, destroy our memories, and use us in any way they see fit, then we are caught up in a poker game being played with marked cards.

Through prophecy, synchronicity, materializations, messages, and other attention-getting devices, someone clearly seems to be trying to tip us off about the marked deck, but we are like the inveterate gambler who, when informed that the game is crooked, shrugs and says, "Well, it's the only game in town."

CHAPTER 16

Ashtrays skitter across the room. Doors wrench themselves from their hinges and zip up stairways, like giant Frisbees. Heavy pieces of furniture float to the ceiling, while doorbells ring when no one is pushing their buttons, and telephones jangle incessantly, even when their wires have been pulled from the walls. Helpless human beings levitate from their chairs and beds, soaring skyward, while their desperate relatives and friends try to haul them back to Earth.

This epidemic of phantasmagoria has been increasing in recent years, spreading to every society, no matter how remote, and inspiring dramatic cultural changes. The bogeymen are back, scaring the bejesus out of whole populations, and creating a new folklore of demons, flying-saucer critters, and bug-eyed monsters.

When the "Force" first broke loose in the mid-1800s, learned scientists muttered in their beards, crying "hoax," and hoping the whole weird business would soon go away. A couple of teenaged American girls, the Fox sisters, started it all when they held conversations with mysterious knocking sounds. They called it "spiritualism." The scientists called it "humbug," and said the girls were making the sounds by cracking the joints of their toes.

Following the Civil War, spiritualism became a national mania, and the Force happily obliged by creating phantom orchestras from coast to coast. This was a weird game played in thousands of parlors, in which musical instruments were placed on a mantel or shelf in a dimly lighted room. Given proper encouragement, fiddles and horns would begin to play by themselves.

In modern times, these eerie manifestations have been blamed on poltergeists ("noisy ghosts") and discombobulated spirits of the restless dead. But a handful of courageous scientists have made some exciting breakthroughs in the past 20 years, and we are finally beginning to understand the true nature of the Force that produces these phenomena. It doesn't come from wandering "shades" or diddling demons: It springs from our bodies.

Some of us radiate mysterious forms of energy that can cause an ashtray to fly, a disconnected phone to ring, or a toilet to flush by itself. It is even possible that we may, in time, learn to harness this Force and use it for our own corrupt purposes. There are already legends aplenty claiming that the Egyptians mastered the secret of levitation, and when building the pyramids, were able to float the huge slabs of stone into place with the wave of a hand.

The inhabitants of Easter Island still insist that their ancestors moved the 40-ton statues found there by levitating them with the force called "mana" – a magical power. Imagine what mana would do to our modern construction industry!

Each generation has produced a small group of people who have the conscious ability to move objects by the power of thought, or with the energies radiating from their bodies. We call this "psychokinesis" (PK). While we wasted decades testing psychics with dice-throwing games (more about this later), Soviet scientists have been conducting complex, methodical experiments with PK subjects.

For example, Nelya Mikailov, Russia's most famous PK operator, has voluntarily submitted to years of tests. She is able to move all kinds of objects, even when they are under glass or plastic. In one series of incredible tests, she was able to separate the white of an egg from the yolk after it was broken in a glass tank six feet away from her. Skeptics couldn't explain that as being the work of hidden strings or magnets.

However, magnetism may play some part in psychokinesis. Genady Sergeyev, a neurophysiologist in Leningrad, discovered that Ms. Mikailov has a magnetic field surrounding her body that is roughly one-tenth the strength of the earth's own magnetic field. During the test, she not only radiated intense energy fields, but all of her bodily functions went haywire. Her pulse soared to 240 beats per minute, and she would lose over two pounds during each test.

She also became temporarily blind, and suffered from insomnia for several days after the more intense tests. Obviously the output of energy is enormous. Spirit mediums sometimes lapse into a condition close to death when they attempt to make an entity materialize. Scientists think that such materializations are constructed from the medium's own energy.

An American, Mr. Ted Owens, sneers at Mikailov's demonstrations with raw eggs. Owens, who calls himself "PK Man," claims to be able to conjure up hurricanes and earthquakes. He has been endlessly examined and tested by government scientists and major universities.

Remember the flight of Apollo 13 back in 1970? Bucking popular opinion, the geniuses behind our space program had decided to disprove, once and for all, the myths around the number 13 (by not skipping directly from Apollo 12 to Apollo 14).

But as Apollo 13 lifted through the clouds, it was struck by a bolt of lightning that disabled it. This made the astronauts very uncomfortable, forcing them to cancel their plan to land on the moon. Ted Owens took credit for that lightning bolt, having predicted it in advance, *and in writing* – proof that you should never fool about with Mother Nature *or* with PK operators.

Ted's real specialty is predicting the outcome of football games, and then allegedly blasting the opposing players with his powers, causing broken legs and fractured skulls until the score meets his approval.

Although psychokinesis is a rare talent, it does seem to be stimulated by stress, particularly among teenagers. When the late Dr. Nandor Fodor carried out in-depth investigations of the poltergeist mystery, he discovered that things begin to go bump in the night when a child just entering puberty is involved. Usually there is great stress in the family – a father who is too strict, a mother who is too neurotic.

Later investigators have confirmed Fodor's findings. When the child is removed from the household that is suffering from a mysterious haunting, or the stress is relieved in some fashion, the manifestations cease abruptly. The child's energy is somehow feeding an invisible monster, just as adults often give off a destructive temporary energy when angry or under stress.

There are countless cases in which a vase, or glassware, suddenly explodes – all by itself – while two people are having an angry confrontation. When we're in a mean mood, we release waves of biological energy.

Levitation, literally the ability to fly, is linked to PK and the emotional release of energy.

The Vatican recently named Joseph of Cupertino as the patron saint of the space age. Poor Saint Joseph, a monk with rather limited intellect, lived in the 17th century, and had the disconcerting habit of floating in the air, often in front of large numbers of witnesses. Usually it happened while he was praying and was in that state that religionists call "ecstasy" – a very emotional state, akin to a medium's trance.

It was not unusual for him to suddenly rise from a large congregation of worshipers and float gracefully over their startled heads. On one occasion, a Spanish ambassador and his wife saw Joseph take wing. He flew over the altar of the church, circled a religious statue, and made a perfect landing.

In the Himalayas, holy men spend their entire lives trying to concentrate their bio-energy, and involuntary levitation is often one result. Historic accounts of flying yogis, nuns, and priests are numerous. Apparently, this bio-energy can turn off the forces of gravity. (We still don't understand what gravity is or how it works. It seems to permeate the universe in very slow waves. The PK force may screen the subject from these waves, just as a wall of lead can block a wave of radioactivity.)

The first known case of levitation in America took place in 1693 when, according to the famous clergyman Cotton Mather, a young woman named Margaret Rule began to fly around her bedroom with some regularity. She would often float all the way to the ceiling, and remain there while groups of strong men grappled with her and tried to haul her down. Flying under your own power was definitely frowned upon in those days, and the girl was accused of being a witch.

One Daniel Dunglas Home (pronounced Hoom) is remembered as the greatest wonder worker of modern times. If he was a fraud, then he was the greatest hoaxer and the greatest magician of all time. He not only levitated, but also produced a wide variety of inexplicable manifestations. Leading scientists and the most skeptical reporters of the 19th century attended his séances, and went away baffled. Though he was born in Scotland in 1833, his family moved to Connecticut when he was a boy.

In his early teens, Home began to experience poltergeist phenomena: mysterious rappings on the walls, objects floating in the air, and furniture sliding across the floor toward him. By his 20th birthday, he was already famous, recognized as one of the greatest mediums in the age of Spiritualism. He could cause a heavy oak table to rise in the air by merely touching it with is fingertips. Here's a description of one of Home's table-tilting séances, as observed by a R.T. Hallock, a medical doctor:

> On the table around which we were seated were loose papers, a lead pencil, two candles, and a glass of water. The table was used by the spirits in responding to our questions. The first peculiarity we observed was that, however violently the table was moved, everything on it retained its position.
>
> When we had duly observed this, the table, which was mahogany and perfectly smooth, was elevated to an angle of thirty degrees and held there, with everything remaining on it as before. It was interesting to see a lead pencil retaining a position of perfect rest on a polished surface inclined at such an angle. It remained as if glued to the table. The table was repeatedly made to resume its ordinary position and then, again, its inclination as before, as if to fasten upon us the

conviction that what we saw was no deception of the senses.

Later, during the same séance, Dr. Hallock and a man named Charles Partridge climbed onto the table. Their combined weight was over 350 pounds. At Home's command, the table rocked so violently that both men were thrown off. Defying gravity became one of Home's regular feats. He usually performed in a lighted room and, on many occasions, he apparently caused heavy objects to rise in the air in full view of everyone.

Sometimes, he himself would ascend to the ceiling. At one well-witnessed séance, he allegedly floated out of a hotel window, high above the street, and returned by floating in another open window.

Unlike many of the mediums of the period, Mr. Home did not perform for money. His demonstrations were usually restricted to members of the royal family, celebrities, medicine men, and scientists. Early in life, he discovered that wealthy ladies were attracted to him, and he married well. He didn't have to waste his time and energies performing any kind of useful work. Nor was he much interested in glory and publicity. He traveled in the loftiest circles and lived well.

An accordion that played by itself became one of Home's most popular stunts. He would hold the instrument in one hand with the keys hanging downward, and the accordion would play any song, even foreign music. Other members of the séance could hold the accordion, with the same mysterious results. With today's technology, an accordion could be rigged electronically to play by itself, but such electronics did not exist in 1852.

Sir William Crookes, one of England's foremost scientists, the man who discovered thallium and who invented the Crookes tube – forerunner to the X-ray tube – investigated Home thoroughly. He built a special cage to house the accordion and make it impossible for Home to manipulate it with hidden wires or other trickery. The instrument continued to play by itself in the cage. Crookes even planted a trusty assistant under the table, to study the lower end of the accordion. He later reported:

> Very soon, the accordion was seen by those on each side
> to be waving about in a somewhat curious manner; then
> sounds came from it and, finally, notes were played in succes-
> sion. Whilst this was going on, my assistant under the table
> reported that the accordion was expanding and contracting...

> Presently, the accordion was seen by those on either side of
> Mr. Home to move about, oscillating and going round and
> round the cage – playing at the same time. Dr. Huggins now
> looked under the table, and said that Home's hand appeared

quite still, whilst the accordion was moving about emitting distinct sounds.

D.D. Home died at the age of 53 in a villa in France. There has been no one like him since.

In the 1970s, the U.S. government made a faltering attempt to catch up with Soviet research by sponsoring some of the work being done at the Stanford Research Institute (SRI). Under the auspices of the Central Intelligence Agency, SRI launched a few abortive boondoggles that advanced the bank accounts of a few selected Ph.D.s. We were not only short of talented parapsychologists, we were also hamstrung by the dreary, unimaginative methods developed back in the 1930s by J.B. Rhine, a college professor of unlimited patience.

Rhine spent 30 years testing PK subjects with the longest, dullest, most boring crap game in the history of the human race. Hundreds of shooters threw the dice millions of times, and not one of them won a nickel. When it was all over, scores of people who had not even been present wasted tons of paper and spent pointless years arguing that the dice had been loaded. Several books were published about this, the world's longest floating crap game, and almost nobody bothered to read them – because they were boring.

Dr. Rhine had set out to prove, scientifically, something that every gambler has known since dice were first invented: namely, that some people can make the dice come up any chosen number when all the conditions are right. Not surprisingly, many people *were* able to toss the dice so that certain numbers came up far beyond the expected laws of chance.

After Rhine's endless crap game became known in scientific circles, other Ph.D.s tried to top him. A psychologist in Belfast, one John Beloff, won the booby prize for originality. He suggested using nature's own dice: atomic particles. Two French schoolboys, who had previously been proven to have PK powers, served as the guinea pigs. Under tightly controlled laboratory conditions, they were asked to speed up or slow down the beeps of a Geiger counter simultaneously exposed to uranium. In other words, they were assigned to manipulate the smallest particles of matter in the same way that a gambler on a lucky streak can control a pair of dice. They were successful.

While we have been playing with dice and atomic particles, the Soviet scientists have been trying to find practical applications. Time-travel is suddenly within our grasp, because experiments have shown that mediums, levitants, and PK subjects are very special people living in a kind of time warp. Their minds are able to cross some mysterious frontier where the past, present, and future all blend together. A medium's mind is an instrument, tuning into a future that already exists, in some form, outside of our space-time continuum.

Modern scientists studying bio-energy and "the Force" are shaping a new physics: discovering and interpreting alternative rules for our overall existence. The old physics (e.g., what goes up, must come down) are on the way out. Current studies into the mysterious universe of mental telepathy and extrasensory perception may one day put Ma Bell out of business.

D.D. Home, Saint Joseph, Ted Owens, and countless others have proven that the human body is capable of generating some mysterious force that can negate gravity and manipulate physical matter. If all this energy could be unleashed in a controlled manner, we could change the world almost overnight. We could peer around the corner, into the future, and avert wars and catastrophes.

Everything is interrelated. The red-eyed monsters of our forests, the sea serpents, the howling phantoms of the night, the strange lights that streak through the black skies, the children who bend keys and make dinner plates fly, and those haunted by dreams of the future are all part of the same fabric, the same cosmic explosion. We are careening into a new age of magic, where psychokinesis and levitation may be normal – where the Force is with us all.

CHAPTER 17

DOOM – *HIGH TIMES #92* – APRIL 1983

It's going to be the biggest going-out-of-business sale since Adam peddled his rib and traded his bachelorhood for a bite of an apple and a toss in the hay. Our entire planet is going to be auctioned off in a mere 16 years. The human race – or whatever is left of it – is going to pack it in. It's going to be an ugly scene, and if you don't have a lead-lined cave in your backyard, it'll be your last barbeque – with you as the barbeque. Fried eyeballs and roasted buttocks top the menu. It's going to make Hiroshima seem like a Boy Scout wiener roast.

Who says?

All of the great prophets of history, that's who.

Michel de Nostredame, better known as Nostradamus, head honcho of history's peeping toms – the seers and doomsayers – even pinpointed the date. He said there's going to be very bad news in early July 1999, when a "king of terror" will come out of the skies. Since his death back in 1566, many of his prophecies have come true. So we should probably take this one seriously. And July 1999 is as close to us as the epic years of 1960s, which changed all our lives.

Predicting the end of the world has, however, been a cottage industry for at least 2,000 years. Major religions have been founded on the premise that the end is just around the corner. Countless generations of believers have trudged up the sides of mountains to sit on the summits and wait for the sky to fall.

Back in the last century, a Baptist preacher named William Miller received a news flash from God, and soberly announced that the Second Coming of Christ would take place on October 22, 1844. His followers, known as Millerites, unloaded their worldly goods and grimly waited for the great event. When nothing happened, they simply regrouped and continued their vigil, forming the Seventh-Day Adventist Church.

They are still waiting, as are the Jehovah's Witnesses. Founded in 1872, the Witnesses pass the time peddling their magazine, *The Watch Tower*, from door to door.

Somehow, the Christian theologians have managed to turn the end of the world into a glorious event, anxiously awaited by billions of people, generation after generation. The basic concept is that all of the dead, in all of the cemeteries, will rise up on the appointed day. How's that for the ultimate nightmare?

Meanwhile, the skies will open up and be filled with luminous objects, and Christ himself will descend from a luminous cloud. All the good guys, those who have led exemplary Christian lives, will be whisked off to Heaven, where, as Mark Twain once pointed out, they will be given harps (even though they don't known how to play musical instruments), and wings (even though they don't know how to fly). Thus, heaven will be filled with the discordant sounds of billions of people aimlessly strumming on harps while they flutter about and crash into each other with their untried wings.

Actually, though, according to the biblical prophecies, only 144,000 will go. Everyone else will end up shoveling coal in you know where.

The real end of the world might be even more dramatic. Scientists estimate that if the earth should collide with a meteor only one mile in diameter, the concussion would kill every living thing on the planet. We've have had several close calls in every decade.

There's all kinds of space junk out there, posing a constant threat to us, and we can't do a thing about it. Remember comet Kohoutek? When it was discovered in 1973, some astronomers estimated that it would hit the earth, and quite a few people went to sit on the mountaintops and wait for the end.

An all-out atomic war probably would *not* wipe out mankind. There would still be many survivors in remote areas of South America, Africa, Asia, and the Pacific islands. Of course, they might cough a lot, and radiation would bring about many changes. The prophets have often described what sounded like atomic wars, although most prophecies are phrased in such a vague way that they never make sense until after the event has occurred.

Very specific predictions usually don't happen at all. For example, Mother Shipton wrote that the world would end in 1881. That's about as specific as you can get, so her fans all prepared to meet their maker in 1881. Like the Millerites of three decades earlier, they were disappointed.

"The future controls the present," Sir Fred Hoyle, the famous astronomer, once observed. In some strange and fascinating way, prophets seem to be reporting their memories of the future. Tomorrow already exists in some fashion, and by freeing their conscious minds through hypnosis or other techniques, they can cross that fourth-dimensional bridge.

Nostradamus produced his predictions while in a trance state. Others have used Ouija boards, crystal balls, or simply relied upon dreams. Still others have claimed telepathic contact with some all-knowing force that exists beyond our space-time continuum.

But the most interesting prophets of all are those ordinary people who suddenly have extraordinary contacts with entities who seem to know everything about our future. These entities have masqueraded in many guises throughout history. They look just like us, dress in contemporary clothing, and usually travel in threes. The Bible calls them "angels." In earlier times, they were often regarded as gods.

The Phoenicians, for example, had a goddess of fertility named "Astarte." The Christian holiday "Easter" is named after her, and the fertility symbols of eggs and rabbits are holdovers from the pagan holiday that celebrated the spring equinox. An entity identifying itself as "Ashtar" has been visiting humans for thousands of years, showering us with predictions (many of which have come true), and even dictating books. These books usually purport to be histories of the human race.

An Arab businessman is said to have had encounters with a prophesying angel around A.D. 600. His name was Muhammad, and the angel dictated a book called the Koran, which became the bible of the religion Muhammad founded – the religion of Islam.

By the 19th century, these mysterious entities were posing as East Indians or ghosts from Lost Atlantis (interest in Atlantis ran high around the turn of the century). Then, in the 1940s, they assumed a new role. They became visitors from *outer space*.

Dr. Charles A. Laughead, a (British) medical doctor on the staff of Michigan State University, started communicating with these assorted "outer space" entities in 1954, largely through trance mediums, who served as instruments for Ashtar and his cronies from that great intergalactic council in the sky. A number of minor prophecies were passed along, and they all came true, on the nose.

Then Ashtar tossed in his bombshell. The world was going to end on December 21, 1954, he announced convincingly. He spelled out the exact nature of the cataclysm: North America was going to split in two, and the Atlantic coast would sink into the sea. France, England and Russia were also slated for a watery grave.

However, all was not lost. A few chosen people would be rescued by spaceships! Naturally, Dr. Laughead and his friends were among the select group. Having been impressed by the validity of the earlier predictions,

Dr. Laughead took this one most seriously, and made sober declarations to the news media.

On December 21, 1954, he and a group of his fellow believers clustered in a garden to await rescue (by the Council of Nine). They had been instructed to wear no metal, and they therefore discarded belt buckles, pens, clasps, cigarette lighters, and shoes with metal eyelets. Then they waited.

And waited.

And waited.

Two years earlier, in 1952, two men were driving through the mountains near Parana, Brazil, in the state of Sao Paulo, when they encountered five saucer-shaped objects hovering in the air. Later, one of these men, Aladino Felix, revisited the spot, and this time, a UFO landed. He was invited aboard, and had a pleasant chat with the saucer captain, a being who looked very human and very ordinary. Felix went away convinced that the Venusians were paying us a friendly visit.

Then, in March 1953, there was a knock at the door of Felix's home, and he answered. He was told that "a priest" wanted to talk to him. Since Felix was an atheist at the time, he was a bit surprised. He was even more surprised when he walked out to the meet the man. It was his old friend, the saucer pilot! The "Venusian" was decked out in a cashmere suit, a white shirt with a stiff collar, and a blue tie.

This was the first of a long series of visits, during which the two men discussed flying saucers, their mechanics and propulsion, and the state of the universe at large. Mr. Felix kept careful notes of these conversations, and later put them into an interesting book titled *My Contact with Flying Saucers*. It was written under the pseudonym of "Dino Kraspedon," and it enjoyed modest sales among the growing cults of ET believers.

Dino Kraspedon's real identity remained a mystery until 1965, when he surfaced on Brazilian television as a self-styled prophet named Aladino Felix. He warned of a disaster about to take place in Rio de Janeiro. Sure enough, floods and landslides struck a month later, killing 600.

In 1966, he warned that a Russian cosmonaut would soon die. Cosmonaut Vladimir M. Komarov became the first man to die in space on April 24, 1967. In 1967, Felix appeared on television to grimly discuss the forthcoming assassinations in the United States, specifically naming Martin Luther King and Senator Robert Kennedy.

The startling accuracy of his major and minor predictions impressed many people, of course. When he started predicting an outbreak of violence, bombings, and murders in Brazil in 1968, no one was too surprised when a wave of strange terrorist attacks actually began.

Police stations and public buildings in Sao Paulo were dynamited. There was a wave of bank robberies, and an armored payroll train was heisted. The Brazilian police worked overtime, and soon rounded up 18 members of the gang. A 25-year-old policeman named Jesse Morais proved to be the gang's bomb expert. They had blown up Second Army Headquarters, a major newspaper, and even the American Consulate.

When the gang members started to sing, it was learned that they planned to assassinate top government officials and eventually take over the entire country of Brazil. Jesse Morais had been promised the job of police chief in the new government. *The leader of this ring was Aladino Felix!*

When he was arrested in August 22, 1968, the flying-saucer prophet declared: "I was sent here as an ambassador to the earth from Venus. My friends from space will come here and free me, and avenge my arrest. You can look for tragic consequences to humanity when the flying saucers invade this planet."

It was a story almost as old as the human race. Following contact with these mysterious entities (known to occultists as "ultraterrestrials"), ordinary people are often swept up into disastrous events. Their whole lives are frequently destroyed. Their families are scattered, their careers are ruined, and they suffer all the hardships of the biblical Job.

In the fall of 1967, when Dino Kraspedon was publicly issuing his uncanny predictions in Brazil, another group was battening down the hatches in Denmark, preparing for the end of the world. A man named Knud Weiking began receiving telepathic flashes in May 1967, including a number of impressive prophecies that came true. (Just prior to the capture of the U.S. "spy" ship *Pueblo* off Korea in January 1968, Weiking had warned: "watch Korea.")

Weiking began receiving messages from an entity named "Orthon," and was instructed to build a lead-lined bomb shelter and prepare for an atomic holocaust on December 24, 1967. This seemed like an impossible task, since 25 tons of lead were needed, and the total costs exceeded $30,000. But donations poured in, and voluntary labor materialized. The shelter was built in about three weeks. On December 22, Weiking and his friends were "told" to leave the shelter and lock it up. A telephone blackout next occurred, lasting throughout the Christmas holidays, and cutting off all of the participants from one another.

Meanwhile, mediums, telepaths, "sensitives," and UFO contactees throughout the world were all reporting identical messages. There was definitely going to be an unprecedented event on December 24, 1967. "Ashtar" was talking through Ouija boards to people who had never before heard the name. Another busy entity, named "Orlon," was spreading the word, too. The curious thing about all these messages was that they were phrased in the same manner, no matter what language was being used.

It was as if they were all the work of some mischievous phonograph in the sky. They all carried the same warning. People were reporting strange dreams that December – dreams involving symbols of Christmas (such as Christmas cards scattered through a room). There were also reports of dead telephones and glowing entities prowling through bedrooms and homes. Many of these messages, dreams, and prophecies were collected by a British organization calling itself Universal Links.

The stage was set for doomsday. Thousands, perhaps even millions, of people had been warned. At midnight on December 24, the messages said, a great light would appear in the sky. Mr. Weiking, nonplussed but not discouraged, later gave the press a message he had received, which, he thought, explained it all:

> I told you two thousand years ago that a time would be given, and even so, I would not come. If you had read your Bible a little more carefully, you would have borne in mind the story of the bridegroom who did not come at the time he was expected. Be watchful, so that you are not found without oil in your lamps. I have told you I will come with suddenness, and I shall be coming soon.

It was all a dry run!

One of the millions of dry runs staged since we crawled out of our caves and stared at the sky...

You would think that mankind had learned a lesson from all these ultra-terrestrial pranks – that we wouldn't play this foolish doomsday game anymore. But there are always new victims ready and willing to face the unknown terror of the end of the world.

In September 1982, a young couple in Scottsdale, Arizona, Michael and Aurora El-Legion, hit the contactee road to spread the latest message of impending doom. Straining whatever finances they had, they traveled from town to town, appearing on local radio and television programs, lecturing to anyone who would listen. In New York City, they hired a huge hall, and about 30 people showed up.

Their message was hardly different from that of the Denton family who toured the United States in the 1860s. Like William Denton, Michael had been receiving warnings while in trances. The end of the world was at hand. In fact, the El Legions predicted that it would occur around 2 a.m. on October 18, 1982. At that time, they promised, millions of flying saucers would appear in the skies, all over the world, and rescue all those who deserved to be rescued. If you are still here, you are obviously one of the rejects.

There are literally millions of people all over the world who have the gift of prophecy and are haunted by dreams that later come true, or by sudden visions of future events. Usually, such people avoid publicity and share their unnerving talent with only their family and immediate friends.

Unfortunately, they are responsible for many of the rumors that spread in troubled areas such as California. Millions of Californians deserted their state (no less than four different times in the 1970s alone) because of rumors that it was about to sink into the Pacific. One recipient of psychic warnings did go public, moving her family to Oregon after announcing that California was doomed on a specific day in 1970. On that date, *she dropped dead.*

Traditionally, prophets who try to exploit their talent quickly lose it. When they place themselves under pressure to come up with new predictions on a regular schedule for a newspaper column or TV show, they usually begin to produce gibberish. They are often forced to steal from other prophets. There's an old saying that prophets are without honor in their hometowns.

There's a new saying that there's no honor among prophets. Jeanne Dixon, best known for her prediction of the death of President Kennedy, borrowed heavily from Nostradamus in her biography, *My Life and Prophecies*, much to the delight of the skeptics. She gave herself away by paraphrasing from Henry C. Roberts' translation of the French seer – a version sneered at as being inaccurate by most experts.

Translating the poetry of Nostradamus is no easy task, however. The learned doctor deliberately used vague imagery to disguise his meaning. He wrote about a vegetarian named "Hister, the hysterical" who would wage war and wreak havoc in the 20th century. Apparently, he was referring to Adolf Hitler. And translators were baffled for generations by this verse:

There will be go from Mont Gaulfier and Aventine

One who from the hole will warn the army.

The booty will be taken between two rocks.

The renown of Sextus Cornerstone will fail.

It didn't make any sense until 1783, when the Montgolfier brothers demonstrated the first hot-air balloon. The operator was stationed in a basket below the hole in the balloon. Within a few years, hot-air balloons were being used by armies in the Napoleonic wars.

The second part of the verse seems to refer to Pope Pius VI (the Sextus Cornerstone) who was kidnapped and held prisoner by Napoleon. Many of his predictions dealt with Napoleon. He foresaw World War II as well, and even got some of the names and dates right! For example, here's how he predicted that the Germans would never succeed in capturing Gibraltar, in spite of aid from Spain's right-wing dictator, General Franco:

The Assembly will go out from the caste of Franco,

The Ambassador not satisfied will make a schism:

Those of the Rivera will be involved,

And they will deny the entry to the great gulf.

How could Nostradamus have known that the head of German intelligence, Admiral Wilhelm Canaris, would advise Franco *not* to support the Nazi regime? Canaris, a straightforward military man, disliked his Nazi bosses, and was eventually executed for plotting against Hitler. (Some have even claimed Canaris was really a British agent.)

In 1980, a new translation of Nostradamus became a runaway bestseller in France, convincing millions that World War III was just around the corner – that Paris would be atom-bombed, and that many other horrors would be unleashed:

Live fire will be left hidden death,

Within the globes, horrible frightful.

By night a fleet will reduce the city to rubble,

The city on fire, the enemy indulgent.

The heart of an atom bomb is a globe filled with plutonium. The outer sphere is composed of high explosives which, when detonated, explode inwardly (implosion) and compress the plutonium, creating a critical mass and atomic fission.

Arab armies will sweep into France from Italy, according to Nostradamus, while Armageddon gets underway in the Middle East. Prophecies of Armageddon, the last great battle, have been around for thousands of years, of course.

The New Testament spells it all out, asserting that the ultimate war will take place after the Jewish people have been restored to their original homeland. The founding of Israel in 1948 took care of this little detail. The very name "Armageddon" is derived from the name of a plain in Palestine. It is possible that the real meaning is that the Arab leader who drags us all into World War III may be born in Palestine. Nostradamus sees it this way:

> He shall also invade the fair land of Palestine, and myriads shall be killed.

> As he exerts his force, the land of Egypt shall not escape.

> He shall lay hands on the treasures of gold and silver and the valuables in Egypt,

> The Libyans and the Ethiopians following his train.

The Bible and other prophetic literature suggest that Russia and China will be sucked into the Middle Eastern fracas. Even the Hopi Indians have an ancient prophecy about a yellow-skinned hero in a red cloak, who will one day come thundering out of the East.

Our mysterious ultraterrestrials have been passing along messages about Armageddon for hundreds of years. Everyone everywhere has heard of it, and most people accept it as unavoidable. Students of prophecy now see the stage being set in the Middle East. The conflict over Palestine, the emergence of the Jewish state, and the world's insane dependence on Arab oil all form part of the larger pattern.

The sagging worldwide economy and the steady collapse of the international monetary system were all predicted long ago. Rising anarchy, hunger and hardship, unemployment and depression, will make whole nations susceptible to the appearance of Hitler-type leaders.

Meanwhile, a curious phenomenon has been taking place all over the world. People everywhere are suffering from a sickness of the soul. There is a universal feeling that these are the "end times" – that the end of everything is close at hand. It has even spread behind the Iron Curtain. Soviet authorities recently blamed the sudden rise of religious fervor, and a growing sense of hopelessness, on the influence of the sinister CIA. How they arrived at such a conclusion is anybody's guess.

The widespread dry run of December 1967 was trivial compared to the growth of the worldwide sense of impending doom in the 1970s. It has permeated whole countries, and even small children everywhere sense it and discuss it. Ironically, the same negative spirit gripped the world in the 1880s, when millions of people became convinced that the world was going to come to an end in the year 1900. Another dry run, perhaps?

Nostradamus' incredible track record (he even predicted the date of his own death – July 2, 1566) has focused attention on his uncanny prophecies for this century, particularly his biggie:

> In the seventh month of 1999,
>
> A great king of Terror comes from the sky
>
> To receive the king of Angolmois.
>
> Before and after, Mars reigns by good fortune.

Who will be the "king of Angolmois"? Some interpret this to be a Mongol from China. The poem that struck terror in the hearts of Frenchmen in the early 1880s made reference to an Oriental invasion:

> The Oriental will leave his seat,
>
> He will pass the Apennine Mountains, to see France;
>
> He will pierce through the sky, the waters and snow,
>
> And he will strike everyone with his rod.

After all these battles and bloodbaths, nature will strike a terrible blow. There will be earthquakes, floods, and generally rotten weather conditions, according to Nostradamus:

> There will be, in the month of October, a great translation made,
>
> Such that one would think that the liberating body of the earth
>
> Had lost its natural movement in the abyss of perpetual darkness.
>
> There will be seen precursive signs in the springtime,
>
> Extreme changes ensuing, reversal of kingdoms, and great earthquakes.
>
> Then by great deluges, the memory of things will suffer incalculable loss.

It does sound as if the whole planet is headed for grand cosmic problems. Despite warnings of ecological collapse from various scientists, world political leaders have become more right-wing, retrograde, and disinterested. Some seem to advocate a return to the Middle Ages, or at least to the hard times of Charles Dickens.

Everything seems to be shutting down in the 1980s. The whole human race is following a timetable that was laid out thousands of years ago. Since 1945, we have been constructing thousands of these globes envisioned by Nostradamus – globes filled with plutonium, and capable of turning the earth into a cinder.

The "Me Generation" of the 1970s has bred the "Blank Generation" of the 1980s.

The question is no longer: Is the end of the world at hand?

The question is: When the end comes, will anybody care?

CHAPTER 18

Dear Bob:

I vaguely recall exchanging a few letters with you several years ago. Perhaps I discussed the Allende matter with you at that time. I did see your interesting article in *Fate* a year or two ago, but I have not seen the booklet you have published.

The purpose of this letter is to outline, once and for all time, my own observations and sometimes-innocent involvement in the Allende affair.

First, Morris K. Jessup personally regarded the Varo document as a joke. He openly scoffed at it. Shortly before his suicide, Jessup wrote a long, rambling letter to Long John Nebel, a New York radio personality, and similar letters to a few others, including Hans Steffan Santesson, editor of a science-fiction magazine. These appeared to be the typical "pre-suicide" letters of a depressive personality.

While there are some odd things about the way the authorities in Florida behaved in handling his death, there is absolutely no doubt that Jessup ended his own life because of career setbacks and family problems (at least it appeared this way). Just before he killed himself, he turned over his correspondence with Allende, and his personal copy of the Varo document, to Mr. Santesson.

He had made many notations of his own in the margins of the Varo book, all of them questioning the validity of the comments made by Mr. "A" and Mr. "B," and generally ridiculing their efforts. He felt the whole thing was a waste of time and money, and that Allende was a mental case.

In 1966, Santesson turned over the Jessup file to Ivan Sanderson, because the latter was writing *Uninvited Visitors*, a UFO book, and had been receiving letters from Mr. Allende. On a visit to Ivan's farm that year, I sat up all night reading this material with great fascination. My conclusion, like Jessup's, was that the Varo book was the work of a schizophrenic – a dual personality.

But I was also intrigued by the accuracy of several of annotations concerned with magnetism and other matters then virtually unknown to the general field of ufology. (You must remember that in 1966, ufology had been paralyzed for years by ignorance, lack of methodology, and overemphasis of meaningless side-issues, such as their futile battle with the U.S. Air Force.)

Ivan was quite enchanted with the story of the disappearing ship in the Philadelphia Naval Yard, and used some of Jessup's material in his book. After the book was published in 1967, Sanderson began to receive phone calls from a man claiming to be Allende.

Meanwhile, Brad Steiger published a quickie paperback book on the Allende affair, and was soon inundated with letters from people around the country, all claiming to be Allende. He also got a letter from a woman professing to be Allende's widow. There were obviously a lot of nuts out there, and Ivan Sanderson was enthralled by all of them. I was amused by the scene, and Hans tried to remain neutral.

Sometime in the late 1960s, I referred to Allende in some of my magazine articles. I soon began to receive letters from Mr. Allende himself. I was openly skeptical, and asked him to prove his identity. He sent photostats of his seaman's papers, tax records, and other documents, including a signed postcard he had received from Jessup.

Around that time, he had visited the Lorenzens in Tucson, Arizona and spent an afternoon with them. He presented them with a copy of the Varo book and freely admitted to them that he had written all the annotations. In writing to me and describing his visit, he complained about Coral Lorenzen's legendary rudeness, claiming that she and her family left him sitting in the living room while they all went into the kitchen to eat dinner.

In a rather haughty letter to me later, Coral confirmed this visit, and boasted that she "always knew the whole thing was hoax."

But here is a very important point that you and all the others have mangled for years: *Varo was behind the "hoax," not Allende or anyone else.*

Jessup, Sanderson, Santesson, myself, and everyone else knew that Allende had written the annotations. Allende admitted this, on many occasions, to many people. One set of notations was written in his handwriting. The other set was probably written with his other hand, and thus disguised. The introduction of the Varo document tried to make a bigger mystery out of the whole thing. The Varo secretary who typed the thing up is the perpetrator of the real hoax.

Allende's letters to me, mostly mailed from Mexico, were clearly the work of a very unstable personality. For example, one 15-page letter begins with high praise, declaring that I was the best thing ever to happen to ufology, etc. But as the letter progressed, Allende began arguing with himself. By the last page, he was calling me names and telling me that he would never write to me again under any circumstances.

You must realize that I have received thousands of truly crackpot letters over the years, so I am something of an expert. Allende's letters confirmed my earlier conclusions – that we were dealing with a rampantly schizoid personality. However, you must also realize that I could never state this in print, because no editor would dare print it. The fear of a libel suit would be too great.

While researching my book on the atomic bomb and the nuclear mess, I discovered that the Manhattan Project took over part of the Philadelphia Naval Yard in the 1940s, and that one ship was loaded with atomic lab gear. Civilians in the area at the time must have been mystified by the bearded scientists, most of whom spoke with Hungarian accents and clutched briefcases.

The Manhattan Project security force (Defense Industrial Security Command, now called the Defense Logistics Agency) probably circulated false stories – cover stories – about what was going on there. These stories undoubtedly reached Allende's ears, garbled and over-dramatized.

During the war years, a magician named Joseph Dunninger was very famous. He had a very popular radio show, and was a master of publicizing himself. He brashly announced to the press that he had figured out a way to make ships invisible, and that he was donating his idea to the war effort. His claim made the front pages of all the newspapers, just as he knew it would, yet nothing further was heard of his wonderful discovery.

However, one man apparently tucked it away in his memory. Years later, his poor, confused, schizoid brain would combine the Dunninger claim with the Manhattan Project's cover stories, and a legend would be born.

Disappearing ship stories were popular "scuttlebutt" during the war years. One of the most widely circulated of such stories was the tale of the Liberty ship that vanished inexplicably from Naples Harbor, even though all entrances to the harbor were closely guarded by warships. According to the story, the ship and its entire crew vanished one night and were never heard from again. A journalist friend of mine even tried to write a novel based on that particular rumor. (It was never published.)

So you can see there are several possible sources for Allende's claims. Considering the man's mental state, I'm sure that his letters to Jessup were sincere, and that when he annotated Jessup's book and mailed it to the naval office, he thought that he was offering some valid information. He never expected it to snowball into a wastebasket.

But the naval office passed it on to the nest of UFO believers at Varo. Later, Allende presented himself at Varo and was given copies of the book. (He sent me correspondence he had with Varo's president.) He told them that he had written all of the notations.

Now let's jump ahead to 1975. I had a series of meetings with Charles Berlitz that year. He told me he was writing a book about Allende. I told him that the whole thing was a sad, demented affair, and that it would be best to leave it alone. But I lent him my Allende file.

Then I got a letter from a young schoolteacher from the Midwest (Mount Perry, Ohio, north of Athens). He said he was researching the Allende business, and asked for advice. I wrote to him and told him that he should contact Charles Berlitz. I even sent him Berlitz's home address and private phone number. He was, of course, William L. Moore.

Moore contacted Berlitz and, together, they contrived a book on the Philadelphia Experiment. The book made money. Moore was able to quit his teaching job and become a fulltime writer. I literally changed his whole life!

Yet I never heard from him again. He has never written to thank me for introducing him to Berlitz, and has never contacted me when he passed through New York. We have only had one accidental encounter, while he was visiting a mutual friend.

The material in my Allende file was never mentioned in the Moore-Berlitz book, nor was any of the other wealth of negative material to be found in Sanderson's files, etc.

Allende was supposedly dying of cancer in 1970. But he is probably still out there somewhere, writing long, dissociative letters to anyone who mentions his name in print.

Gray Barker is still selling reproductions of the Varo book for an unseemly price. Anyone who offers the true facts about the non-existent Philadelphia Experiment will be shouted down as a pawn of the Air Force conspiracy. But like 90% of the UFO lore, there never was anything to it.

However, Carl Allen was not a conscious hoaxer. If anything, he is one of ufology's biggest victims.

-John A. Keel

CHAPTER 19

He's exposed fakirs in India and charmed cobras in Times Square. He's chased UFOs, Bigfoot and the dreaded "Men in Black" – and lived to tell the tales. John Keel has spent much of his life being a "world's foremost authority." If you mentioned his name back in the 1950s, the response would have been, "Oh, isn't he that guy who knows everything about black magic and the occult?"

By the 1970s, Keel's name had become synonymous with UFOs, as his fascinating ideas revolutionized the way we looked at those mysterious things in the sky. But Keel was no armchair theorist. He spent years circumnavigating the globe, peeking into the most arcane corners of the Third World, researching their ancient magical beliefs and rites. Along the way, he became world-famous for his exposes of the Indian rope trick and the fine art of cobra charming.

When he returned to the States in the mid-1950s, Keel lectured extensively, then settled back in his adopted hometown, New York City, where he served as head writer for Goodson and Todman, the TV impresarios, working on their hits "To Tell the Truth," "I've Got a Secret," and "The Price is Right." After writing all of Merv Griffin's early ad-libs, he packed up and moved to Hollywood, where he spent a year "hating every minute of it."

Keel returned to New York in 1965, just in time for the big blackout. Intrigued by a UFO flap near his birthplace in upstate New York, he began researching an article for Playboy. For the next 15 years, Keel became known as "Mr. UFO." He published five books on the subject, lectured all over the world, and advanced the groundbreaking theory that UFOs were not extraterrestrial, but had their origins in the psychic and the occult.

Rather than being benign, enlightened "space brothers," Keel noted that the forces behind the UFO phenomenon exhibited the mentality of a malicious toddler. He finally posited a Jungian-tinged theory of the collective unconscious in "The Eighth Tower," where the UFO forces are seen as pale reflections of our own twisted psyches, shimmering eternally in space and time

Put simply, after thousands of hours of field research and hundreds of interviews with UFO contactees, Keel concluded that the UFO phenomenon could not be extraterrestrial in nature. Rather, he theorized that UFOs were part of the chimerical activity that has plagued this planet since its inception – a modern, updated version of faeries, monsters, and other things that go bump in the night.

Besides his 12 books, Keel has also managed to find time to write over 200 slapstick comedy movies under contract to the Trans-Lux Corporation. He is currently working on three books, one of which will "solve all the mysteries of the universe." In our interview, Keel reflects on his years spent chasing down annoying puzzles and ancient mysteries.

JIM CUSIMANO AND LARRY SLOMAN INTERVIEW JOHN KEEL –
HIGH TIMES #102 – FEBRUARY 1984

When did you begin your career?

I sold an article to a magicians' magazine when I was about twelve years old. They sent me a check for two dollars. Then I started writing for things like *Mechanics Illustrated.* When I was sixteen, I sold to *The New Yorker.* I thought I was really a hotshot, because *The New Yorker* was considered the toughest magazine to get into.

You were doing this from your family's upstate New York farm?

Yes. It was my way of getting away from the farm. I was going to write my way out.

What did your family think of it?

They hated the whole idea. They wanted me to be a farmer, like them.

So when did you finally leave the farm?

When I was seventeen. I came to New York with seventy-five cents. It was four hundred miles. I hitchhiked to New York. It took two days. I slept on park benches and all that. In those days, it was much different. The Village was much different than it is now. It was very easy to meet people; within a very short time, I knew everybody in the Village. I was the editor of a poetry magazine down there. Then I started a newspaper called *Limelight*, a weekly tabloid about Village artists and writers.

Had you written for the pulp magazines?

I had written a lot of stuff for the pulps. I used to write by the pound. I'd write detective stories and science-fiction stories. I sold a lot of science-fiction in those days, all when I was eighteen or twenty years old.

The comic books then were booming. What happened to the comic books was that an idiot psychiatrist, Dr. Frederick Wertherm, came out with an article in an obscure magazine, saying comic books were bad for children, and that Batman and Robin were homosexuals – all this bullshit! And he ruined the comic book business. Overnight, this article got an enormous amount of publicity, and they had to change all the comic books. For years afterwards, you couldn't buy anything except *Donald Duck* and *Archie*.

At that time, television was coming in. I worked in television, at WABD, down at Wanamaker's Store on Astor Place. Everybody worked for nothing in television. The cameramen, the directors, everybody was working for nothing, just to get started in it. And I was writing all kinds of stupid shows. They had really dumb shows in those days, because they had no money. Their biggest expense, their big deal for a production, would be to release balloons. We were going crazy trying to think of ways to use balloons, because they were cheap.

Then you got drafted?

I got drafted in 1951, when the Korean War broke out.

Where were you sent?

They sent me to Europe. But first they sent me down to Indiantown Gap, Pennsylvania. Every day, they would tell us that the hills there were just like the hills in Korea. And they had us running up and down these hills playing soldier.

The Army was a charming thing in those days. Most of our officers were southerners, and most of the guys that I was drafted with were black, and from the north. After we finished basic training, they sent all the black guys to Korea, and all the white guys to Europe. And this was an Army policy! The Korean War was fought largely by black guys – talk about racial prejudice carried to an extreme.

What did you do in the army? Didn't you get into intelligence or psyops?

Well, they told us how terrible it was going to be in Europe –

that we would live in tents, and that we would travel in these cattle cars to our destinations, and so on. They shipped me to Frankfurt. I had no idea where I was going. They just put numbers on my orders.

We got off the train, all of us GIs. The others were being loaded into trucks, so me and my buddies were looking around, saying, "Where's our truck?" Just then, a limousine pulled up and this German driver got out. He was dressed like a Nazi stormtrooper. He called out our names, and we got into the limousine, and he started driving through the night from Frankfurt.

We asked him, "Are we going to live in a tent?" And he said, "No, you'll live in a castle." He drove us to this castle outside of Frankfurt, which housed a radio station, the American Forces Network. We actually lived in a castle.

You were working for the Armed Forces Radio?

Yes. It turned out it was the biggest radio network in the world. They had stations all over Europe. Within a year's time, I was the chief of continuity and production. I was the head of the whole production setup for the whole network. It took me about a year to work my way up to that position, mainly because nobody else knew anything about anything. I was the only one that had any experience, from writing for *Superman*.

And then I wrote my own way. I dreamed up assignments for myself, and sent myself all over Europe. I produced the soldiers' singing contest all over Europe. I went through France, Holland, and so on, finding singers in the Army, to record them for the radio program. When there were disasters, like in the Po Valley in Italy, I would fly down and cover the disaster.

Then, on Halloween in 1952, I dreamed up a radio show from inside Frankenstein's castle. There really is a Frankenstein castle there, and it was a huge success. It scared the hell out of everybody, and the British newspapers wrote it up. *Time* magazine wrote it up, and they were comparing me to Orson Welles. So the next year, in '53, I had to top myself when Halloween rolled around. I suggested to the colonel who was in charge of the network that he send me to Egypt.

I'd do a broadcast from the Great Pyramid. He said, "Sure," and they sent me and a whole team down to Egypt. We did a broadcast from inside the pyramid. I spent about eight or ten hours inside the Great Pyramid.

What happened when you came back?

I took my discharge in Europe. I decided that I would like to go and live in Egypt for a while. And then, from there, I worked my way around the world.

When did you start writing magazine articles?

While I was still with the Army. I have six scrapbooks at home filled with clippings from *Stars & Stripes*. They would write me up every week, because I was the only one that was doing anything. They would carry all of these John Keel stories, and pictures of me. I was a celebrity there. I remember going into a nightclub in Berlin; they turned the spotlight on my table, and had me stand up.

When did you write "Jadoo?" How did that come about?

Well, first I did all of the traveling in India and so on. Then, when I got to Singapore, the British threw me out. I had ended up broke in Singapore. They called me an "adventurer" and threw me out. They made me take the first ship out, which was going all the way back to Europe. It was a Swedish boat, and it took forty days to get back to Europe.

You describe some incredible adventures in "Jadoo," like the time you woke up in a brothel in Iraq, and saw a prostitute disemboweled by her brother!

Yes, well, I guess they still do it. If a woman becomes a prostitute, she disgraces her whole family. And if the family catches up with her, they'll kill her. The brothers will kill her. I saw that happen.

There are some great things in that book, such as your meeting with the infamous "Ali Baba."

Yes, he was later killed by the Iraqi army. He was a bandit who lived in the desert. He made the mistake of killing a jeep full of tourists. If he had killed a jeep full of Arabs, they wouldn't have cared. But, my God, he was interfering with the tourist business! And it was a group of American tourists, which made it even worse. And so, about a year after I had spent some time with him, the Iraqi army tracked him down, and they killed him and his entire band.

Wasn't it in Iraq that you visited that community of devil worshipers?

Yes, the Yezidi tribe in Iraq. I think they have been wiped out, too. It was a tribe of primitive people in northern Iraq, who believed that God was good, so you didn't have to worry about him. However, the Devil was bad, and you had better appease him at any cost. And so, they sort of worshipped the Devil. "Don't bother us, Devil, because we think you're the greatest." I spent some time with them. They had little ceremonies that were kind of weird. But it wasn't anything like you'd see with the people practicing black magic in other parts of the world. It was just sort of a harmless form of religion.

Weren't you buried alive in India?

For just a few minutes. That was a very unhappy experience. They didn't use a coffin or anything. You would lie on the ground and they would put a board on top of you and cover you with very porous dirt. Some of these fakirs can be buried for days at a time. You can breath through the soil, especially if it is a shallow grave. But it is very claustrophobic.

I did all these things so that I could be photographed doing them. Then when I got the pictures, I could easily sell articles from them. I have photographs of all of this stuff. I photographed people eating snakes alive, and doing all kinds of weird things. There were groups of people in India that used to walk down the street beating themselves with whips. There were many strange things like that.

How old were you then?

I was twenty-four or twenty-five years old.

And you were just making a buck? Would it be wrong if you we said you were a hustler?

I wasn't a hustler. If I had hustled, I would have made more money than I did. I was broke most of the time, waiting for checks from my agent. What I thought I was doing then was building a career. Once you become famous for doing something, you've got to keep on doing it. If you are going to climb the tallest building in Chicago, then you've got to climb the tallest building in Los Angeles, and the tallest building in New York. It doesn't matter if you can do card tricks, too. They don't want to see the card tricks. They want to see you climb buildings – whatever it is that got you famous. I was constantly searching for new things to add to my repertoire.

Looking back, do you think you were then more of an adventurous person?

Yes, I was willing to take chances that I wouldn't take today. I did things and went places that I wouldn't think of doing now. I was never in very robust health. I did a lot of things in spite of my physical condition. I climbed mountains, mostly because they were in the way. I was trying to get over them.

I did a lot of things just because it was necessary at that time to do them. I suppose I had the soul of a hustler. But I was not hustling, per se. I was trying to go from point A to point B. If there was a village of snake charmers in between, then I was spending time with the snake charmers.

Didn't you become a celebrity in these places?

Yes. In India, the newspapers gave me enormous coverage. For some reason, they loved Robert Ripley of *Believe It or Not!* in India. He must have been a big tipper. And the newspapers decided that I was another Robert Ripley. They followed me around, calling me the "new Robert Ripley." Well, that helped me enormously.

Tell us about the Indian rope trick. That was a big stunt you exposed in "Jadoo."

Basically, the trick is that the boy climbs up the rope, and the magician tells the boy to come down, but the boy says, "No." So the magician climbs up the rope, and then pieces of the boy start falling down to the ground. Then the magician climbs down the rope. He gathers up these pieces and puts them in a basket. Then the boy jumps out, whole. That's the Indian rope trick in a nutshell. There are about ten different ways of doing it.

Didn't you attempt to do it yourself?

I attempted to do it on a very small scale. I invited all of the newspapermen in New Delhi to come and see this thing, but everything went crazy. The string broke. The newspapers gave me enormous publicity, but I would say that most of them were very kind about it. It was a total fiasco.

In essence, a lot of these things that you were doing had to do with debunking primitive magic.

Yes, mostly debunking.

On the other hand, there were authentic miracles, like the tricks the Tibetan lamas did.

Yes, I saw a lot of weird things up there. There was a monastery in Tibet where the lamas were studying certain disciplines. They'd go naked through the snow, in bitter cold. They seemed to have such control over their bodies. There was one discipline where they learned to run very fast. It's hard to explain how they do it, but they become messengers. They can travel like the wind, practically, covering great distances in short periods. And they did levitation.

You actually saw levitation?

I did see one actual levitation. There was a man sitting cross-legged in the air. This is a lot more common than Westerners believe. I suspected a magic trick at the time, but there doesn't seem to have been any way to fake it. He had one hand on a stick, keeping his balance on the stick. Mechanically, such a hoax would be beyond the means of most Tibetans. I know that other people photographed it. I couldn't because, by then, I was broke and had sold my camera.

There are all kinds of amazing things. I saw one man who could gradually pull his eyeballs all the way out. They'd just hang down his face. They will do these things just as a trick, to beg for money. There was one man who could hang enormous weights from his genitals. This was the way he made his living! He had this thing rigged up; it was like a bag, and he'd fill it with stones and tie it to his genitals. This bag weighed fifty or seventy-five pounds. Everyone would say "wow" and give him money. Then you would see a man standing on one leg, who claimed to have been standing on that one leg for thirty years straight. And people would give him money for standing on one leg.

What was the heaviest thing you saw in your travels?

The thing that will shake you the most is to see that millions of people are suffering. People are dying on the streets of Calcutta – people living in a kind of poverty you can't imagine. I remember almost crying over the state of these people, knowing that I could "escape" and be in New York or Chicago the next month. But these people were there for the duration of their lives.

I was in a village in the desert that had a little muddy hole in the ground. It was their village well. The chief of the village said, "Did you ever see such water in your whole life? Have you ever seen so much water, and such great water?" I had to drink some of it, and it was like drinking urine. For them, this bad waterhole was the center of their entire life. Those were the things that shook me up the most.

There were other things, like walking through the jungle in India; they call it the "bush." I saw this huge thing that I thought was an anthill. You see these big anthills. As I got right up to it, and it turned around – it was an elephant. The elephants move with total silence through the jungle. I don't know how they do it, but they don't snap any twigs or rustle the leaves. They just sort of glide through, and fortunately this was a peaceful elephant. But sometimes they can be rather nasty. The Indians call them the "elephant people." They are almost human. They are very intelligent.

You know, I have seen the ants on the march. You lie awake at night, and it sounds like it's raining out. But it isn't raining – it's the ants, eating as they go along. Eating everything in their path. And they are huge, vicious ants.

How did "Jadoo" do?

It did pretty well. The publisher was very aggressive. They promoted the hell out of it. There was a period in 1957-'58 when you couldn't pick up a newspaper without seeing a picture of John Keel, charming cobras and all this other stuff.

Didn't they have you in a window doing promo?

Yes, I was in a window of a pet shop near Times Square. Every day at three o'clock, I'd get in the window and charm my cobras. I brought three cobras and two boa constrictors back from India.

Were they defanged?

No. They die if you do that.

These were cobras that were actually dangerous?

Yes. The window was only about six-feet square, so there wasn't much room for me to move around. And the snake, of course, was always trying to get at you. That's why you really can't charm a cobra. He's just biding his time, waiting to strike at you.

Well, how the hell do you charm cobras?

You have to learn how to do it.

That's what I'm asking. How did you keep them from getting you?

You learn from his actions when he's about to strike. And he's not going to strike until you are within range. He'll strike at a distance of about one-third of the length of his body. So, if he's six feet long, he can strike about two feet. So you have to be two and a half feet away. When you're in a window that's only six-feet square, you don't have much leeway. So huge crowds used to gather every day, and watch this stupid kid get in the window and risk his life. I had the flute, and the snake was in the basket, just as one would imagine.

It wasn't just bullshit?

Of course not! You just move your hands back and forth with the flute. The snake is following the movement of your hands. If you stop moving, the snake strikes. I had a whole act I worked out. The people watching were terrified, because a cobra is a very awesome thing when you see it alive, in front of you.

After I would do this, I would go home and fall apart. While I was doing it, I was perfectly calm, and could do it. But I would get home and collapse. It was a crazy time.

How did you get the snakes into the country?

Simple. I packed them in a box marked "cobras." At five o'clock one morning, the airport phoned me and said, "We've got a box here that says it's full of snakes. We want you to come out here and get it." I said, "Well, suppose it's full of diamonds." And he says, "It says they are poisonous snakes. And we believe it." So I had to run out to the airport and pick this box up. They only cost me about three dollars apiece in

India. This guy I knew used to go out and collect them, and sell them to zoos. He made very little money.

Are cobras smart?

No. They have no personalities. They live entirely by instinct. A snake is totally devoid of intelligence or personality.

You started your research into flying saucers when you did a Playboy article about a UFO flap in your hometown in 1965. Before you went up to Buffalo to investigate during the flap, were you at all interested in flying saucers?

Oh, sure, I'd been interested in it since I was a kid, because I had read Charles Fort then. I was one of the few people who attended the first flying saucer convention in 1948. They had a convention on Fourteenth Street here in New York, and there were about thirty people there. I remember it rather well. I can't remember who staged the damn thing, but I do remember that everybody was shouting at everybody else. It was a screaming match; even in 1948, they'd all decided that the government was withholding information about the flying saucers, and that something should be done about the Air Force.

So, in 1952, when I was with AFN in Germany, I did a radio program about flying saucers, and it was very well received. We got mail from all over about that – people in Europe testifying to what they had seen themselves. There were a lot of sightings in 1952 everywhere in the world, especially in Europe.

How much of an influence did Fort have in shaping your ideas?

Oh, I'm sure he had an enormous influence, because Charles Fort wrote about all sorts of unusual things. The biggest influence of my childhood would be the various books about Harry Houdini. I was more interested in magic than I was in Fortean things. I wanted to be a stage magician. Of course, there was no way to make a living in magic anymore.

So you wrote this article for Playboy.

I wrote a lot of other articles, too. I did an article for *True* magazine on flying saucers, and after the issue came out, I went up to the editorial offices. The editor showed me three or four big bags. He said, "This is the mail that's come in on your article; you want to take it home with you?"

There were eighteen thousand letters about that one article. Today, of course, you get three letters from an article like that. But this was the height of the UFO thing in 1967. We could only read samplings of those letters. Most of those people described really unusual contacts – bizarre things, like "missing time." I'm sorry that I had no way of preserving those eighteen thousand letters.

When you first started investigating and actually doing work in the field, on UFOs and contactees, you held the theory that they were extraterrestrial?

Well, I went in there with a belief, not a theory. I accepted the extraterrestrial belief, because everybody else accepted it. The extraterrestrial explanation was a belief that sprang out when everybody reasoned that since the UFOs don't belong to the Russians or to the United States, they have to come from Mars or Venus or something like that.

They were seen as spacecraft – machines.

They're always called spacecraft, even today. You pick up the UFO fan magazines, and they're always talking about the craft. But what people are mostly seeing are lights, not objects. The solid objects are very rare, and when you really investigate those cases, they often fall apart.

I had a friend who saw objects and photographed them. What turned out on the photographs was entirely different from what he saw, which often happens with the UFO contact. He had seen these huge things rising up out of fields and so on, and a lot of other people saw the same things.

What have you seen?

I've seen a lot of the lights in the sky; a *lot* of them. I've seen – I've lost count – maybe fifty or seventy-five of these very special lights. If you see one, you know how different they are from any other light. Once you've seen these lights, you know that it can't be a star or any other thing that's in the sky. It's a special kind of light that there's no way to describe. People usually try to describe it as a diamondlike light; it's a very special kind of thing. The strobe lights on airplanes don't come close to the diamond lights.

When I first got into this, I used to drive out to the airport at night, and sit there and watch the planes entering and leaving. I became familiar with every kind of light that the airplanes carry, so that I would be able to recognize them. When I was down in West Virginia, in Point Pleasant, these diamond lights were flying like an airline, on a regular schedule. They'd say, "Well, if you want to see a flying saucer, come out at eight o'clock on Wednesday night; they go over every week at that time."

And you would go out at eight o'clock on Wednesday night, and there would go one of these strange lights; sometimes they seemed to be very low in the sky. One night, we tried to chase them with a private airplane. We couldn't chase them because they would just take off, zip, like that, and be gone. We tried all sorts of ways of finding out something about them.

Did you ever see any other physical evidence, like burnt ground?

Oh, yes, we had the rings (crop circles). In earlier times, they used to call them fairy rings. These are circles in the fields. Sometimes they are "burned" in. The grass is just knocked down, or pressed down, like something round has landed there. The weirdest case was in Kanauga, Ohio (right across the river from Point Pleasant). A lovely farm dog had been crushed to death in the center of one of these circles. The local veterinarian said that every bone in the dog's body had been crushed. It was like some very heavy thing hand landed on this dog. There was a circle of crushed grass around it.

Our first modern animal mutilation?

Well, there were a lot of animal mutilations in those days in Ohio and West Virginia, and I was checking those. They seemed to be related to the UFOs, but I couldn't figure out how. There was one case where a cow in Ohio had been cut in half, like a big pair of scissors had just cut it right in half. I couldn't figure out. Suppose you wanted to do that to a cow, how would you do it? I mean, you'd have to build a huge buzzsaw or something, and run it through the saw. The cut was absolutely clean; there was no blood oozing. There should have been a lot of blood from something like that, but there was nothing.

And about four years ago, a man in Mexico turned up in the same unfortunate condition. Some people were driving on a highway down there, and something hit their car. They stopped the car, and it was one-half of a man's body. Then, some distance away, they found the other half of a man's body. It had been cut right in half. He was an elderly man. They don't know what happened to him, but it's pretty scary that these things happen at all.

I also remember some people in New Haven, West Virginia, who had a loveable little puppy. They let it out one night, and as soon as it went out the door, it let out a little yelp. They went outside, and the dog was lying dead. There was a little cut in his body, and the heart had been removed. This was in a minute or two of it heading out the door. I examined the body of this dog, and I don't know how the hell it was done. Somebody or something made a little cut, reached in, and removed the heart, all in the space of a few seconds. There's no animal that would do that. You can't blame owls for that. No way.

We don't know what happened to that poor little puppy. There are a lot of dog disappearances during UFO flaps. Often the dog will go running out of the house, barking at something in the field. The owners will see something in the field, and the dog will never come back. It's a mystery where they go.

Well, how long did it take you to begin to link the UFOs to all the other activity?

Well, that was a gradual thing. I remember I gave a speech in June of 1967, after I'd been in this about a year, in which I had begun to stress that you had to look for these ground--level effects – that they were all linked with the UFOs. This did not sit very well with the ET believers, because their belief is that the extraterrestrials are benevolent and kind, and have our best interests at heart. Yet, here I was talking about cows being cut in half.

So they didn't want to believe you?

The believers in extraterrestrial visitants did not want to believe that the UFOs could do any harm to human beings or animals. Of course, there's a lot of evidence to the contrary now. We have catalogued many dangerous effects to animals and human beings.

We have several cases of people getting too close to a UFO

and dying of leukemia within days – sometimes only three days. They didn't have leukemia before this happened. You can get leukemia from radiation. There are a number of cases of that now; obviously these things are casting off a lot of radiation.

There's a blind woman here in the New York area, who swears she was blinded by a UFO. A few years ago, she saw this brilliant light and it blinded her. We have other cases where people have been somehow deafened by the noise made by UFOs – a high-frequency sound.

There was a police officer in Wanaque, New Jersey, who was unable to speak for an hour or two after he saw one of these things. There are side-effects to the vocal cords, ears, and eyes. A lot of people get conjunctivitis from the glare of these things. It's like looking at a welder's forge.

Is there a certain type of person that sees UFOs?

Well, we've done a lot of work trying to isolate if there is selectivity. It seems that people with certain kinds of backgrounds are more apt to have these experiences than others. If you have Native American or Gypsy blood, for example, you're more likely to have these experiences. It may simply be that other minorities don't report these things. If you break it down according to national population, five percent of all sightings normally should be by Jews, ten percent should be by blacks, and twenty percent should be by Catholics. But it doesn't break down that way at all. Catholics see them far more often, particularly those who are "lapsed" or "fallen" Catholics. Non-practicing Catholics will see these things, but practicing Catholics won't. It's like a whole system of selectivity.

I got a list from the Social Security Administration of the most common names, such as Smith, Jones, Brown, Johnson, and so on. You would assume that because there are four million Smiths in the country, that you would get a lot of people named Smith reporting UFOs. That is not the case. The people with rare names, like Wamsley, report in. There are only *two* Wamsleys in the New York City phone directory! Yet, here we have several cases of people named Wamsley being involved. Reeves is another one; unrelated people in different parts of the country, named Reeves, will have these experiences.

So, by 1967, you had established yourself as pretty much an authority in this field. Why did you decide to be this interested?

It's an obsession, pure and simple. When I got into it, I realized how little work had actually been done, and I thought it was time that somebody really did a systematic job on it. I was really obsessed by it, as most people are when they get involved in it. I really believed that I could solve the entire thing. I naively thought I was smart enough to solve it.

You came the closest to solving it, by suggesting that UFOs are not extraterrestrials, but linked to psychic and occult phenomena. Not that your answers are necessarily the right answers, but they're the most coherent. By linking the UFO phenomenon with the whole tapestry of human history, you gave it a perspective that was completely missing.

Well, there are a lot of European books that have been written, in which they glorify me, and say that I've "solved" the mystery. But I don't feel that I solved it. I feel that I compounded it/ I've found a lot of other mysteries within the mystery. There may not be an ultimate answer. Dr. Jacques Vallee says that there isn't – that it's unsolvable.

You can only go so far. It's like we're ants, trying to understand a universe that we can't perceive. I think our basic vision of the universe is wrong. We assume that the laws that work here on Earth are also working out there in the Andromeda galaxy. We can't really judge the universe at all, anymore than the ant can judge his immediate environment. So in that way, it's sort of hopeless. A lot of people who read *The Eighth Tower* said that the feeling that they got from it was that it's all hopeless. But, in a way, I was just making fun of the phenomenon.

In that book, I was pointing out that the end product of our civilization, without question, is going to be a computer. If we don't blow ourselves up first, we're going to overpopulate ourselves to death; we're well on the way now.

When the human race dies, however it dies, the one thing we're going to leave behind is the computer. And that computer is going to be ticking there, maybe for centuries, until more men appear. They will worship this damn computer, because this computer will be smarter than they are. They'll want to know where it came from, and what it was all about. The result of all the misery we've gone through will be a small cube of transistors and batteries.

Maybe there's a computer like this already in existence somewhere. It may be causing all kinds of mischief, some of it beyond our comprehension. Maybe there is one in a cave somewhere, left by some ancient civilization. The earth is five billion years old. We know that man is at least five million years old, but we only know what man has been up to in the last five thousand years.

Of course, there are all these theories that the process of evolution happened more than once. But, in fact, you argue against evolution.

A lot of scientists have dropped evolution, as it is very hard to prove. You can prove it up to a point. You can prove that once a species is born, it changes and adjusts to its environment, but we don't know the process of creation. If we knew it, we would start creating things; we'd be building Frankensteins. But we don't know how it's done.

If man was born in a natural way, it had to be a simple way, one that we could duplicate. You wouldn't need much, really, but a few chemicals and some electricity; but we haven't been able to duplicate it. And that indicates that something more is involved. I would suspect that early man probably was put here from somewhere else.

This would be my conclusion: evolution requires a long series of accidents and coincidences. The right chemicals would have to be at the right place, at the right time, so that when the lightning bolt hits, the ingredients are all there. It's very hard to argue that this could happen naturally.

Now I see that the religious people are quoting me as a great authority, because I "came out against evolution." But they ignored everything else that I had to say, which was very anti-religious. Most of my books are, you know, about exposing faulty beliefs. If you can expose UFOs, you can expose religion, because the mechanism of belief in both is the same.

So, forgetting for the moment that there might be a computer that was hidden somewhere, causing the UFO and Bigfoot sightings, and animal mutilations...

Well, that's not even a theory, that's just a gimmick that I used in *The Eighth Tower.*

Oh, okay. But you talk about the superspectrum, the energy belt, and various UFO phenomena as transmogrified puppets. In a sense, they are created or manifested with a very low intelligence. They go around being kind of stupid, sly, and mischievous, destroying people's lives. What do you think is really behind it?

Well, Carl Jung's theory was that it was collective unconsciousness. The easiest way to describe it is that you take one ant, having no intelligence whatsoever. The ant is totally stupid; he has no powers of perception. He's got two little antennae, and he can maybe sense the air movements around him, but that's about all.

But if you take a million of these ants and put them together, they are – or become – highly intelligent. Each one becomes a cell in a larger brain; then, the ants can do incredible things. In battle, they do like an Army general would. They plan. They organize. If they come to a river, they can cross it, collectively – something an individual ant couldn't do.

Now take the human race; each one of us may be a cell in this larger mind, the superconscious. Carl Jung suggested that it is this superconsciousness that is controlling everything. Each one of us is part of it. In a way, the religionists are right. They say that we are part of whatever you want to call God. It is like a world soul.

But your book suggests that the world soul is inherently evil; it's a demiurge ruled by Satan.

Well, if you look at it in human history, the influence has always been very evil, and continues to be very evil.

That's a very Gnostic conception of the earth.

It goes back to the old religious idea of the battle between good and evil. Evil is usually winning.

Where does good come from?

That's another philosophical thing. Good is sometimes a negative force in our world. For example, if Hitler had won World War II, we might not have invented the atom bomb. So which would have been worse? I mean, it's like the lady and the three doors; there's a tiger behind all three doors.

So there was a shitload of UFO activity around 1965, '66, '67.

Actually, the UFO wave started in 1964, and continued until about '68. Those were four years of very intense UFO activity. Then in 1973, the UFO activity was renewed until '75. During that period, we had major animal mutilations all over the country. At that time, I wrote a few articles about the animal mutilations, and the UFO buffs were screaming and yelling, "Keel is trying to invent this whole thing!"

Then the mutilations would begin in their own area, and they'd investigate them, and they'd begin to see that I was right. There *was* a relationship to UFOs. Then there was a long, deathly silence from a lot of UFO buffs, especially those who had been big believers in extraterrestrials before that.

Then we lapsed into another period, between 1975 and about '80, when there wasn't much UFO activity at all. Then in 1981 and '82, there was a lot of UFO activity, but it got virtually no publicity whatsoever. There were a lot of these cars stopping on highways, and abductions, and all kinds of sightings – an enormous amount. But the old reporting networks that we had in the '60s had collapsed by then. There aren't that many ufologists running around anymore.

Are there newer manifestations of the same phenomenon?

Yes, last year we had a lot of them – abductions in particular. Somebody is driving along the road late at night. Their car stops for no reason at all. They see a UFO coming towards their car. Suddenly, the next thing they know, it's three hours later.

You did that Mothman book based on your research in West Virginia in 1967. Was that your primary focus in the field?

No, there were a lot of things in Long Island and New Jersey, closer to home; I was involved in a dozen cases at once at any given time. I was involved, eventually, with hundreds of contactees. They were writing to me because of my articles. People would travel three thousand miles to spend an hour with me, because they were so troubled by what had happened to them. Nobody else would listen to them.

Give us a profile of what you saw among these people.

Well, for one thing, I saw a common physical characteristic. It had gradually dawned on me that most of them looked pretty much alike. The men all had a certain look about them, and the women all had a certain look about them. It's hard to place, but they all shared certain genetic traits. They all looked sort of Nordic, like they were from Sweden or Norway.

The men would be darker than the women. The women all tended to be blondes or very fair. If you had a hundred photographs of these people and put them up on the wall, you would say, "My God, maybe they're all brothers and sisters or something; there's some relationship there." This is something that I tried to get people interested in, because it would cost money to do a genealogical study of these people. I could never get anybody interested in it, because everybody was still convinced that we're dealing with extraterrestrials. But there's a genetic tie-in with all this.

There were a lot of other things that they had in common. I was always looking for what used to be called the "devil's mark," where they would have a scar somewhere on their body. They often didn't know how they got the scar. Other investigators have since rediscovered this. It was common for them to have a scar on the leg or on the thigh, or on the back of their neck. They would always say that they'd had it since childhood, yet couldn't remember how they got it.

And this is from the Middle Ages, the devil's mark?

Yes, if you had it in the Middle Ages, it was off to the firepit with you. They'd burn you at the stake. That was one of their tests.

Brad Steiger has since made a career out of this, with what he calls the "star people." He's decided that there are a lot of star people on this planet, and he's published several books about it. He gets a lot of mail from "star people" all over the country now. They're people who have somehow been branded – like we would brand cows.

So you're suggesting some kind of cosmic experimentation?

Not cosmic experimentation. I mean, there's a lot we don't know about our own planet. There may be people left over from some previous age, hiding in a remote place.

Could you help any of the contactees you saw?

Some you can help. For a lot of them, however, there is nothing you can do.

How can you help some of them?

Just by talking it out with them. One of their big problems is that nobody will listen to them. They just brush it off. A lot of people are convinced that if they have lost three or four hours, something terrible has happened to them – something that is affecting their lives. I tried hypnosis on them, until I found out that that was useless. Hypnosis is totally useless.

So when did you get into the "Men in Black," the strange men who visit UFO contactees and threaten them to keep silent about their experiences?

I think that started with my Long Island cases. I began to hear about these guys who were running about talking to witnesses, even when the witnesses hadn't reported to anybody. It's one thing for a witness to get his name into the newspapers and have somebody come around; it's another thing for the witness to see something on Tuesday night and, on Wednesday, have somebody coming around to say: "Don't talk about it." The witness doesn't know what to make of it.

I began to hear a number of these stories. Up to that time, I thought the Men in Black had been something contrived by Gray Barker. He had written a book about Men in Black called *They Knew Too Much about Flying Saucers*. I thought that it was partly or wholly fiction. But then I heard thousands of Men in Black stories.

Have you observed any Men in Black yourself?

Well, I've seen the cars out on Long Island. I got a mysterious phone message to meet somebody at the place called Mount Misery out there. As I drove up this narrow dirt road, I came upon a black Cadillac sitting there, facing me. As I approached it, it flashed its lights on and off. There were two men in black suits in the front seat. The road was so narrow that I had to go up a short distance before I could turn around. So I passed this Cadillac, turned around, and came up behind it.

I was going to park behind it and get out to talk with these two men. But as I drove up, the Cadillac started to move off very slowly. I followed them up and down these roads on Mount Misery, which is the highest point in Long Island. It is a rather bleak area. They turned down this side road, and I followed them. It was heavily wooded on both sides. The Cadillac disappeared, but there was no place for it to disappear to.

It didn't disappear before your eyes.

No, it went around the bend, and when I went around the bend, there was no Cadillac and there was no place for it to go. So, that was one of my experiences with the black Cadillac. A number of times, I would arrive at somebody's house, especially in West Virginia, and they would tell me that ten minutes earlier, this guy in a Cadillac, in a black suit and everything, had been there to see them. He had just taken off ten minutes earlier.

Why a Cadillac?

I don't know, but after I did a couple of articles about the Cadillacs, they switched to Volkswagens.

What was the next level? After the Men in Black, what comes next?

Well, you get involved in all kinds of conspiracies; they're really games. I got involved in an investigation here in New York in which there was a building on Park Avenue that was – I learned later – filled with CIA fronts. For some reason, I was maneuvered into going into this building, into a certain room, and learning all this stuff that I had no need to know about.

Obviously there were some very strange things going on in this building; there was an organization there with very peculiar name. I'm not going to tell you the name because it's still in existence. In checking around, I found out that this organization had a Cadillac rental agency in Elmhurst, Long Island. I went out there and they had something like forty Cadillacs.

In order find out something about this outfit, I went there to rent a Cadillac. But they wouldn't rent me a Cadillac, even though renting Cadillacs is what they were supposed to be doing. A year or so later, I was out in the same area again, but the agency was gone. It was a huge place, so it's odd that it would shut down so quickly.

What did you make of that?

Well, this strange organization in New York maintained a Cadillac agency on Long Island. They had tie-ins with all sorts of bizarre things.

You said before that you were being maneuvered into the game. Who was playing the game?

I was being maneuvered by somebody – just the way the investigators of the Kennedy assassination were manipulated. I don't know if you followed this too closely over the years, but people who were obsessed by the Kennedy assassination kept getting sucked into these games. They would go to hotels to meet with mysterious strangers that were going to tell them the "whole truth" behind the Kennedy assassination.

They would meet with these guys, and these guys would give them a very elaborate and convincing story. When they would try to check it out – I'm talking here about professional reporters checking things out – they'd find that these guys didn't exist, and that none of the things in their story existed. You have to ask, "Why do they do this?

Do you think these are human agents, government agents, or occult societies?

It's more occult than anything.

A secret occult organization?

It's very possible. But what are their motives, and where is their money coming from? In our animal-mutilation cases, there are a number of Men in Black incidents. There was one case, in either in Texas or Oklahoma, where all of the local farmers were up in arms because their cows were being mutilated, night after night.

They decided they were all going to arm themselves to the teeth, and really go out every night and be vigilantes, and catch these mutilators. So these guys are driving around with the local sheriff and his men. They see a truck coming along, and there are two guys in the truck in Air Force uniforms. They stop and talk to the guys in the truck, and the men in the truck say that they're in radio contact with an airplane overhead, which is searching for the mutilators. This whole vigilante gang was told that they should follow the truck.

So these heroes go off following this truck through the night. Of course, the truck leads them away, and the mutilations take place that night in some other spot. Then the truck and the men in the truck disappear, way out in the wild somewhere. It goes around a bend in the road and disappears.

A lot of this sounds like CIA disinformation or "dirty tricks."

Yes, but to what point? Why would the CIA be playing games like that?

Did you ever feel threatened?

Well, there was a period when I felt very threatened. I was getting letters in the mail, threatening to kill me, and I was getting threatening phone calls. At one time, it looked like they were setting up a contactee – so that the contactee was going to turn up dead – in such a way that there would be the evidence pointing to me. It looked like they were going to set me up for murder.

I wrote several letters to people, like my agents and other people, explaining all the circumstances if this should happen. It never happened, but I was really scared. And I was very scared for this particular contactee.

Weren't your phones also being fooled with – tapped and so on?

Yes, everybody's phone was being screwed with at that time – anyone who was involved in this.

Here's an example of setups that they would use. I would get a phone call, and somebody would be threatening me. Then a voice in the background would say, "Hang up, Larry, somebody's coming in now." Then the phone would be hung up.

I'd say, "Larry, Larry… How many Larrys do I know?" Meanwhile, Larry would get a threatening phone call saying that they were going to cut his tongue out or something. Then he would hear a voice saying, "Hang up, John, there's somebody coming in now." Such things provide "evidence" that something criminal is going, so that accusations and disagreements can ensue.

Do you think some of this may have been done by practical jokers?

No, because some of it was too involved. There was one night, in particular, when I kept notes. I talked to a lot of people the following week. It had happened to about twenty people in one night, in different states of the U.S. Whoever was doing it was paying for a lot of long distance calls; it seemed like an organized effort. Obviously, at that time, the only one you would blame would be the CIA. But why would the CIA be bothering with all these people? Why would they be playing this kind of stupid game?

Did you ever think that you, yourself, might become a contactee?

I don't think that was any great concern of mine. I went through different stages. At one stage, I was determined that I was going to track down whoever was pulling all these tricks. I felt that sooner or later, they would tip their hand in some way; but they never did.

However, a lot of the UFO buffs fell for this stuff. They would either drop out of the field, or they would become very antagonistic towards each other. There was a very active UFO group in Boston that was at each other's throats because of these phone calls and interferences with mail. They were all blaming each other, which was exactly the intended result. The whole group dissolved because of this crap.

When did your own involvement in UFOs begin to trickle off?

By about 1970. After I finished *Operation Trojan Horse*, I needed to do something else, so I took a job in the government. I went down to Washington for a year. When I came back from Washington, I went up to Woodstock for a while, doing other things.

I feel that my own thinking has gone way beyond where it was at that point. I've evolved a lot of ideas since then, but most are just too complex to even talk about. Eventually, I may do books about them.

Like what?

It's sort of a cosmology, a more elaborate discussion of what has happened to man, from the beginning, and how we've been directed to this point.

I was going to ask you for a little sketch of Keel's occult history of the world.

Well, we've allowed ourselves to be misdirected and misguided by these evil forces throughout history. Essentially, we worship the wrong gods, and now it's all beginning to come home to us.

We're going to need some new system of belief, but we're probably not going to get it, because we're going to revert to an animal state as the population increases. It's already happening all around us. There are a lot of people in New York living on an animal level. They're out there mugging and stabbing people. It's happening worldwide; we're reverting back to a very primitive state. What else *can* illiteracy bring us?

When survival becomes the main consideration, it only takes a couple of weeks to take a civilized human being and turn them into an animal. The Army proves that over and over again. It takes just two weeks to do it. If your food and water supply were cut off tomorrow morning, in two weeks from now you would be out there killing to get something to eat. The instinct for survival is strong.

It's starting to happen in the major cities. What we have is a superfluous population. We have people who just cannot fit into society, and who our society can't or won't support. They will have to get by the best way they can.

This what we're facing now: growing *terror*. The breakdown of the educational system is probably responsible.

You see growing terror, rather than an Armageddon-type nuclear disaster?

Yes, because the nuclear nightmare has been hanging over our heads for decades already. It's lost its impact.

But if you talk about this "superspectrum" that manipulates people, events, and physical reality, why can't you see them manipulating the U.S. and Russia into a nuclear war?

I just don't think it would work that way. I don't think it's in their interest to do something that total.

But hasn't the history of the earth been civilization continually destroying itself?

Yes, but on a small scale. Destroying the entire human race is not in their interest. This phenomenon tends to ruin individual people's lives. For instance, there was a very well-known psychiatrist in West Virginia (Dr. Alan Roberts). In fact, he was the *only* psychiatrist in West Virginia. Roberts was sitting watching television, and suddenly, he heard a voice in his head, telling him to go outside. There, he saw a flying saucer, which he later came to believe had been piloted by Indrid Cold. So, Roberts became a fanatical believer in the ETs, to the point where it ruined his career.

There was a well-known physicist famous in the field of metallurgy. He had his own company. He was driving along one night, and he had a UFO experience. The upshot was that he sold his company, dedicated his life to UFOs, and it ruined his whole life. It happens again and again.

My old friend Ivan Sanderson was a marine biologist and zoologist. He investigated the UFO cases, and said that he felt this force had the intelligence of a four-year-old. These cases reminded him of ape behavior. He really nailed it. The UFO buffs like to think they're dealing with superior beings with advanced technology, but they are really dealing with four-year-old mentalities (a good match, perhaps).

Can you sum up your theories now on the whole UFO phenomenon and its associated manifestations, such as Mothman, Bigfoot, etc.?

Well, ultimately, nothing has come of it. For thirty-five years, everybody expected something to come of it, but it hasn't changed the human condition in any discernible fashion. It's put us through a period of mild consciousness-raising, but in the end, nothing has changed. It's had little or no effect on us.

Do you feel that the ultimate weapon against it is mockery — making fun of it?

My one favorite phrase has been "belief is the enemy." If you can only believe in something, it has to be wrong. But if you have facts to back up that belief, then it's not a belief; it's something you have come to know. You know that a Volkswagen exists, because you've ridden in one, or maybe been run over by one. But you don't know that UFOs exist; therefore, you are forced to believe that UFOs exist.

Haven't the UFOs discredited themselves by now?

Yes, a lot of people have lost their faith in the UFOs; that is why the subject is dying. There were people, beginning in the early 1950s, who chased them for years. They thought the phenomenon was going to change everything, yet it changed nothing.

Do you see the phenomenon changing again?

Yes, it changes with us. It changes with the times.

Do you think that these ultraterrestrials have an existence independent of us?

No. If they blew us up, they would cease to exist, too. It's an interrelationship; everything points to that.

The ones changing the tune are basically parasites.

They can either change the record that is playing on the Great Phonograph in the Sky, or they can place the needle somewhere else. They've done it throughout history. They've set up the belief for the fairy commonwealth, which was a big belief in Europe for two hundred years. Then, all of a sudden, everybody decided that faeries don't exist. Today, nobody believes in faeries, except people in Ireland and Scandinavia, where they still see them.

So we're back to that Great Phonograph that you talked about in "The Eighth Tower." There's a beginning, middle, and end to each song. Once the record has played to the end, it has to start over again at the beginning. "They" are compelled to keep telling the same story, over and over again. They may even debunk themselves, so that they can start over again.

Yes, that's the circle. Even if they change the record, it won't be that different than the previous one, at least in its basic tonal range, bandwidth, etc.

Has anything happened since you've stopped devoting your life to this? Anything new that really has surprised you?

No, I don't think so. There are haven't been any real surprises for me in years. Once you're steeped in the subject and know all about it, it becomes predictable; there is nothing really new. There may be something new in the next century, when you have the problem of a larger population that is increasingly superfluous. Think of the mischief the UTs could cause with robots and computers – a grand stage for trivial actors to make themselves conspicuous: "Look at me, look at me."

CHAPTER 20

Did T. Lobsang Rampa actually go buzzing through the solar system in a flying saucer? Or was he just another deluded psychopath dredging up a good yarn from the dark depths of a twisted mind?

If he were a nut, he would have plenty of company. Men, and some women, have been circumnavigating the cosmos for thousands of years, leaving extensive records of their travels behind for us to puzzle over. Even Enoch, the traditional son of Cain and father of Methuselah, is supposed to have visited other worlds, where he had such harrowing experiences that they became a part of religion and folklore.

According to the Books of Enoch, which were once part of the Christian Bible, he was sleeping alone in his house one night when he was suddenly awakened by "two men, exceedingly big, so that I never saw such on Earth… They were standing at the head of my couch and began to call me by my name."

The two giant entities plucked Enoch from his bed and escorted him into outer space where, during the next sixty days, they gave him a guided tour of ten different worlds. Some were occupied by deliriously happy people, while others were gloomy and dark, filled with Gregori – wretched gray beings with withered faces, who mumbled and marked in dreariness.

Enoch saw worlds of dazzling light and energy, too. He was the first space traveler. He was also the first abductee. Although he supposedly underwent those adventures more than 4,000 years ago, copies of his "books" (scrolls) were smuggled out of Russia about 1,500 years ago. Since then, thousands of other people have claimed almost identical experiences. Indeed, the beginning of Whitley Strieber's *Communion*, the big bestseller of 1987, is uneasily similar to Enoch's account.

A great Swedish seer, Emanuel Swedenborg, went floundering around the cosmos in the 1700s, leaving behind a score of ponderous books written in Latin. Many of his experiences were undoubtedly what we now call "out of body" experiences. It doesn't seem to be a dream, but there are many dreamlike qualities. Earth time loses its meaning in these adventures…

Swedenborg claimed that he had visited Jupiter and other planets. He often fell into trances that lasted as long as three days. During some of these trances, Swedenborg became the victim of missing time. That is, the brain was unable to account for long periods of time or supplied confabulations (false memories) to fill in the gaps.

This "missing time" phenomenon has been happening wholesale in the 20th century; whole cults have sprung up around the confabulations produced by the percipients. Lacunar amnesia, the medical term for this, has become a serious study for many doctors and psychiatrists. Hundreds of technical books have been written about it.

Did Enoch and Swedenborg actually visit heaven, hell, and all the myriad worlds in between? It's not very likely. But their minds did take trips stimulated, perhaps, by mysterious forces that are actually able to distort our reality. They seem to be able to control the human race.

These forces have been given a thousand names over the centuries and have been credited with all kinds of wonders, miracles, and catastrophes. Swedenborg astonished his friends with precise prophecies of future events. He was even able to accurately describe events that were occurring hundreds of miles away at that exact moment.

Several years ago, I was mysteriously drawn to a cemetery on Long Island after a rash of strange phone calls and eerie instructions from various UFO contactees. Following their directions, I found myself standing among the tombstones of a family named Denton. But I didn't understand why.

So later, on one of my many visits to the musty bookstacks in the cavernous New York Public Library, I decided to see if I could locate any information on the Denton family. I was flabbergasted by what I discovered. Back in the 1860s, shortly after the Civil War, the Denton family of Wellesley, Massachusetts began to visit Venus and other planets! They did it psychically, with their mind's eye.

Papa Denton wrote a series of bestselling books. They took advantage of the "New Age" craze that was sweeping America in the aftermath of the Civil War, and the amazing rise of Spiritualism. Everyone everywhere was suddenly aware of Swedenborg's "internal man."

Before the century ended, most were chatting with spirits, Atlanteans, Indian guides, Ashtar, and assorted space entities. Astral projectionists everywhere were zooming around to the backside of the moon and frolicking on the satellites of Jupiter.

The next New Age revival took place in the aftermath of World War I. The boys who failed to come home in 1918 began conversing with their loved ones through spirit mediums, and Spiritualism again became the rage.

Spiritualism began in 1848, and has had many revivals since. Harry Houdini saved his flagging career by exposing some of the many phony spiritualists who claimed they had visited distant planets.

Following World War II, there was another big revival of interest in things spiritual, and a whole *new* New Age movement sprang up in the 1950s. These New Agers were preoccupied with flying saucers and the space brethren, who were issuing stern warnings about our atomic follies. We were told to "shape up, or ship out." And, some of us went!

There were growing numbers of contactees, all over the world, who claimed they had been flown to other planets in flying saucers. Thousands of others were complaining about being seized by hypnotic trances and losing time. The phenomena were so widespread and so bizarre that no government could deal with them. Investigating the manifestations was an impossible task. Even more impossible was the task of interpreting what was going on.

In 1947 in England, a struggling British writer named Cyril Hoskin told his astonished wife that he had decided to change his name. A few months later, Cyril Hoskin became "Carl KuonSuo" by court order.

Then, on June 13, 1949, while climbing a ladder in his garden, Carl KuonSuo fell and cracked his head, suffering a mild concussion. When he recovered, the Englishman was gone and had been replaced by a Tibetan with full memories of growing up in Tibet!

Now, I have read every book about the place. You might say that Tibet was my hobby. I visited that far country in 1955, when it was still a very hazardous journey, and very few Americans had ever been there. I read Rampa's book, *The Third Eye*, with a skeptical eye, and yet found most of it quite compelling and convincing. He wrote knowledgeably about Tibetan beliefs in reincarnation and astral projection, those perennial New Age favorites.

If *The Third Eye* had been a flop, no one would have paid any attention to its humble, robe-bearing author. But its media success brought Rampa under heavy harassment by the media. He often complained that he was never permitted to answer his critics. The newspapers would not give him any space, and only one TV station offered to interview him, provided he follow the script they wrote!

For the rest of his life, he repeatedly insisted that all his claims were true.

My Visit to Venus is made up of chapters deleted from one of Rampa's other works. It was discovered by Gray Barker, who rescued it from total oblivion. It is possible, of course, that it is total hogwash. It is also possible that it is a description of an out-of-body experience, like so much of Lobsang's work purports to be.

Certainly, it is at least as valid as Swedenborg's visits to Jupiter, Enoch's travels among the Gregori, and William Denton's excursions to Venus. It may be that there is a curtain of magnetic frequencies between our reality and some other, greater universe that only few are privileged to see.

-John A. Keel

CHAPTER 21

Since the beginning of the modern period of ufology in 1947, John Keel's writings have influenced the development of almost every aspect of the subject. Firstly through articles in pulp and 'men's' magazines, then through his seminal "Operation Trojan Horse" (1970) and "The Mothman Prophecies" (1975), Keel boldly criticized prevailing theories.

Two other books, "Strange Creatures from Time and Space" (1970) and "Our Haunted Planet" (1970) show him to be a Fortean skeptic by inclination, prepared to discuss and investigate the most fantastic ideas and phenomena, while carefully committing himself to nothing – except to challenge dogmatic belief on all sides.

We caught up with John in London, England, between his lectures at the UFO conference in Sheffield and the conference in Salisbury. We talked about Japanese terror balloons, crazy UFO people, a lost photo of a pterodactyl, and his first successful book, "Jadoo" (1957), detailing his search in the Far East for authentic miracle men.

MIRACLE MAN: BOB RICKARD TALKS TO ANOMALIST JOHN KEEL
– *FORTEAN TIMES #65* – 1992

John, you created a storm of controversy by suggesting that many of the classic UFO sightings from the late 1940s were, in fact, Japanese Fugu balloons. What were they?

The Japanese sent about 9000 across the Pacific towards the close of the war, carrying anti-personnel bombs and incendiary devices. The damned things were the size of a three-story house, and made of bamboo and laminated paper. It was the toughest paper ever made; damned near indestructible. They were masterpieces of artistic craftsmanship.

Most of them self-destructed or were damaged by storms. We have records of about 300 possible sightings and about 500 maybes. All the information on these balloons has been readily available to people. There's one historian on the West Coast who has interviewed all the Japanese scientists involved. He has complete records on all the recoveries and sightings.

There are still specimens on display in about seven U.S.

museums, but I can't get the UFO buffs to go near them. I think there can be no question that one of these came down at Roswell, New Mexico. The debris found in July 1947 fits the description and the timescale.

I've had three letters from people who swear they saw a manned balloon of this type, and were told to keep quiet about it. Of course, a small Oriental-looking man in a flying suit is a classic description of many UFO occupants, so I've wondered whether this is how it all started. However, the experts on these Japanese balloons say they were never manned at all.

If one reached Roswell, as you claim, are there any records of them going further across the USA?

Yes, one reached Michigan, and the remains of one was found in 1990, in the Black Hills of Dakota. There are photographs of a deputy sheriff being dragged into the air when he grabbed a rope dangling from one of these things. It just happened that the one that landed in Roswell happened during the two-week period when flying saucer mania was at its peak.

Where do you think the Budd Hopkins school of ufology is heading? Does it have any future?

Of course not. It's based on recovering memories of abductions by hypnosis, and this is highly unsatisfactory – as we know from the research into claims of reincarnation. They're dealing with the unconscious mind without reckoning on it being a trickster.

Why can't they see that?

They've been told this a thousand times. I've talked to Budd about this, and he refuses to read a book on hypnosis. This is the man who holds therapy groups for abductees. If they start talking about, say, poltergeist experiences, he stops them. He doesn't want to hear about that. He just wants to hear about the "Greys." If someone has a dream about the Greys, that's interesting; but if it's a dream about poltergeists or ghosts, he doesn't want to know.

When you think about it, very few professionals have gotten involved with ufology over the last 45 years. I heard recently about a bonafide psychiatrist (John Mack) who has been paid a $200,000 advance to do a study of abductees. He has only looked into a couple of cases, and he is already emotionally involved. This is the key problem; people become emotionally involved. Objectivity is hard to come by when you've been subjected to years of cult literature. Your brain turns to mush.

You must get a lot of crank calls. Whispered hints of events that will shake the world...

They all talk like that. They even give a date. "On June 10th, it's gonna happen, Keel." And I say, "Yeah. Sure." The religious nuts in the States are currently predicting the end of the world in October. When it doesn't come, they'll say it's because they prayed very hard and averted it. Even some longtime ufologists – who ought to know better – fall for this crap every year.

How do you explain the great deal of interest generated by Whitley Strieber?

First of all Whitley, was already an established writer – a novelist whose books had sold in high numbers; some had been made into movies, which had made even more money for him and the publisher. So, he had a great track record. When he wrote his first UFO book, *Communion*, everyone turned it down despite his record.

He told me that something like 16 publishers had turned it down. Even agents didn't want to handle it. They told him that if he were smart, he'd leave the subject alone. They said it would ruin him, and that all the UFO people are crazy. He went ahead anyway and, of course, the book sold very well.

He was quite generous with the UFO crowd. He gave away something like $25-30,000 to individuals and groups. Then they all turned on him, like the snakes that they are. Whitley is thin-skinned, so he couldn't take all the nonsense they wrote in their little journals. Finally, he wrote a three-page letter to everybody, saying the UFO buffs were the meanest, craziest people he'd ever met in his life. He didn't want anything further to do with them.

But then he started his own newsletter on UFO abductions. He took subscriptions for it, and it wasn't bad. But now he doesn't respond to phone calls or letters on the subject. He showed us expensive x-rays of human heads, claiming there were anomalies (implants) there, but that no one would allow the surgeons to go in and find out what these little black specks were.

You would need a control study, however – x-rays of the heads of a thousand people who've never been abducted. The problem is, the ET believers think everyone has been abducted; so they would never go for that.

Anyway, Whitley has learned a bitter lesson from it all, as so many other people have over the years. When I first got into this seriously, in 1966, everyone warned me that the people involved were all nuts. I said I was going to do it the right way. If someone writes me a letter, I'm going to answer it no matter how crazy it is. Even though I did just that, it seemed to create more suspicion. No matter what you say, it's the wrong thing. "He must be with the CIA. He is one of them!"

Now, when college professors and the like come to me, I give them the same advice. Of course, they never take it. I always warn them to be very careful; UFO organizations, their leaders and their followers, are nothing but trouble.

How did you get into journalism?

When I was about 12 to 13 years old, I wrote a letter to the editor of my hometown newspaper, in upstate New York. He thought it was very funny and called me in, and invited me to write a weekly column. I was flabbergasted and thrilled. The column was called "Scraping the Keel," and it lasted for a number of years.

Did your interest in UFOs come out of that period?

No, as a kid, I was interested in everything. My father was a compulsive reader and passed the habit on to me. I worked my way through the whole public library in that little town. In 1944, when I was about 14 years old, I discovered the writings of Charles Fort. He began as a young newspaper-man, too. I wasn't at all surprised. I even wrote a couple of columns about Fort at that time.

I remember going to a meeting on UFOs, in 1948, on 14th Street in New York. Tiffany Thayer may have organized it, but I don't recall meeting him. All I remember is about 40 people crowded into a small room, yelling and screaming at each other about government suppression and such.

Nothing much changes, does it? You've addressed many such meetings over the years.

I've always hated public speaking. I've given some dreadful speeches in my day. UFO audiences are often very hostile; that's their nature. Forteans are much more congenial. The UFO buffs only want confirmation of their beliefs, with no persuasion or argument, just lots of anecdotes. Most of them are cranks, who don't want any hint of logical or scientific thinking. They can't deal with that at all. It's like talking to a group of religious fanatics.

How did you come to be in the Far East and have the experiences you wrote up in "Jadoo?"

In 1951, just after the start of Korean War, I was dragged kicking and screaming into the Army. I had already done a little radio in New York, so I was sent to AFN (American Forces Network) in Frankfurt, Germany. I immediately began doing Fortean things on the radio there, like a broadcast from Frankenstein Castle on Halloween.

It was such a success that I had to outdo myself in the following years. I suggested to the colonel in charge of the station that he send me to Egypt to broadcast from the Great Pyramid. To my surprise, he agreed, and arranged it all, including the finance. We taped the show in the King's Chamber on some of the world's first tape recorders. It had great acoustics.

I was so impressed with Egypt. There is such a tangible presence of ancient Egypt. It called to me, as though my ancient ancestors were from there. It's magical what happens to you there. It's hard to explain. I decided to return as soon as I could. When I left the Army, I was offered a civilian post at AFN. Here I was, at 23, with a big staff and in charge of script production for the whole network. I made enough money in a year to fulfill another boyhood dream, so I quit and traveled to India, via Egypt and Baghdad.

I got as far as Malaya, where the British threw me out. Then I settled in Spain; I stayed in Barcelona for three years and wrote *Jadoo*. In those days, the dollar was king. I had to return to the States to do all the publicity for *Jadoo*, or I'd still be in Spain today. I was on radio and TV quite a lot. This was the height of my fame. I was about 28 years old.

Jadoo reads like the travel diary of Indiana Jones. On your travels, you heard the cry of a Yeti in Sikkim; you saw a wandering stool in a Tibetan monastery; you conversed with a levitating hermit, and a yogi who could pull out his eye; and in Cairo, your life was in danger from illicit mummy dealers.

Travel writing is a genre that has declined since the advent of easy jet travel. Anyone can get to faraway places now and see things for themselves. Travel writers, in the early days, used to take a little fact and write mostly fiction around it, or make fabulous claims...

There was William Seabrook in the 1930s, who went to Haiti and almost single-handedly kick-started all the interest in voodoo and zombies. He lectured for years after writing one book. Another example is Richard Halliburton, who claimed to have swum in the pool at the Taj Mahal. You know, it's a reflective pool only, just three inches deep! Halliburton bought a Chinese junk to test his theory that the Chinese sailed to America, and was never heard of again...

He's probably a castaway on a Pacific island, with Amelia Earhart. For Forteans, the most interesting travel writing, like "Jadoo," has a mystical dimension. Alexandra David Neel's accounts of Tibet spring to mind, or Paul Brunton, who was the first to have claimed to have slept in the Great Pyramid.

I met Paul Brunton once; he must have been about 65. He was almost upset that I had virtually retraced his steps, including going into the King's Chamber. It was as though he was afraid I was going to expose him or something.

You learned a few simple tricks from the fakirs – how to poke a needle through your cheeks, and you were even buried alive for half an hour. You said that anyone can train themselves to do these things, including reading minds.

Yes. I once met a schoolmaster who had trained his class to distinguish colors with their elbows. Apparently, anyone can do this with a few hours of training. For some reason, the skin cells "see" or respond to changes in color.

The janitor of a building I once lived in was a full-blooded Indian, and he was very psychic. I saw him sit in front of a Ouija board and make it fly around by itself. He wasn't even touching it. He was a classic drunken Indian; he'd drink and go on terrible rampages. The talents are there, but we have to find and develop them.

A skeptic group in California started a craze for firewalking parties. A few minutes of confidence-building ritual, and then off they go, over the glowing ashes...

I heard that at one of these, a smart-ass psychologist wouldn't take the few minutes of training. He stepped onto the coals and was badly burned. He had to be taken off to hospital. A lot of people were making a lot of money "teaching" firewalking.

You have written – in Fate magazine and elsewhere – of your search for a photograph of a giant bird. Did you ever locate it?

That's just it: many people remember seeing it, and no one has been able to find it. I don't remember the source. My feeling is that it was in a men's magazine like *Saga* or *True*... In my mind, I can see the entire photograph: a group of men standing in front of a barn door. The caption said they were college professors, but they were all dressed like cowboys. They were seedy types, some wearing top hats. Nailed to the barn was a huge winged creature – like a pterodactyl or giant eagle – with a wingspan of around 36 feet.

After reading my original article in *Fate*, some people went scrambling around in libraries trying to trace the picture. The story goes that the original account was in *The Tombstone Epitaph*, the Arizona newspaper. But people have gone through every single issue of the *Epitaph* without finding it. It's a real mystery, because in the late 1800s, photos in newspapers were a rare innovation. Mark Hall now thinks the picture never existed, but too many people remember seeing it.

Perhaps it was a part of a cigarette advertisement or something, and that's why no one saved it. Otherwise, it doesn't make sense. You know how keen Forteans usually save every little scrap of paper; this is one that ought to have been clipped by somebody.

Speaking of thinking you've seen something... Andrija Puharich, in "Beyond Telepathy," refers to a case of a fakir performing the "Indian rope trick." The audience sees the rope thrown up, and the fakir following the boy up and

throwing down his dismembered limbs. However, the film record of the event
showed the fakir and boy standing motionless to one side throughout the whole
performance. This man had somehow influenced the audience hypnotically,
and the whole event had taken place in their imaginations only.

That's a legend that goes back to the 1800s, right after cameras were introduced. It's one of those stories that everyone believes happened, but for which there's no evidence. Puharich heard this story from Charles Laughead, a British doctor who was very prominent in ufology in the late 1950s, with his belief in the Council of Nine. He took his group to sit on a mountaintop, waiting for the UFOs to come down; but they didn't come. This was the basis of Festinger's book *When Prophecy Fails.*

What about mystics like Sai Baba? Do you think his phenomena are merely showmanship?

I've known a number of magicians who've gone to study Sai Baba, and who've watched him very closely. Sometimes he'll produce a handful of ash – there are dozens of ways a stage magician can do this – and other times, he'll open his fist and produce a jewel, which he'll then give away – a ruby or something quite valuable. But none of them have come up with any real expose of Sai Baba, even when they've said they don't believe the remarkable things attributed to him. No one has caught him using any of the common gimmicks.

After all your years of investigation, do you think there are still questions to be answered?

I think a lot of questions *have* been answered. It's just that people have not recognized the answers, or have ignored them. You had a letter in a recent issue, where someone had observed it raining only in one spot in the street. I saw something similar in New York City in 1972, on the corner of 5th Avenue and 42nd Street. It was one of the busiest corners in New York, near the city's Public Library.

On a beautiful sunny day, probably in August, not a cloud in the sky, I walked past that corner and it was raining on that corner. People were scurrying by, but no one was looking up. I stopped and looked around for 10 or 15 minutes, but couldn't figure out where it was coming from. It was not a burst water tower.

I have a theory about all this. Most anomalous phenomena are, in fact, demonstrations of "black magic" powers, or something intended for just one or two people. It won't make any sense to the rest of us.

CHAPTER 22

If you live in one of the hundreds of areas where multicolored luminous blobs zip around the night skies like giant fireflies with a glandular condition, you probably don't need a magnetic detector.

But if UFOs are a rare sight in your community, there are only three ways to tell when they are coming. The first method applies only to psychics. If you have some latent or active psychic ability, you may instinctively sense when a UFO is nearby. Many people do. These mysterious objects seem to have a strong connection with the psychic world around us.

The second method is networking. In many places, people simply phone each other and spread the word that UFOs are buzzing around. When CB radios were popular, the CB bands were cluttered with UFO reports during UFO waves or "flaps."

If none of the above applies to you, you might try building a UFO detector. They are simple to make, and they really do work. During the great waves of the 1960s, several companies manufactured and sold such detectors.

Everybody in the flap areas seemed to have one perched on their mantle or kitchen table. When the alarm bell sounded they all scrambled for the door, running outside so they could utter the familiar cry: "There goes one!"

How does a UFO detector work?

It is basically a switch that is activated by a sudden change in the magnetic environment.

We are all wading around in invisible magnetic fields generated by the earth, by radio and television signals, and by pulses from power lines and telephone lines. An outside magnetic influence suddenly entering our well-established magnetic environment causes a major disruption. The image on your TV screen may go bonkers as it does occasionally when an airplane flies directly overhead.

In thousands of recorded UFO cases, there are incidents where major electromagnetic disruptions occurred. Automobiles stalled. Electric meters ran amok. Compasses and other sensitive instruments reacted violently.

So you need only build a gadget sensitive enough to detect a sudden change in your magnetic environment, and it should work on UFOs. It is really nothing more than an enhanced compass with a bell or buzzer attached.

You will need the following items:

1) A wire clothes hanger.

2) A pair of pliers that can cut wire.

3) A couple of feet of insulated copper wire.

4) A strong alnico magnet, like one of those circular magnets you use to stick notes to the refrigerator door.

5) An old doorbell or door buzzer that works on a cheap nine-volt battery.

6) A battery (nine-volt batteries seem to work best) and battery holder.

7) A small board or wooden block to mount the whole thing on.

Take your pliers or snippers and cut the coat hanger so you can bend it into a C-shaped wire about ten inches high. Make a small hook on the upper end and mount it on the board with thumbtacks or nails.

Now take a piece of insulated wire and strip an inch or so of the insulation from one end, and make a loop. Tie the magnet to the other end. Hang the loop on the hook on the vertical wire. Make a larger circular loop about one inch in diameter on another piece of coat hanger.

Mount this on the board. The magnet now hangs down into this second loop. Strip the insulated wire where it hangs in the center of the loop. Now connect the lead wires, bell, and battery. When the magnet swings, the wire should strike the loop, complete the circuit and cause the bell to ring. (To save your battery, remove it when the UFO detector is not in use.)

Now all you need is a UFO. Put your detector where it won't be disturbed by normal vibrations, gusts of air, etc. Some people put them under a large glass jar for protection.

When a UFO visits your area, the powerful electromagnetic waves they usually emanate will cause the magnet to swing against the wire ring.

Warning: This could happen at three in the morning and wake up your whole household.

If your house is already haunted by mundane spooks, be prepared for non-UFO alarms. Parapsychologists have found that compasses and other electrical devices respond when a ghost is present. If you live in a large city, there may be so many electrical interferences in your building that the UFO detector will be useless. For example, the elevator could set it off.

Readers who understand electronics can build a much more sensitive magnetic field distortion detector with transistors, resistors, and capacitors. Several designs are available. I recommend the one that appears in the best-selling book *Build your own Laser, Phaser, Ion Ray Gun & Other Working Space-Age Projects*, by Robert E. Iannini, Tab Books, 1983.

CHAPTER 23

"Long ago, in days of yore, I was part of the Independent UFO Network team, which staged a series of successful conferences showcasing some of the biggest names in the world of ufology, including Bill Moore, Stan Friedman, Budd Hopkins, and Jenny Randles.

"But for the conference we organized in August 1992, we had the biggest name of all: American journalist and author, John A. Keel. As far as I know, this was his one and only U.K. appearance. Ever since I was a child, I had been a fan of his writings, particularly his account of investigating the bizarre Mothman and sinister Men In Black flaps in West Virginia.

"For a teenager growing up in bleak 1980s South Yorkshire, Keel's books were a source of inspiration and escape into a world where anything was possible, and indeed probable. Keel's accounts of his adventures in West Virginia, chasing red-eyed, winged monsters, sinister MIB in dark Cadillacs, and cool, gentlemanly spacemen like Indrid Cold simply blew my mind.

"Although Keel's presentation at the IUN conference was centered upon Roswell, rather than the anticipated Mothman, it gave us the opportunity to interview the man we felt had been one of the key influences of a generation."

-Dr. David Clarke, 2009

Ever since I was about 11 years old and read Keel's first book, "Jadoo," I was obsessed by him. I later found out others felt like that, too. He's one of the few people to have revolutionized how we think about ufology and strange phenomena generally. I had long wanted him to speak at a U.K. UFO conference.

Although debilitated by jetlag, the effects of diabetes, and the unwanted attentions of the Men in Black from BUFORA, Keel still managed to give a stirring speech to the troops, which left many people leaving the hall shaking their heads and muttering, "Well, that wiped the floor with Bill Moore's explanation for Roswell."

This was the first time Keel had ever publicly spoken in the U.K. I spoke to Keel at length over the three days he spent in Sheffield, and learned many things, some of which I agreed with, some of which I didn't. But what struck me was his overall grasp of ufology, his perspective, and his sense of humor. When the conference was over, I managed to get a formal interview with John. Here it is.

CHRONICLING THE STRANGE: INTERVIEW WITH ANDY ROBERTS – *FORTEAN TIMES* – 1992

Could you tell me how you first became interested in Fortean subjects?

I read Charles Fort when I was very young, when I was about 14 or 15 years old. I was reading *Amazing Stories* in those days, too. They were getting letters at *Amazing Stories* about things people had seen in the sky – before 1947.

I was writing a newspaper column at that time for my hometown newspaper. I did a couple of columns on lights in the sky. I was around when the whole UFO thing broke. I was standing in a carnival in my hometown, in the middle of the midway. A friend of mine came up and said, "Hey, Keel, have you seen this newspaper story about this guy out West who saw some strange things over the mountains?"

It was like a shock to me. I thought, "Oh my God, it's starting." I remember thinking that – that it's now starting. And indeed, it was the beginning, for that was the Kenneth Arnold story.

Do you think the Arnold sighting and the subsequent UFO hysteria was a bit of a reaction to WWII? The world had been used to Earth-threatening excitement for several years, and then peace broke out.

Yes, but it was also what we called the Silly Season. In the newspaper business, in those days, the summer months were very slow news-wise. So they would seize on something like that. One year it would be Loch Ness Monster sightings; the next year it would be UFOs. We don't really have a Silly Season any more; we have the Silly Season year-round now.

What did you believe UFOs were at that time?

I assumed, after reading Fort, that they must be spaceships. Fort didn't really come right out and advocate the ET thesis, but he said there was something there, and that it had been around for a long time. He'd traced reports all the way back.

Fort was very persuasive if you could get past his style. He had an odd style of writing – a humorous style that a lot of people, to this day, don't quite comprehend.

When did you start traveling?

JK: That was years later, after I left the Army. I decided that I would take a wild chance, and use the money I had saved to go around the world, which I had always wanted to do. I especially wanted to visit India. So I took my savings and left Germany and went back to Egypt, where I had done a broadcast from the Great Pyramid.

Any particular reason why you went back to Egypt?

I felt a strong relationship to Egypt. A lot of people feel this way. It's rather mysterious; you almost feel like your ancestors are from Egypt. I've heard other people talk about it too. I felt no kinship at all to the modern Egyptians, but I felt something about the land of Egypt. I really felt a strong relationship to it. So, I lived there for almost a year.

Was it during this time that you saw the UFO at the Aswan Dam?

I saw a UFO at the *old* Aswan Dam. They later built a new one. But I was down there and there were a lot of people around. About two hundred people visiting the dam saw this circular thing that was spinning. It appeared in a clear blue sky in 1954. Later, I found out there were sightings all over the Middle East at that time, and 1954 was a very big year in France and Britain.

This thing I saw was like the Saturn-shaped objects. The center of it was not moving, but the outside was spinning. It was a very odd thing, and everyone had a different answer. You had 200 witnesses, and you had 200 different answers! I thought it was about 200-300 feet in the air, but some people thought it was 1000 feet, or 5000 feet. You don't know the size of a thing if you can't judge the altitude of it.

Right there, in two seconds, I was convinced that flying saucers existed! After that, there was no way anybody could ever tell me that there's no such thing as flying saucers.

Where did you go from Egypt?

I lived in Egypt for a while, and then I moved on across the desert. I arrived broke in Baghdad, which had become my normal condition, because I had an agent in New York who would send me money – sometimes the money would be delayed. I was broke in Baghdad.

I quickly learned, whenever I was broke, to check into the most expensive hotel. Because I was an American and had that famous green passport, they never questioned me. They just thought, "Hey, he's an American; he must be filthy rich!" So I would check into the best hotel and eat in their restaurants until the money came through. I never got questioned once! From Baghdad, I took the long trip down through the Persian Gulf to India. I spent a great deal of time in India, because it's a fascinating country.

In "Jadoo," you traveled through India, sort of debunking the so-called paranormal events such as live burials, snake charmers, the rope trick, and so on.

I always had a childhood interest in magic, and I continue to have an interest in magic. I wanted to find the famous street magicians of India. When I did find street magicians, they were all doing card tricks that they had bought, by mail, from London! It was very hard to find anyone doing the famous Indian tricks. I searched for the Indian Rope Trick, and found various forms of it being performed, but they were not the authentic Indian Rope Trick. They were little faked tricks for the tourists.

What was so special about snake-charming?

Snake-charming had always fascinated me as a kid on the farm. I started studying herpetology and reading books on the subject. I had a neighbor who used to go out and catch rattlesnakes, and sell them to some company that needed rattlesnakes. I used to go out with him. So at a very early age, I learned quite a lot about snakes and reptiles.

I actually studied snake-charming with some of these snake-charmers, except there's not much to study. The charmer is just blowing a pipe, and moving his hands back and forth; the snake is just trying to strike at his hands. The snake can't hear, so it's all showmanship. The audience thinks the snake is dancing to the tune of the pipe, but the snake is just trying to kill the piper!

Did anything unusual happen to you in India?

I had many Fortean-type experiences in India. One strange thing, which happened more than once, was that strange people would come up to me and say that they'd been "waiting for me to appear." This was probably baloney. They were probably saying, "There's an American tourist! Let's take him for big bucks!" I had to get very sophisticated very fast.

I went into the Himalayan Mountains because at that time, in the 1950s, there was a lot of publicity about the Abominable Snowman. There were a number of expeditions into the mountains looking for the Snowman. *The Daily Mail* in London sent an expedition, and I figured I might be able to get a photograph of the Abominable Snowman and sell it to either them or *Life* magazine. I went to the little country of Sikkim, and crossed the border into Tibet – not too far, because the Chinese could easily tell I was not a Tibetan. But at least I could say I'd been to Tibet.

When you got into the Himalayas, you seemed to become less skeptical. You had some experiences with remote viewing, which the monks do.

I was very impressed with what some of these monks, or lamas, were doing. They seemed to know every move that I was making. It was like I was being watched through the whole trip. I would arrive at a monastery, and they would be expecting me. They would already have dinner ready! I was quite impressed with a lot of that.

They weren't even surprised to see me, even though in some of these areas, they had never seen a white man before. At that time in Sikkim, there had only been 400 white men seen throughout their entire history. Nepal was practically inaccessible then, and Bhutan was inaccessible. You could cross into Bhutan and never come out again.

How do you think they did it? Was it because of the time they spent training their minds?

Yes, because what else is there to do there? I had the experience of running into a lama on a snow-covered mountain. He was almost stark naked, but he didn't mind the cold at all.

Did you actually see the Yeti?

I was with some of the people who lived there, when across

the lake, we saw a large, brown figure moving around in the brush. The natives said that it was a Yeti. Now it could have been a bear, or it could have been anything, but they told me it was a Yeti, probably because they knew it would make me happy. So that was my Yeti! I saw the famous Yeti footprints, which are huge. If you see the footprints you say, "Well, maybe I don't wanna meet this guy."

Do you believe Yeti exists in the physical realm?

I did then. The stories about the Yeti there seemed very demonic. They believed it was bad luck to see one of them. Everybody who lived in those areas had a story to tell about the Yeti. Nowadays, I'm not so sure the Yeti is a real animal; but at that time, I was absolutely convinced.

I know you don't want to talk about the Mothman, but I'll just ask one question. I'm still puzzled by one bit of "The Mothman Prophecies," where you relate the story of how you called at a house to make a phone call, and because you were not from the area, people misidentified you as the Devil! Is that a device to make people see that everything isn't as it seems?

As you know, the book was written several years after the events. It was very difficult to get a New York publisher interested in it. I needed a strong opening, and this was a true story.

My car had run off the road on a very rainy night, and I was dressed in a necktie and a full suit. You didn't see that very often then on backroads in West Virginia. I went around pounding on doors, to get somebody to call a truck for me. It turned out that the people who finally made the call were among the people that were on the bridge that later collapsed.

The day after I knocked on their door, they told everybody that a strange man in a black suit and a beard (which was rare in those days) had called, and that he must have been the devil. Years later, I found that people were still telling that story of the devil who had come around to those houses on that backroad.

I think that says a lot about human beings. The majority of your West Virginia sightings seem to have been just odd blobs of light, into which people read something else. Are you saying, then, that we live in an environment that still has many hidden, but natural, mysteries, which we interact with and interpret?

Yes, we seem to be surrounded by an almost invisible world, which can manipulate us in any way. In fact, I just got a letter, before I left New York, from a man named Henry Belk. His family is very rich; they own a chain of 400 stores in the south. For many years, Belk has been investigating psychic surgery – that's his thing. I was astonished to get this letter. He said that after all these years investigating psychic surgery, he had decided that the psychic surgery was being done by an invisible force. The surgeon was just an instrument for it. Henry is evolving a whole theory about invisible entities and so on. He is very scientifically oriented, so it's a surprising thing for him to propose.

Do you think that this phenomenon is conscious, or merely reactive?

When I was investigating UFOs, I realized that somebody was playing games with us. In fact, there's a chapter in *Operation Trojan Horse* about the cosmic jokers. You get involved in a situation that seems very real, and then as it progresses, if you're smart enough, you realize somebody's playing a joke on you – that it has no meaning at all. Of course, some people are too dumb to realize this. With them, it will just keep growing and growing, because this phenomenon feeds on stupidity.

Can you give us an example of how it manifested itself to you?

Yes. "They" had me running around New York, looking for a mysterious gold cross. If I could find this gold cross, I would save the world! So for a while, I was playing these games. A very well-known American ufologist named Ted Bloecher spent 30 years of his life researching UFOs. He would be in a small town, and he'd go to the newspaper and go through their UFO reports.

He finally got involved in some contactee stories in New York State, where there were landings and contacts. He got deeper and deeper into these, and then it finally occurred to him that somebody was playing with him. It wasn't real, and the phenomenon would mold itself to his expectations. So he quit ufology. He has made statements to people that he's very sorry that he spent 30 years on it. He regrets now that he wasted 30 years, when he could have been out chasing women or whatever.

Do you think there was any connection between the collapse of the Silver Bridge and whatever else was going on?

Well, some of the people who died on the bridge were people who'd seen the Mothman. It was all very strange. There were millions of coincidences and strange, interrelated events. For example, there was a family in West Virginia with the rather unusual name of Wamsley, who were an integral part of the Mothman mystery. Several people in this family had seen the Mothman. Even in Budd Hopkins' first book, he talks about the first UFO sighting in New Jersey that he got interested in – and it's the Wamsley family in New Jersey! A couple of the Wamsleys in West Virginia went down with the bridge.

There do seem to be things interacting with us on this planet, which we can't understand.

We're not smart enough to figure it out!

In several of your books, you mention that you've been contacted by witches and magicians that have had similar experiences. Do you think that's perhaps because witches and magicians can manipulate these energies by the power of emotion?

They have studied the same thing, but they haven't studied it from a ufological point of view. They've studied in from almost a religious point of view. Incidentally, after all the publicity Mothman received, the town of Point Pleasant was inundated with witchcraft cults. The walls of the power plant where the Mothman was first seen are now covered with graffiti from witches and magicians – pentacles and that kind of thing.

Are humans actually meant to understand the universe and its mysteries, or are we fighting a losing battle?

I think the human race is going very slowly, step by step, towards some goal that we don't understand. As you know, many of our ufologists are now dead. They died without knowing anything about all this. Some of them carried it a little step forward. It may take another hundred years, or another five hundred years, before we know what this ultimate goal is.

Have you any guesses about what the ultimate goal might be?

Our physical bodies are very limited, very fragile, and not

worth very much. But our spiritual existence – whatever it is – is the key. If there are such things as evolution and reincarnation, then they are due to the endurance of this fragment of energy, which we each carry around with us.

Do you think it's connected to the earth in any way? In your talk last night, the first slide you showed was of the earth from space. That is the first time I've ever heard a spontaneous round of applause during a lecture at a U.K. UFO conference.

Yes, I think the earth is involved. The American Indians believed that they were part of the earth – that the earth "owned" them. They didn't own the earth; it was the other way around. And I think that's probably true. I think the Indians and so-called primitive people had a great understanding of all this. Much of it was, unfortunately, lost when the white man came over. In South America, we destroyed their written records in the name of religion. There were written records on Easter Island, and the first thing that the Spanish priests did was destroy those written records – for being the "work of the devil."

You once said, in the pages of Fortean Times, that we are "the source of the phenomenon." Are we simply contacting ourselves?

It's like that question about the sound of a tree falling in a forest. If we weren't here, would the UFOs still be here? I think the UFOs are definitely connected directly to us. We're only seeing what they want us to see.

Who are the "they" then?

It's a force. I tried to define it in very simple terms in my book, *The Eighth Tower*. I also went into the problem of mystical illumination, which has always fascinated me, because it happened to me when I was eighteen. When I was in New York as an eighteen-year-old, I was living in a furnished room. I woke up one night, and the whole room was bathed in this very peculiar light. I thought the building was on fire! Then a flood of material started coming into my mind. And suddenly, I understood everything. I swear I understood the meaning of everything – how the world was created, and how it was going to end. I knew it all!

So I said, "This is terrific. Boy, I'll write this all down tomorrow, when I wake up." The next day, of course, I couldn't remember anything! I remembered the experience, and the room being bathed in the light, but I couldn't remember any of the material; but it must have entered my unconscious mind.

For thirty years, I thought I was the only person in the world that had had this experience. I never mentioned it to anybody. Then I started reading some of this stuff about cosmic illumination, and started meeting other people who'd had the same experience. I realized that many people, in each generation, have this experience. Many of them don't necessarily do anything with it, but for others, it changes their whole life.

In what way?

They become teachers, scientists, politicians. I think John F. Kennedy probably had that experience. Unfortunately, if someone like JFK has the experience, it dooms them; he got into his position of president too soon. Otherwise, he would have changed the world. If he had lived, there would have been no Vietnam. There would have been a major space program, because he would have diverted all the money for warfare into the space program. That was his plan. We would probably be on Mars now.

Do you think contactees self-destruct because they think they have "the secret," and want to do something with it too fast?

No, contactees only get part of the experience. For contactees, it's mostly a false illumination. They only get part of it, and so they get crazy; they misinterpret it. There are a lot of people in religion who have this experience, and put it to good use. It's the reason a lot of priests and nuns and holy people get into religion. They have this experience, and so they spend their lives helping other people.

Mystical illumination is a very important key to this. There are books on it, written by people who've had the experience, and who've studied the literature. There are many people who have the experience, yet don't necessarily remember seeing a light, or seeing anything. It just happens to them. They change, overnight, and don't know why.

What do you think about the current fascination in the U.S. for the extraterrestrial hypothesis?

Well, it's been a propaganda campaign by a very small group of proselytizers. It's a new religion, this notion that there are extraterrestrials out there. Science, on the other hand, has backed away from the whole extraterrestrial thing. In the 1960s, many scientists thought there was a very good chance that there were extraterrestrials; Carl Sagan, for example, founded exobiology. Arthur C. Clarke has made a number of statements in the past few years, saying that he no longer believes there is any chance for extraterrestrials to exist.

The ET premise has principally been promoted by the movies and the UFO buffs. The average person in the street now sort of accepts it, because they haven't given much thought to it. They've seen the movies, or they've heard UFO buffs on radio or TV, and they say, "Well that makes sense; we're being visited by extraterrestrials." They just simply accept it without thinking.

Do you think the U.S. government has the faintest idea about UFOs, or is the only cover-up one of ignorance?

I think they're pretty dumb about this. I've spent a lot of time trying to find files that would contain significant material. I've known a lot of people in the government and in the military. There are a lot of official people who are interested in the subject, but there's never been any unified effort to study it or discover anything. And how do you study it without actually making contact with the UFOs?

The ET believers have dreamed up a whole fantasy world, where they think the government has made deals with the UFOs. That's just the UFO buff's way of protecting himself. If he didn't think that way, then he would be in a very vulnerable position. So he says that the reason we don't know anything about UFOs is because the government is keeping it quiet. The only alternative to that is: *the reason we don't know anything about UFOs is that they don't exist.*

In "Operation Trojan Horse," you issue a warning to people wishing to become ufologists, basically warning them off the whole idea. What brought this on, and do you still hold the same position?

Yes, in a lot of my speeches, I end up with a statement like that. I usually point out that individuals and civilian organizations don't have the expertise or the money to do anything, and that it's a waste of time to try to investigate these things. The best they can do is go sit on a hill, watch the lights in the sky, and say, "Hey, there goes one!"

In order to really investigate this, you might need twenty million dollars to build the right instruments. That is a big project. I don't think even the government has ever undertaken it. And I don't think any other government has ever undertaken it. The governments around the world all assumed the American government was going to do it.

Remember good old Idi Amin? Well, in Uganda, they were seeing UFOs all the time in the 1970s. Idi Amin had his ambassador to the UN stand up, in the UN, and say, "Hey, *do* something about this!" It was a famous speech at the UN.

Of course, the UN officials said, "What are we going to use for money, and where are we going to find the experts?" When you think about it, there isn't a single real expert on UFOs in the world, because nobody has that kind of experience. You can be an expert on submarines, because they're tangible; but nobody can really do that with UFOs.

So if a UFO landed tomorrow in Trafalgar Square, who would the British government call in to study it? It would be a big problem. As I said, they would probably have to call in aeronautical designers. You wouldn't call in physicists and astronomers. If there were beings on board, you would call in your very best medical people – forensic pathologists and biologists. The last person you would call in would be a ufologist, because he'd be useless. He'd stand there and stare, and say, "My god, it's real!"

Are they real?

I'm talking about the lights and things. People do see something, because I've seen them myself; but I don't think they are machines.

One final question, which I'm sure an awful lot of British ufologists have wanted to ask you for a long time. Just why didn't the moon come up on the night of April 3rd, 1967? (Note to baffled readers: consult your copy of "The Mothman Prophecies.")

I got the information from the local newspaper. I put that in the book almost as a joke, because it was a humorous incident. But it was real. People were saying, "I had seen the moon the night before, but then, the next night, there was no moon."

THE MOTHMAN PROPHECIES: A BIG JOB – SCI-FI ONLINE – 2003

What do you think of "The Mothman Prophecies" film?

I was pleased with the Hollywood interpretation. They got a lot of the stuff in the book into the movie, but with slight variations. It revived a lot of memories of that period, which was a very traumatic period for me. I have no real complaints about it. It's Hollywood, and it's done well; that's my feeling about it.

I worried, at first, how they were going to do the scene with the bridge, but they did the collapse of the bridge beautifully. I thought Richard Gere was good in it. He did not try to imitate me; that would have been too big a job. *[laughter]* I thought Alan Bates was very good in it, slinking around alleys, hiding from whatever he was hiding from.

Ever felt like you were being stalked?

Sure. There's a chapter in the book about it. They worked a lot of that stuff into the movie. And did it very well, I thought. Because a lot of this stuff sounds totally insane – the telephones ringing when they were unhooked, the mysterious voices on the phone. I really went through all of that.

How close did you come to really experiencing the Mothman?

I never saw the Mothman, but I saw people minutes after they had had an experience with it. And they were in a state of total terror. I just happened to be in the vicinity at the time.

It's taken a long time since you wrote the book for Hollywood to come calling.

It took 30 years. I had many, many offers and would-be deals. Agents would call me up, and say, "How soon can you get out here?" I'd say, "As soon as I get your check." That would bring the conversation to a close. They all wanted something for nothing. They all had great deals – for them, but not for me.

See, I have one of the best agents in the country – maybe in the world. I'd say, "Well, you'll have to talk to my agent." And that would bring the conversation to a dead halt. They didn't want to talk to agents.

I know authors who've been tricked like that. Everyone's heard of *Close Encounters of the Third Kind*. It's a title from a college professor's book. The author, J. Allen Hynek, only got a total of $1700 out of that, which is absurd. But they conned him into it. They promised him the moon – a world of publicity, cardboard figures of him standing in front of the theater, and all this stuff. And of course, none of it came true.

So what made you go for this deal?

I'd had countless calls from young writers who wanted to write it, some of them well known. This young man (Richard Hatem) called me, and he understood the book. He'd probably read it 10 times. He gave me a pitch, so I put him in contact with my agent, and they worked out the deal. Then they got involved with Mark Pellington (director), who was instrumental in putting the whole package together. I wish I could complain about something, but I can't. They pulled off a very difficult project.

Have you any idea why these things happened in Point Pleasant and not, say, somewhere else?

Well, it does happen in other places; you just don't hear about it. I just happened to be there, and kept careful notes. If I hadn't been there, you'd never have heard about it. But I was there to record the whole thing, step by step.

As I was recording it, I didn't know what the hell I was doing, or what was going on. So I withdrew from the whole thing. I had so much trouble with the telephone that I took it out. I didn't have a telephone for 10 years.

I've been afraid many times. But I've also spent a lot of time in cemeteries at midnight, and I've been inside the great pyramids alone. I've done a lot of interesting and dangerous things. I trekked through the Himalayas alone. I'm six foot two, and the Tibetans are five foot two, so I'm not that courageous or anything. I'm just stupid. I take chances. A lot of people don't take chances. They'll sit in the corner of their insurance office all their lives, and be happy with that.

INDEX

abductions, 205, 220-221
Abominable Snowman, 9, 47, 235
Abominable Swamp Slob, 47
Adamski, George, 102-104, 117
Adkins, Brenda Ann, 56
Africa, 13, 99, 135, 146, 151, 173
Alabama, 50
Alaska, 67, 110
aliens, 114, 128, 162-163
Allen, Carl, 186
Allende, Carlos, 183-186
Amazing Stories, 232
ambrosia, 101, 104-106
American Forces Network, 190, 197, 223
Amin, Idi, 242
amnesia, 114, 162, 216
Amundsen, Roald, 69-71, 84
Antarctic Ocean, 34
Antonio, Jose, 105
ants, 20, 195, 202, 204
apes, 48, 50, 52-53, 57, 213
Apollo 13 mission, 166-167
APRO, 60, 94-95
Arabic, 15, 18-19, 24-25
Arabs, 15, 19-20, 174, 180
archaeologists, 97, 100, 117, 154-155
Arctic Ocean, 67, 69-70, 72, 78-79, 88-91, 93, 100, 147
Argentina, 147
Arizona, 38, 177, 184, 225
Armageddon, 180
Ashtar, 161, 174, 177, 216
Asia, 100, 173
assassination buffs, 134
Astarte, 174
astrology, 138
astronomers, 30-32, 35, 37-38, 116-118, 154, 156, 173, 242
Aswan Dam, 233
Atlantis, 101, 111, 174
Atomic Energy Commission, 117
aura, 96, 126, 139

aurora borealis, 109
Australia, 30, 121, 146
Austria, 91-92
automobiles, 48, 55, 64, 75, 108, 115, 118, 133, 135, 138, 148, 160, 207-209, 228, 231

Babylonia, 100
Baghdad, 20-22, 223, 234
Bahamas, 111
Barker, Gray, 186, 207, 218
Bates, Alan, 243
belief, 37, 78, 101, 104-105, 122, 128, 161, 198, 200, 203, 212-214, 219, 226
Bell Laboratories, 156
Beloff, John, 170
Ben Eielson, Carl, 67
Bender, Albert K., 40
Bennett, Floyd, 67
Berlitz, Charles, 9, 111, 186
Bermuda Triangle, 9, 147-148, 157
Bhutan, 235
Bigfoot, 50, 111, 120, 187, 203, 213
bitumen, 18
black magic, 115, 187, 192, 227
Bloecher, Ted, 43, 237
blood, 14, 126, 152, 199, 201
Blum, Peter, 124
brainwashing, 112, 115, 162
Brazil, 98, 104-105, 175-176
British intelligence, 179
British Museum, 153
Brown, Gordon, 53
Bruns, Walter, 70
Brunton, Paul, 224
Buddha, 28
BUFORA, 231
Burma, 28
Byrd, Richard E., 67

Cadillac, 115, 133, 135, 207-209
Cagle, James, 54
Cairo, 14-16, 18, 20, 224
California, 30, 32-33, 37, 50-51, 97, 102, 104, 121, 178, 225
California Institute of Technology, 33

Made in the USA
Middletown, DE
23 March 2015